*Planning, Prediction, and Policymaking
in Foreign Affairs*

Perspectives on International Relations

Series Editor STANLEY HOFFMANN, *Harvard University*

Planning, Prediction, and Policymaking in Foreign Affairs

Theory and Practice

ROBERT L. ROTHSTEIN
The Johns Hopkins University

Little, Brown and Company
Boston

This book was sponsored by the Institute of War and Peace Studies, School of International Affairs, Columbia University.

Library of Congress Catalog Card No. 72-5938

First Printing

Published simultaneously in Canada
by Little, Brown & Company (Canada) Limited

Printed in The United States of America

To William T. R. Fox

Foreword

Perspectives on International Relations is a new series of volumes on important issues in contemporary world politics. In the past twenty years the development of international relations as a discipline has been both exuberant and uneven. Fierce battles have been fought, either on normative issues (such as the idealist-realist debate of the late forties and early fifties) or on methodological issues (such as the battle between the "scientific" approach and the "traditional" one, both misnomers). Enormous pretensions have been expressed, due to a burning desire to submit, as fast as possible, an enormous mass of facts to the illuminating discipline of general theory. The elaboration of such theory has led either to the varieties of "systems theory" characterized by a high degree of generality and, frequently, abstraction, or to a proliferation of hypotheses both analytic and normative for limited parts of the field, such as strategy and integration. At the same time, authors have continued to produce broad, essentially descriptive surveys of the whole field—which has grown so much, now that we live in the first truly global international system, that such compilations of data prevent, rather than promote, further analysis.

Today we need neither stratospheric nor fragmentary theories nor broad theoretical surveys, but studies in which the authors concentrate on important aspects of the international system, combining empirical treatment and theoretical analysis. The selection of these issues for this series is unashamedly eclectic: no other thread binds them together than my conviction that an understanding of contemporary world affairs requires an examination of these problems—some of which have often been discussed, while many others have not been sufficiently studied. Insofar as there is any conceptual framework, it is the loose one provided by historical sociology: a conception that accepts the notion of an international system, recognizes the considerable autonomy of the system's elements, acknowledges the important role played by the system's units—the states—in shaping it, and emphasizes the scope of the relations between these units as well as the means they use to reach their goals. History provides the raw material, the touchstone, and the object of such research, but the research itself aims at making sense of, introducing order into, discovering meaning in the data examined.

Another object of the series is to help the readers establish what might be called a balance sheet of the old and the new in the current international system. On the one hand, the competition of states continues in familiar, often depressing ways, according to a logic of behavior that has recently been described brilliantly in Raymond Aron's *Peace and War.* Here, the actors are the states, pursuing goals largely shaped by the contest itself, by the well-known means of diplomacy, strategy, and war. On the other hand, because of a variety of factors—risk of nuclear annihilation, economic interdependence, the pressure of domestic affairs in "socially mobilized" nations—there are new kinds and new rules of conduct that often bring international politics into closer resemblance with internal politics. Here, the actors on the world stage are often private forces, national or transnational; the competition rules out the use of force and entails complex bargaining. Also, a study of the way in which foreign policy is elaborated in the state reveals that to a considerable extent the goals are determined, not by calculations about the outside world, but by internal needs and bureaucratic politics. For both sets of reasons, the concept of the state as the central actor thus deserves reexamination. The only way to determine the importance of the "new" game, its impact on the traditional one, and the degree to which it is the traditional contest which continues, although in muted and devious ways, in the "new" game is to look at the current international system from a variety of angles. No sweeping answers can approximate the truth, as long as detailed assessments have not been made.

The books in the series are being written by a variety of scholars—some already well-known, others at earlier stages in their careers—all of them much too wise and too much in control of their subject matter for any editor to try to impose a common set of concepts on them. Some volumes will undoubtedly be more analytic or theoretical than others, but all of them will be "subjective" in the sense of offering the reader the categories, conclusions, and biases of distinctive scholars, based on their approach to a large body of material.

My hope is that the volumes will prove doubly useful: they should provide specialists in political science, scholars in international relations, and readers generally interested in the field with either an analytic balance sheet on a given issue or an original treatment of it; and they should also supply students with something in between the survey texts and the frequently abstruse grand theories.

The topics that have been selected for such treatment belong to four categories, the first being *the states*. If we accept the view that—despite important nonnational or transnational actors—the states remain the motor of international politics, we must know more about how this motor works. One volume will examine the domestic determinants of foreign policy. Another will look at the fuel itself, and discuss the transformations of power in the postwar international system, i.e., in the nuclear age. Another will analyze one of the most interesting aspects of the "psychology" of international politics: the shaping and the impact of perceptions, especially those of leaders. Robert L. Rothstein's book studies the problems of prediction and planning in foreign policy.

A second set of volumes will focus on *the strategies of the actors* in the system. Several will look at the superpowers, at their relations with one another, and at their respective alliance systems. Another book will study the role of small- and middle-sized powers in the system.

A third set of books will examine *the chessboards* on which states play the games of conflict and cooperation. Some volumes will focus on the game: one will be devoted to the use and control of force; one will reflect on the increasingly more important interaction of revolutions and international politics; and one will look at the political economy of international affairs—a field deserving as much attention from political scientists and sociologists as strategy received ten years ago. Other volumes will be more concerned with world order, i.e., with the regulation of the "game." One will discuss the political uses of international law; J. S. Nye's book, the first in the series, examines the record of regional organizations.

As the fourth category, there will also be some volumes designed to put the present international system in *perspective*. One study will examine comparatively the international systems that have emerged, developed, and disappeared in history. Another will turn toward the future and deal with the normative aspects of the international system—both political (what should the future international system be?) and ethical (how should nations behave in it?). A third will analyze political philosophy in its reflections on world affairs.

In this series we do not pretend to offer the reader a complete view of, or a thorough and impartial evaluation of, the discipline. These works should, however, make the reader aware of, first, the changes in world politics that are increasing its resemblance to domestic politics and, second, contemporary forms of the continuing "state of war" among states. Our aim is not to flood the mind with new information, but to expand it.

In this second volume in the series, Professor Rothstein examines problems important to students of international affairs: What are the relations between theory and practice and especially between the academic study of world affairs and policymaking? As he points out, this is a particularly timely investigation, since after twenty-five years in which, in this country, statesmen and scholars have been intimately associated, there is now a widespread demand for divorce. The policymakers, faced with increasingly abstract and occasionally vituperative academics, deny that the scholars have anything of value to contribute to the daily drizzle of decisions. The academics, especially after Vietnam, denounce not only the mindless callousness and self-deception of the practitioners' pragmatism, but also the corruption of their own standards by service in, or advice to, the government. Professor Rothstein is engaged in a vigorous and subtle battle to prevent such a divorce and to dispel oversimplifications. He wants theorists to engage their minds in practical problems, but without abandoning their standards. He denies that there is any wisdom in "pure" practice. His book will be of great interest to all those who are concerned with decisionmaking in government and with the role planning plays. His emphasis on the difficult problem of how to train future practitioners is as sound as his critique of recent writings on the American foreign policymaking puzzle is acute. Not everybody will agree with his proposal for a radically new kind of planning staff, but nobody will deny its originality.

This is not just a book for those who are curious about prediction in government. Professor Rothstein also examines the limits and the prospects of prediction in what he accurately assesses as a rapidly changing international system, which can no longer be understood with the state-centered concepts of political Realism. He avoids both the error of those who believe that "traditional wisdom" will always be a sufficient guide to the future and the excesses of the more intoxicated among the futurologists. He wants prediction to be taken seriously, and makes us aware of both the need for it and the difficulties around it.

STANLEY HOFFMANN

Preface

Planning has never been a fashionable activity within the American political system. Many critics have asserted that planning is either impossible or unnecessary. In this book I challenge both propositions. There are surely important things for which we can plan, and planning may provide one means of avoiding a grim future.

To argue for planning in foreign affairs is also, of course, to argue for change. Many obstacles in our policymaking system, our bureaucracies, and our belief systems make the creation of a long-range planning staff problematic. We shall discuss these obstacles and how they might be bypassed or overcome. Even if we manage to establish a new planning staff, it will not function successfully unless the persons appointed and those who appoint them believe in planning and are willing to expend resources to protect the staff against those who would erode its power or independence. Thus, merely to describe what has happened to planning in the past and to analyze what it might contribute in the future are insufficient. We must also deal with what theorists and practitioners in foreign affairs believe about planning, on what grounds they feel that it is possible to cooperate, and how these beliefs might usefully be altered.

An academic who spends time in Washington, or who is responsible for educating future practitioners, confronts serious questions about the relationship between social theory and social practice. These questions have been tacitly settled—usually in favor of a particular interpretation of what the "science" in social science implies—in graduate departments which exclusively develop theorists and theory. But that settlement looks precarious, and the few convictions on which it rests much less compelling, when we question the responsibilities that theorists within a social discipline have toward its practitioners. Why has the relationship between theorists and practitioners virtually disintegrated? What can be done to alter this?

Does how—or whether—we answer these questions make any difference? I believe it does, for the answers we accept determine critical matters for both the theorist and the practitioner, from the problems they will work on, to the results they will honor. One need not agree with my interpretation of what theorists and practitioners can and cannot do for each other to appreciate the importance of a sound interpretation of theory and practice. We shall discuss these matters in Chapter 1 and especially in Chapter 3.

A concern with the proper relationship between the realms of theory and practice seems inevitable in a serious study of planning. My experiences in teaching a course on contemporary theory to future practitioners and in attempting to convince highly regarded officials that theory was not useless simply because it could not predict next week's headlines have, however, affected the form of this discussion. More attention will be paid to proper education of practitioners and practical judgment than would probably be necessary in a narrowly conceived analysis of planning.

I feel that when historians review this period, international relations, among other disciplines, will be indicted first—not for having been behavioral, traditional, or eclectic—for a vain effort to act as though the best thing that the theorist and the practitioner could do for each other was to ignore each other. If this book succeeds in its purpose, it will indicate why this effort *is* foolish and what a proper relationship between theory and practice ought to be.

My research for this book began with a few convictions about the proper relationship between theory and practice and what these implied about a soundly conceived planning function. A subject that I could once discuss with great economy and enliven with a few edifying aphorisms now seems complex and intricate—a sad cost of understanding almost any perennial social issue. The attempt to understand these issues has taken me over unusual trials and a wide terrain. If this expanded version makes a more useful and less derivative book, this may compensate for the loss of simplicity and elegance.

One occupational hazard of academic life is reading manuscripts of friends and colleagues. I am especially grateful to the people who read my manuscript, for their comments were extraordinarily helpful in determining whether my argument—right or wrong—was comprehensible and where I needed to clarify it.

Professor Stanley Hoffmann of Harvard University not only invited me to contribute to his series but also managed to survive two readings of the manuscript. If the arguments in this book make sense, much of the credit is his.

My good friend Professor Robert Dallek of the History Department at the University of California at Los Angeles one day asked how my work was going; within the week, he was finding out firsthand. His comments were especially useful because their perspective was from another discipline; in addition, his suggestions on order and style were very helpful.

Three friends read the chapter on theory and practice, which is central to the argument of this book, with great care: Herbert A. Deane of Columbia University, M. M. Goldsmith of the University of Exeter in England, and Robert E. Osgood of the School of Advanced International Studies, Johns Hopkins University. I am grateful for their discussion, advice, and support.

My debts to Professor William T. R. Fox, Director of the Institute of War and Peace Studies at Columbia University, extend back to my years as a graduate student at Columbia. For this study, he not only invited me to spend the year at the Institute, but also commented on my manuscript with his usual discernment. I am especially grateful for the latter task, for it was done during Professor Fox's own year off. Some measure of my gratitude for his intellectual support, his encouragement, and especially his understanding may be gathered from the dedication of this book.

The Institute of War and Peace Studies staff members must be thanked for their aid and good humor. Very special thanks go to Anna Hohri, the Administrative Assistant, who shares the responsibility for making the Institute a pleasant and efficient place in which to work. I should like to thank Linda Wangsness, who typed most of the manuscript with great efficiency and a pleasantly disconcerting sense of its place in the general scheme of things, and also Yvette Herbert, who typed a portion of the manuscript with speed and efficiency.

If it were possible without being read out of the fraternity, I should be glad to attribute all failings of this book to someone else, but they surely could not be blamed on any of the foregoing—this would be a much poorer book without their aid. For the errors, the omissions, and the biases that remain, I accept full responsibility.

ROBERT L. ROTHSTEIN

Contents

On the Behavior of Theorists and the Utility of Theories. On the Behavior of Practitioners and the Limits of Experience and Intuition. Research: "Pure" and "Applied." Theorists and Practitioners—Conflict and Cooperation.

Planning, Prediction, and Policymaking in Foreign Affairs

CHAPTER 1

Introduction

THE NEED FOR PLANNING

Whether planning suffers more from the enthusiasm of its apostles or from the zeal of its detractors is difficult to say. We are told, especially by the growing band of "futurologists," that the only alternative to planning is chaos: without planning to avoid the calamities that await us, we can only stumble into a dreadful future. But we are also told, especially by those who defend the virtues of the "old" politics, that planning must fail: it will, indeed, create chaos by fostering the illusion that we can minimize the significance of random events and predict and control the future.

Which group is right? It would be pleasing if we could answer with some confidence that one is right. The truth is, however, that we can assert no answer—unless we are content with a statement of faith. The two positions refer to different matters. The planning enthusiast foresees problems that cannot be dealt with by traditional methods, but perhaps these problems cannot be solved by planning either. The critic of planning insists that *all* our problems, traditional or revolutionary, must be handled by the careful creation of a political consensus and that we must be satisfied with policies that adjust very slowly to new conditions because we lack the knowledge, the insight, and the power to make planning a viable alternative. The debate is never actually joined, for the possibility of planning does not follow from the need for planning. The missing elements are statements of meaning: What do we mean by planning when we assert that it is imperative—or impossible? What kinds of planning are within our means and what kinds are beyond our means? What can bring our needs and our capabilities closer together?

1

We could reach some conclusions more readily—and more confidently—if we had greater experience with the planning process. To assert that planning, especially in foreign affairs, has failed is impossible, for it has never been tried; by the same token, we cannot assert that it will improve the conduct of foreign affairs. (We need not take too seriously the United States State Department's contention that it devotes an important amount of time and skill to planning, for the activities thus described are permeated by the operator's ethos so that any resemblance to planning is coincidental.) We must therefore stop flailing away with metaphors and slogans and turn the debate, so to speak, on its head: instead of imposing on events and processes an abstract image of what planning is, we must analyze the record of planning and speculate how the record could be improved.

To attack the failures of the past (destructive criticism) is much easier than to affirm the prospects of the future—a strategy that has characterized much recent debate on social issues. In the present case, the difficulty of moving from criticism to advocacy is compounded because we lack experience with planning in foreign affairs; this means that we must begin by seeking analogies with the planning record in other areas and disciplines. And that record hardly encourages excessive optimism. Aaron Wildavsky has recently argued, on the basis of the French experience, that long-range economic planning cannot work, for "no large and complex society can figure out what simple and unambiguous things it wants to do, or in what clear order of priority or how to get them done."[1] In addition, the effort to forecast (or prophesy) contemporary trends and tendencies, an effort integral to improve planning, has been exposed to severe criticism.[2] If planning cannot work in economics, which is so much better supplied with theory and data, and if the effort to improve forecasting is futile, what can justify an attempt to understand what planning may contribute to an area as complex and "undertheorized" as foreign affairs?

We can readily admit that there is a gap between planning as an ideal and planning as social process; the road from theory to practice has been particularly hard to traverse not only in the developing areas but also in developed countries like France and Sweden. But is it reasonable to jump from the failures of comprehensive economic planning to a sweeping

[1] Aaron Wildavsky, "Does Planning Work?" *The Public Interest,* no. 24 (Summer 1971), p. 104; see also Harry G. Johnson, "A Word to the Third World," *Encounter* 37 (October 1971): 3-10.
[2] See, for example, Robert Nisbet, "Has Futurology a Future?" *Encounter* 37 (November 1971):19-28.

assertion that planning cannot work at all? It is reasonable, but only if we are committed to a wider system of beliefs about politics that simply assumes that planning must fail. Failure is then to be expected, and one illustration of it is as good as any other. As we shall see in Chapter 2, the futility of planning is an unexamined premise for two of the belief systems with which we shall deal.

The dangers of assuming the failures of planning or inferring it from the failure of planning in another area would be more evident if we knew precisely what critics mean when they assert that planning cannot work. If they mean that planning cannot succeed if it is judged against some set of unimpeachable criteria—such as the achievement of clearly defined goals within a definite time period—they are surely correct. But *no* social process can survive such criteria; they are too stringent, especially for an eminently practical function like planning, once we recognize the weakness or absence of reliable data and valid social theories and the impossibility of controlling or eliminating all uncertainties. Most critics are singularly reluctant to submit whatever alternative they favor to equally rigorous tests. For example, the only standard of judgment that advocates of incrementalism appear willing to accept is the minimal one that a policy has been agreed upon—no matter what the substance of the policy and no matter who has had (or not had) a voice in negotiating it.

Perhaps the central point is that we cannot understand planning by merely asking whether it will or will not work. Planning is an activity that can encompass various activities and is surely not limited to the creation of centrally determined five-year plans and the like. When we ask can planning work, what we want to know is whether a particular activity, carried out by specific men, has any possibility of reducing the uncertainties of policymaking by illuminating and influencing the alternatives we *now* have in order to reach the kind of future we *now* prefer. The means before the planner to achieve this effect stretch from the creation of comprehensive long-range plans to subtle and intangible efforts to effect what we all think about the significance of the future. What works or does not work cannot be inferred from ideologies or analogies—this is an empirical question that must be analyzed in its own terms. But many obstacles, both ideological and practical, impede the effort to understand planning.

Unfortunately the obstacles have been especially profound in foreign affairs. Neither the policy process nor the foreign affairs bureaucracy has encouraged a serious consideration of long-range problems. Moreover, the practitioner's firm conviction that international events are inherently unpredictable has provided additional support for the belief that planning cannot succeed; events that cannot be foreseen must be dealt with as they arise. But we need to worry about planning *only* in environments in which predictability and control are at a premium. Planning may be relatively easy where the rate of change is slow and the costs of miscalculation are manageable, but it is less than indispensable, for habit and improvisation on perennial themes may suffice. It is, however, irresponsible, or simply stupid, to attempt to deal with a revolutionary environment in this fashion.

To understand where we can go with planning in the future, we must know where we have been with it in the past. Thus we will begin in Chapter 2 by analyzing the processes, the institutions, and the professional beliefs that are primarily responsible for the almost exclusive preoccupation with today's agenda and the inevitably sorry record of planning in foreign affairs. We shall then move from an analysis of the past to what might happen if we define planning so as not to equate it to any single activity. We shall suggest that different planning tasks require different staffs, and we shall suggest specifically which tasks ought to be done by which staff. The problems and prospects for a long-range planning staff, its organization, and its personnel conclude Chapter 2. Then by reference to specific tasks and specific planners, we can define what we mean by the argument that planning can—or cannot—work.[3]

To develop an argument for planning in this country is never easy, for mere mention of planning evokes glazed eyes and frozen smiles. In Washington the reaction might be even worse, except superficial politeness is still regarded as a virtue there. I do not believe that planning is a panacea, the adoption of which will guarantee no more Vietnams, a smaller defense budget, and a perfect relationship between our commitments and our interests. Nor do I believe that an emphasis on planning should replace all other means by which we currently make policy. Whatever the inadequacies of the alternatives to planning, they do incorporate some tested virtues; it would be as irresponsible to ignore them or throw them

[3] I shall attempt to deal with the attack on "futurology" in Chapter 4. I am in general agreement with many criticisms that have been made, for much of the literature is appalling. I also believe, however, that much criticism is uninformed and misleading, for it reflects a misunderstanding of how to interpret the utility of social prediction. To merely argue that random events always destroy the accuracy of long-range predictions, or that one could not predict 1970, for example, from what we know *now* about 1930, is not decisive because the aim of such efforts is not a precise blueprint of the real future but rather the provision of some grounds by which we can make more sensible *present* choices. Those choices will themselves undermine the accuracy of any prediction, but this is not nearly as significant as the fact that predictions are absolutely necessary if we are to be able to take account of the long run in what we do now.

away as it would be to act as if they were perfect alternatives without substantial costs and intrinsic distortions.

To insist on a clear and definitive choice between incompatible alternatives (either planning or some other policymaking system, but not the two together) would undoubtedly satisfy some aesthetic imperative. This position is much fancied by ideologues of both persuasions. Nonetheless, it seems excessively destructive to me. We are not about to discard our policymaking system, whatever its defects, for too many powerful interests, as well as individuals, have a very large stake in its perpetuation (and little faith, needless to say, in alternatives). Also planning is both an inadequate alternative (because of the weakness of the theories and data on which it rests) and an untested one. Therefore, the only feasible alternative must involve a demonstration that planning is not *necessarily* in contradiction with our prevailing policymaking system and may indeed become a useful supplement.

The activities involved in planning are not in fact incompatible with any political system—they are indeed unavoidable for any system that does not develop an excessive infatuation with improvising. I do not imply that the day of the great operator, the fabled hero of the bureaucratic wars, will ever end: no policymaking system, planning included, will eliminate the need to have skilled policymakers deal with the uncertainties of the practical realm. The operator (or practitioner), however, who believes that procedural skills alone are sufficient to his task and that he can choose wisely for the future solely on the lessons of the past, is, to put it bluntly, a fool. Both the academic world and the practical world share the responsibility for allowing the fool to assert, virtually without challenge, that he knows all that he needs to know. For the operator to know more and to be exposed to more varied knowledge requires cooperation with the planner. The planner can increase the probability that long-range considerations will be weighed in the balance when decisions are made and also can attempt to ensure that the alternatives in conflict in the bureaucratic wars have been exposed to intellectual analysis—and not accepted because they are familiar and satisfactory to the most powerful interests. The planner can (and must) supplement the traditional play of power and interest with concern for where we want to go and where our conscience dictates we should be.

We have operated with a system of government, buttressed by prevailing ideologies and academic doctrines, which takes the futility of planning on faith. The point at which planning could challenge this system is still far off. Thus, for the moment, the institutionalization of a planning function within the prevailing system must be understood as a relatively modest and supplementary action. Yet, in the long run, its effect may be considerably less modest. For the new planning staff to function well, even within the present system, would probably require so striking a change of attitude, education, and training for our policymakers that it would constitute a major transformation of how we think about policy-making. How far-reaching this change will be cannot be firmly stated, for it is really an empirical question about a development yet to be implemented. Nevertheless, the idea that a new planning staff may ultimately have a profound impact upon the policymaking system does provide important support for the argument that we must spend time thinking about the proper way to educate and train our future practitioners. Practitioners who understand and appreciate the need to consult with their planners may have to be exposed to more than the anecdotes of their superiors and the accumulation of their own experiences.

PLANNING AND THE EMERGING INTERNATIONAL SYSTEM

We could argue for planning independent of any judgment about the problems that we shall confront in the next decades. That argument clearly gains in force if we believe that the problems of the future cannot be handled by ad hoc improvisations and that some methods associated with planning may be more capable of resolving or clarifying such problems effectively. This alludes, of course, to the notion that the growing interdependence of world politics may require an entirely new approach to problem-solving, and perhaps even an entirely new policy-making system. The significance of interdependence is far from self-evident, for the idea is both old and new, and commonplace and revolutionary. Whether it is an idea whose time has come, or merely another restatement of a persisting myth about the fate of the traditional state system, is an open question. This, I believe, is precisely what should interest us now, for so long as the question is not foreclosed summarily by an a priori doctrinal fiat, we confront real choices about our response to a world in which interdependence is a factor that cannot be ignored.

This issue combines empirical and normative elements in an unusually complex fashion. The significant questions are not "Is sovereignty dead?" and "Is the state viable?" These are rhetorical questions that can be left to the scholastics. Another range of questions is crucial: Do we want to encourage interdependence? What factors can influence this (or the converse)? What institutional reforms and innovations do these developments imply? The significance of interdependence cannot be assessed simply by measuring and evaluating it against the power of traditional concepts; we must think about it in relation to an idea of where we want to go, where we can go, and what we can do to narrow the gap. This is a speculative and thus very dangerous enterprise. It also clearly involves my personal judgments about the relevance of traditional ideas and the potentialities implicit in the idea of interdependence. To the extent that these judgments are accurate or acceptable, the assessment also obviously implies something about the need for an effective long-range planning staff.

In the past, when state sovereignty seemed impermeable, and when traditional issues of security dominated international events, the absence of planning could be borne without apparent difficulty. Moreover, real-politik concentrated attention on short-run shifts in the power balance; the presumably persisting and transcendent goal of security was so intangible and amorphous that long-range plans to achieve it were impossible to specify. Perhaps more critically, the costs of dealing with events by short-run improvisations never seemed very high: state behavior was, by definition, unpredictable, but it nevertheless tended to fall well within a traditional pattern of expectations. Unpredictable events were thus rarely unexpected events, for the *kinds* of things that states decided to undertake were familiar and traditional.

This vision of world politics has been obsolescent for decades. However, the lessons learned from the failures of the 1930s, the United States' emergence from World War II with *its* sovereignty enhanced, and the apparent ease with which the behavior of our enemies in a bipolar world could be predicted (they were, by definition, simply doing the worst) helped obscure the need to reexamine basic premises about world politics. But it is clear by now that doctrines based on the indivisibility of sovereignty and the autonomy and dominance of the traditional issue of national security may be strikingly inappropriate guides to the future.

This argument hardly implies that the security issue is no longer important or that it will disappear without a trace like some antediluvian dinosaur. It is an argument, on one level, that the traditional problems of security may be transformed by technological and attitudinal changes that the old formulas cannot comprehend. Thus, how we have been forced to deal with the revolutionary significance of nuclear weapons is symptomatic; in the midst of continuing hostility, all the nuclear powers have recognized the need to give concrete form to their shared interest in avoiding accidents and miscalculations. And it may be, although it is *very* uncertain, that changed attitudes in some sectors of the population about what the state should or should not be doing may have an equally profound impact on foreign affairs.

7

The argument on another level is that different issues may become as important in international relations as security, narrowly defined. We can see the outlines of this in ideas and trends that seem likely to exert a major influence on what we mean by international relations: the possibility that many foreign policy issues will become increasingly domesticated, or that many domestic issues will become increasingly internationalized, or that new and different styles of foreign policy behavior may develop in response to internal social and economic changes. More is at issue than the simple erosion of the line between domestic and foreign policy (that was, in any case, never very sharply drawn). Entirely new ways of thinking about the stakes of politics and the rules of the game may be necessary. At a minimum, we can assert that an international system characterized by these developments cannot rely on the autonomous decisions of single states to achieve stability; rising levels of interdependence will make the reassertion of traditional doctrines an exercise in futility.[4]

Some traditionalists have argued that the contention that transnational issues may become as important as the security issue is simply another revival of the functionalist myth (or dream). This seems to me a dangerously premature judgment, with little to recommend it beyond the belief that nothing changes much in world politics. I believe that these developments, properly interpreted and controlled, could transform the international system in a beneficent and peaceful fashion. This result is hardly inevitable, for increased interdependence may merely mean increased opportunities for conflict over more issues. But to assert that conflict is inevitable because "states will be states," or that these developments will fade into insignificance once they threaten the preserves of "high politics," may throw away an opportunity to influence the future significantly—and only because we assume that such developments are unimportant. We should think seriously about measures that stand some chance of moving these events in a favorable direction. And we need not predetermine the issue by a response extrapolated from historical events that may not be relevant or compelling. It is not necessary to worship our aphorisms—especially *plus ça change, plus c'est la même chose*—with such passion that they become fetishes.

No definitive statement about the significance of interdependence can

[4] For important comments on interdependence, see Oran Young, "Interdependencies in World Politics," *The International Journal,* Vol. 24 (Autumn 1969); Edward Morse, "The Politics of Interdependence," *International Organization,* Vol. 23 (Spring 1969); and especially "Transnational Relations and World Politics," Robert O. Keohane and Joseph S. Nye, Jr., eds, *International Organization,* Vol. 25 (Summer 1971).

be made this early, for serious research into these matters has just begun. The most that can safely be asserted is that these developments will increasingly alter the choices statesmen must make and the costs of the alternatives they are willing to contemplate.[5] One crucial variable is how statesmen perceive and interpret the need to make decisions on matters of interdependence.

This issue has usually been summarized by students of interdependence as the inadequacy of the traditional state-centered view of international relations to deal with a world in which transnational phenomena are increasingly important. Although generally true, this argument requires some amplification. What is missing is not only some indication of the distortions imposed by the state-centered view but also some explanation of why this view has remained so attractive to several generations of practitioners. With comments on Political Realism in Chapter 2, the classic state-centered doctrine, we will attempt to fill some of these gaps. The immediate danger is that the failure to alter the traditional formulas by which statesmen are accustomed to interpret world affairs will guarantee that more interdependence will be equivalent to more conflict—a Pyrrhic victory for the wisdom of the past, for which the rest of us will pay the price. Indeed, it may be true that the only way in which transnational developments will exert a beneficial effect and will not simply provide new occasions for conflict is if we (especially our practitioners) jettison some of our most enduring "eternal verities" about international politics.

Issues of security and "high politics" may be even more interdependent than economic, social, and cultural issues. Both technical and political considerations have made autonomous decisions on innovation in strategic weapons development, the control of nuclear proliferation, the arms trade, and alliance policies increasingly futile. Traditional formulas no longer work well even on traditional issues; that the same general questions *seem* to remain relevant has obscured the unique and untraditional answers we are getting.

The connection between the realm of security and the realm dominated by transnational interactions is more significant than many analysts of interdependence seem willing to admit. So long as the state is run by men armed only with traditional perceptions of state behavior, and so long as the state itself is powerful enough to attempt to use transnational developments only in pursuit of its own security interests—which is to say, the Super Powers and a few Great Powers for years to come--it is the state of the security issue that is likely to determine the state of trans-

[5] See also Joseph S. Nye, Jr., and Robert O. Keohane, "Transnational Relations and World Politics: A Conclusion," in *ibid.*, pp. 724-725.

national issues. Transnational phenomena are not completely autonomous; they may be directed toward cooperative and peaceful ends only when the issues of "high politics" are in a détente, or when statesmen learn to ask different questions about them.

Whatever hope we have of controlling and influencing these developments depends on a serious commitment to long-range planning. The policymaking system will come under increasing pressure to make decisions on both traditional and nontraditional issues for which there are no familiar or simple choices. It is futile and irresponsible to wait until these issues have become so salient that everyone recognizes that something must be done, because by this time everything that can be done is inadequate. Moreover, any attempt to act unilaterally will either fail or, where we have the power to make the attempt feasible, will create so much bitterness and conflict in the rest of the system that we will exchange a few short-range benefits for some unappealing long-range costs. These considerations make an analysis of the factors that inhibit long-range planning imperative.

What can the planner do? He can challenge the relevance of traditional formulas and both research and analyze the directions in which we seem to be traveling and the alternatives we confront. This will surely require new planning at the national level and may also require an even more difficult venture into cooperative planning with other states and organizations. The first step is the creation of a national planning unit that has the intellectual power, the technical skills, and the political support necessary to deal seriously with long-range planning issues.

The necessity of planning hardly guarantees that it will be attempted or succeed. Yet only states with huge margins, or superfluous resources, or a benign faith in a safe future can sit back and take the future as it comes. For the rest—which, of course, means *all* states now—some planning, some attempt to understand and influence *as much as we can* of where we are going, is imperative.

THEORY AND PRACTICE
AND THE POSSIBILITY OF PLANNING

Planning has great practical significance: done well, it provides the criteria by which we work our way through present choices. Also, planning is the primary arena of cooperation between theorists and practitioners within a common social discipline. This means that the failures of planning cannot be attributed solely to the imperfections of practitioners and the practical world. Some responsibility must fall on those social theorists who believe that any professional involvement with practical matters is intrinsically wrong and must be avoided. Since planning is an intellectual exercise—directed at very practical ends—which cannot be carried out in isolation from the analytical skills of the theoretical realm, the attempt to isolate theorists from practitioners dooms planning. The few practical men who might be inclined to plan lack the tools to do it well, and the few theoretical men who might be so inclined lack either the opportunity or the incentive.

Why is it, in a policy-oriented discipline like international relations, that theorists justify an indifference to the practitioners' concerns? And why is it that the practitioner who presumably should welcome all the help he can get is perfectly willing to be ignored by the theorist? We shall attempt to answer these questions in Chapter 3. To do so we must move to an entirely different level of analysis, from the familiar categories of the policymaking process and bureaucracy to some very unfamiliar interpretations of how theorists and practitioners in any social discipline (but particularly foreign affairs) determine what constitutes proper professional behavior.

The way in which these questions are answered has a double effect. First, the answers determine what theorists and practitioners are meant to be doing: the problems they choose to work on, the questions they feel it is important to ask about them, and the answers they are willing to accept. Second, once we understand the nature of theoretical and practical activity, we should be able to understand the areas in which theorists and practitioners can cooperate and the areas in which cooperation is illegitimate or impossible. Inevitably there is some ambiguity about these issues, especially in the social sciences, for the creation of new theories (or new epistemological standards) and the emergence of different practical problems may radically change the context of the discussion. Nevertheless, so long as we can draw a picture of the relationship that is generally valid for a historical period—in our case, the years since World War II—we can understand something that the analysis in Chapter 2 could not tell us: *why* theorists and practitioners have established the priorities they have, and *why* they have made no serious effort to challenge the obstacles to planning in foreign affairs.

What theorists and practitioners do determines *how* theorists and practitioners can cooperate, and how they can cooperate heavily conditions the form that the planning function can legitimately assume. This does not completely determine the fate of planning, for obviously some forms of planning can go on without any cooperation between the two realms. However, a successful long-range planning staff, which must combine the ability to use the most advanced intellectual and technical skills with a concern for the problems of the practitioner, is inconceivable without a sound and carefully articulated relationship between theorists and practitioners. This constitutes the direct connection between the arguments in Chapter 2 and Chapter 3, for the attempt to understand where the boundaries between the two worlds must be set and why they can be ignored only at great cost has important implications for the fate of long-range planning.

Our general thesis deserves to be reemphasized. The obstacles discussed in Chapter 2 are only part of the reason for the failures of planning. The more profound reason, which explains why the obstacles appear natural, and why any challenge to them appears unrealistic, resides in the nature of fundamental beliefs about proper professional behavior for both theorists and practitioners. So long as planning requires cooperation between the two realms, and so long as that cooperation is impeded by professional beliefs that justify ignoring each other's concerns, the function of planning will be ignored or trivialized. We shall illustrate this argument in Chapter 3 and suggest a redefinition of professional beliefs that will facilitate cooperation—and thus planning.

There have been many attempts to reform the policymaking system in foreign affairs. They have failed because they have concentrated too exclusively on institutional reforms or adaptations, and have not made a sufficiently serious attempt to change the beliefs and training of the men who must operate the institutions. This provides another perspective on the relationship between Chapters 2 and 3. The creation of a long-range planning staff may *begin* the process of reforming the policymaking system by introducing into it men with unique skills and a special commitment to worry about the long-range consequences of present actions. Over the longer run, however, this planning staff is bound to fail—or to be transformed into another action staff—unless we also change the professional beliefs of both theorists and practitioners that have undermined all efforts to work together. Chapter 3 analyzes these beliefs and suggests changes that might make cooperation more useful and less threatening.

THE ACADEMIC WORLD AND THE PRACTICAL WORLD

The discussion of theory and practice in Chapter 3 illuminates more than the issue of planning, for it bears on everything that theorists and practitioners do, and therefore on all the ways in which they interact (that is, not only planning but also in advice-giving, or reading each other's books, or exchanging jobs). In effect, Chapter 3 is an essay not only on planning in particular but also on the relationship between knowledge and knowledgeable men and the government. This issue has been dominated by a few conventional stereotypes that are simplistic and misleading, and thus subject—as we are all painfully aware—to manipulation by cynical (or foolish) practitioners and overly ambitious professors.

No one can ponder the record of the last three administrations without feeling a little sick about the role that some of its illustrious academic figures have played. An impressive indictment could be drawn up: blatant lying, histories written to ensure entrée into the next adminstration or to subvert the truth for political purposes, self-interested editing of the "classified" documents one chooses to reveal, excessive enthusiasm for simple-minded theories, instant moralizing and rhetorical posturing against policies that were supported without noticeable strain when it assured one of a "piece of the action." The academic contribution to the period that the late Richard Hofstadter called "the age of rubbish" has not been insignificant.

The recent publication of the Pentagon Papers succeeds only in adding substance to these charges. To discover academic figures conniving at the murder of the Diem brothers, and to find the President's National Security Adviser congratulating the press secretary for skillfully obscuring the truth, is only part of the story. Perhaps more pathetic—and dangerous—is the discovery of a poverty of imagination within the upper reaches of the foreign affairs bureaucracy that transcends any error of omission or commission. We witness men so locked into a set of doctrinal propositions about the nature of international politics and foreign policy that they cannot foresee alternatives to actions that they *know* are doomed to failure. A new political principle seems to govern all choices: the necessary persistence in stupidity.

Some of these errors we can attribute to continued commitment to the metaphysical speculations of Political Realism, a doctrine that has always been especially attractive to practitioners. For example, Realism's presumption that foreign policy is a superior realm understood only by a self-chosen elite of professionals, and its ensuing contempt for the inelegant way in which democracies conduct their foreign policies, leads easily enough to the conviction that lying to the public or obscuring the truth—in the national interest, of course—is justified and necessary. And its exclusive concentration on shifts in the power balance has tended to justify indifference toward the substance of an issue: what has mattered always has been how the issue might affect "the struggle of the giants," and not its intrinsic merits. In fact, detailed knowledge has always seemed unimportant or irrelevant, for the generalist could operate better without it—the virtues of ignorance. Other errors, especially the inability to think of alternatives to marginal adjustments of ongoing policies, we can attribute to the intrinsic weaknesses of a policymaking system whose only standard of judgment has been the ability to create a policy consensus—irrespective of the quality and substance of the policy. We shall discuss these issues in greater detail in Chapter 2. We should emphasize here the degree to which both Realism and the policymaking system ignored the long-run and defined "expertise" in a manner sufficiently narrow to exclude outside doubters and dissenters.

Opportunities to repeat the experiences of the 1960s will reappear. And the results will be equally disastrous unless we establish a clearer sense of what the academic can and cannot do for the government, and unless we begin to alter our policymaking system so that it is willing and able to take substantive and long-range considerations into account. To do so will obviously require active cooperation between the academic world, which has the time and the knowledge, and the government, which has the responsibility to act. Perhaps one of the worst aspects, from this point of view, of the effects rendered by academics like Rostow is that they have made that cooperation most suspect and most difficult just when it may be becoming most necessary. If there is a saving grace in this situation, it is that the cooperation the sometime academics of the Kennedy and Johnson administrations fostered reflects a major misunderstanding of the proper relationship between the two realms; perhaps exposure of the futility of the academic as the practitioner presents us with the opportunity to begin to understand that relationship in a more useful fashion.

Contemplation of the sad record of the last decade has created much sympathy for the argument that contact between the academic and the practical world ought to be proscribed for the general good. This notion has attracted strange bedfellows—radicals who believe that any involvement with the government is evil by definition, behavioralists who believe that the discipline of political science can prosper only by turning away from the practical world, and the practitioners themselves who fear that their role will be usurped and their skills ignored if the academic invades the practical realm. These oversimplified responses to complex issues may be the leitmotif of "the age of rubbish," but they are likely to become increasingly fashionable unless they can be refuted by a meaningful alternative.

The contention that the academic world ought to go back to cultivating its own garden, or that it ought, as one sociologist has recently argued, to return to collecting knowledge for its own sake, is misleading and mischievous. (It may also advocate a return to a past that never existed.) These arguments mistake the nature of the disciplines that deal with the political and social world. Concern for policy problems and a desire to get directly involved in efforts to solve them are inevitable, especially in heavily policy-oriented disciplines. Few social theorists are likely to be immune to the desire to see their knowledge translated into policy positions and their expertise called upon to solve critical problems. Moreover, the knowledge that such disciplines create is frequently too relevant and too accessible to practitioners to be left to mature at its own pace. What this means is that the effort to separate the discipline—and its knowledge—from the practical realm is an artificial solution with little chance of success. Nor is it absolutely clear that the separation would be wise if it could be achieved: what is good or bad here depends on the terms of collaboration between the two realms, not on idealized notions of what the academic world was once like. The attempt to establish a rationale for isolation is understandable but misconceived; the abuse of the relationship in the past does not mean that we can (or should) dissolve it, but that we need to establish grounds for legitimate collaboration.

A significant number of academics have worked for the last three administrations. Besides the economists, they have been the familiar "in-and-outers" merchandising policy opinion rather than knowledge or skills that could be honestly described as theoretical. Their intellectual commitment has rarely been to the academic discipline, that is, to the quest for theory and the construction of a particular body of knowledge. Offering advice and opinion on policy matters *is* a legitimate role, and there is no reason to argue that an academic title disqualifies one from playing it. It is, however, a role that falls within the practitioner's realm. Performance must be judged by standards appropriate to that realm; the performer's last mailing address within a university is of limited significance, for he is doing something that could be done equally well, or badly, by a lawyer or a journalist.

We shall be interested in these academic advisers only insofar as they misuse their previous status and make false claims, or harbor false illusions, about the knowledge they possess and the ways in which it can be used. We shall be on guard against those who are prone to describe the latest intellectual styles as "theories"—for example, the theory of counterinsurgency, or the theory of simple stages of economic development. Our focus will be the contribution that academics can make *in their professional capacity* to the solution of practical problems. This role is *always* distinct from that of the practitioner, but need not be completely antipathetical; some skills may be shared and some patterns of thought may be similar.

The in-and-outers would be more interesting to us if they coherently and consciously attempted to combine the roles of the theorist and the policy adviser. They have not done so, for they share, virtually in toto, the prejudices of the practitioner about the proper relationship between theory and practice. Most in-and-outers have been practitioners cloaking their actions in an academic disguise.[6] It is doubtful that many in-and-outers possess a different kind of knowledge they could pass on to the practitioner; they are merely different faces, momentarily located elsewhere—and waiting, sometimes desperately, to be recalled. Confusion about the criteria by which the performance of these men should be judged is responsible for some misunderstanding about the role of academics in government. They shall be judged here as practitioners—no more, no less—until they bring to that practical role something from the academic world beyond a professorial title.

Some radical critics have insisted that our only hope of reform lies in replacing our "national security managers." The revelations in the Pentagon Papers and elsewhere help to explain the sympathy and understanding this argument engenders—it is a sign of how far we have traveled in recent years that it could be made at all and that it could elicit serious discussion. However, our national security managers—as a class—are not about to raise our unemployment figure; the skill that some highly discredited "managers" have displayed by remaining in positions of status and influence is impressive. The radical critics, insofar as they are serious about their own suggestion, also fail to make clear who will replace the national security managers. The answer is not self-evident, for one can be sympathetic to the attack on the national security managers without believing that a government run by the radical critics would be an improvement. Nevertheless, one would prefer something more profound than a statement of faith in the virtues of decentralization.

The most we can expect, I believe, is that the disasters of the past decade will induce willingness not simply to denounce anyone who has been involved with the government but to think seriously about who our

[6] In effect, the "outers" are never sufficiently "out" not only because they rarely possess different skills from the "inners" (not even the skill to serve effectively as a bridge between the two realms), but also because most of them have been on constant call with the government. For example, Rostow stated several years ago that there had not been a single year since World War II in which he had not done some work for the government. The quality of that work should disturb us most, but it also indicates the degree to which the "outers" were "inners" in disguise.

national security managers ought to be, what they ought to be doing, and how they ought to be trained. Seeking answers to these questions is less romantic, no doubt, than asserting that only revolutionary solutions will work; but it may also lead to concrete reforms that are far more meaningful than calls for extreme action that have no possibility of implementation.

My disagreement with the radical position may be more easily understood as a disagreement about the need for expertise and professionalism in government. Criticism of the performance of our national security bureaucracy—as well as their apologists in the university and the media— is necessary but not sufficient. It would be sufficient if we could believe, as some radical critics apparently do, that replacements for the national security managers will arise by some mysterious process within the system, and that they will be capable of performing more effectively than their predecessors.

I doubt both propositions. People without a vocational commitment to politics are not apt to develop a sustained willingness to serve in government. I do not know how people from other walks of life would perform as government bureaucrats, but I doubt that they would be willing to make the effort except under unusual circumstances, at which time we are likely to be in the midst of a disaster that no one can undo.

Even if outsiders were willing to join the bureaucracy, on what grounds could we argue that they will perform well? Surely common sense, a dubious virtue in the face of extremely complex problems, will not suffice—unless one believes that all political problems are simple and uncomplicated. Some issues can be decided as wisely, perhaps even more wisely, by an intelligent citizen as by an expert. Problems we have faced in the past, and an even greater proportion of the problems we shall encounter in the future, will, however, require trained and expert intelligences to deal with them effectively and in time. This is a somewhat unfashionable judgment these days, because the expert is in bad repute for understandable reasons, and the desire to "farm out" even complex problems to local decision-making bodies is widespread. However, too many problems must be dealt with (at least in the sense of setting the range of alternatives) by experts and, in any case, the interest of the nonexpert is too episodic to be useful. Thus, we have no choice but to worry about how we ought to train our experts, and what relationship there ought to be between their knowledge and political actions that affect all of us.

The dangers of expert judgment—especially its narrowness, its tendency to emphasize means, and its insulation from outside control—are additional reasons to emphasize that a long-range planning staff must be only a part, although a critical part that we have neglected, of the decision-making process. We need to use experts, but we also need to take precautions so that we are not abused by them. I have attempted to take account of this danger not only by stipulating that the planner can ask only for a share of the responsibility but also by arguing (in Chapter 2) for a staff with as many windows to the outside world as is feasible. For the rest, we can only hope for competition among expert views, and for a corps of experts who have been trained to understand their obligations to both the practical realm and the theoretical realm. This last consideration makes an analysis of the professional belief systems of the theorist imperative.

The major part of the argument in Chapter 3 must be critical rather than constructive. Criticism of the terms by which theorists and practitioners currently describe and interpret their relationship is absolutely imperative, for there is no way to make a convincing argument for a new approach without first undermining faith in prevailing interpretations. This is particularly true in the present case, for very few theorists and practitioners believe that their relationship can be—or needs to be—improved. It is, however, extremely difficult, without dissimulating, to move from criticism to the advocacy of specific measures that would guarantee useful collaboration. There has been so little cooperation that we have scant evidence for asserting that cooperation is or is not likely to be useful.

Thus, a beneficial relationship must be worked out once both groups begin to understand that collaboration need not be a waste of time. There is no right (or wrong) relationship that always holds. If there were, we could attribute the failure to cooperate to perversity or stupidity. As it is, we hope to clear the ground of false interpretations in order to plead for meaningful and realistic experimentation and innovation. Establishing the conviction that cooperation might be productive is our first task; filling in the details must be left to the future. We will, however, comment on a few untried ventures that appear especially promising to begin experimentation—primarily because of their record in other fields.

PREDICTION IN FOREIGN AFFAIRS

We will attempt to illustrate in Chapter 4 some points in Chapter 3 by analyzing the problem of prediction in foreign affairs. This is one of the areas in which collaboration between theorists and practitioners is most likely to be fruitful. The attempt to predict the consequences of current actions or to forecast the directions in which we may be heading are intrinsic to successful policymaking and sensible planning. Moreover, prediction is a practical necessity that is done best when it rests on sound theoretical principles or at least uses the best knowledge and methods that the theoretical world can offer. In our analysis of the problem, we will attempt not to predict but to illustrate what the social theorist might perform for the social practitioner. We shall concentrate on what can be predicted, what methods are available, and what limits and weaknesses are intrinsic to the task. We shall be aiming at a primer for the practitioner, so that he can understand the kinds of studies he ought to commission, the results he should expect, and the limits that neither he nor his researcher can transcend. The successful use of knowledge in the social world must rest on an initial understanding of the limits of knowledge as guide to practical activity.

THE ATTRACTIVENESS OF GOVERNMENT SERVICE

The number of students interested in pursuing a government career has declined rather sharply in recent years. For example, the Dean of the School of International Affairs at Columbia University has said that the percentage of graduates joining the government has declined from 32 per cent to 14 per cent. There is also indication of a corresponding drop in the quality of graduates seeking a career in the government. This is understandable when we evaluate the government's performance in the last decade, and is also potentially disastrous. The possibility of improving the government's performance is nil if the quality of the people who are willing to work for it continues to decline.

The academic world is severely limited in its ability to alter the external conditions primarily responsible for the decline in the quality of people working for the government. It is arguable, however, that disenchantment with public service is due not only to the sad performance of various academics in official roles but also to the way in which the discipline has felt it ought to educate future practitioners. This issue has been lost to sight in the ferment over the nature of graduate and undergraduate education. The education of future practitioners is of great practical significance over the long run and is an issue that the academic community has the decisive power to affect.

We shall return to this subject in the Conclusions. If we can establish an interpretation of the relationship between theorists and practitioners that rests on something more than mutual contempt, then the determination of what each group thinks is useful should alter. If this change occurs, it will significantly affect the way in which we educate practitioners. In brief, courses that concentrate on instilling a sense of the meaning and uses of theory may come to share equal billing with policy courses or courses designed to facilitate survival in the bureaucratic wars. Teaching future practitioners how to think about their realm may seem as important as trying to teach them what to think about the latest crisis. Changing the education of future practitioners will affect not only the kind of people who will find government service attractive, but also the attitudes and knowledge that they carry with them; presumably government service will look more enticing to our best students if it no longer seems contemptuous of all intellectual values.

Reorienting the educational process for future practitioners may not seem glamorous or exciting, nor is it likely to make the front page of *The New York Times*—all of which is important when many doubt that there will be a long range worth worrying about. Nevertheless, the academic world must be satisfied with what it can do, not with what it dreams of doing. We cannot all be advisers to the prince, nor does the record indicate we should be. Still, determining who our leaders will be, and what they will know and take for granted, only seems to be a more humble task than whispering in the ear of the men in power.

CHAPTER 2

Policy Planning in Foreign Affairs

INTRODUCTION

With so many obstacles to planning in foreign policy, it is a wonder that any of it gets done. In fact, the obstacles are so strong and so pervasive that it has become a mark of sophistication in Washington to understand that planners are influential only to the extent that they do not plan—that they get a piece of the action, so to speak, on the sly. And yet, the alternative to planning is a rather naïve faith in a world dominated by events that are both unpredictable and manageable.

The foremost obstacle to serious planning is the policymaking process itself, not only in its institutional aspects but also in the attitudes and beliefs that have grown up around it. The State Department and the Foreign Service constitute another major obstacle to planning. The State Department has some similarities with other large organizations, but it also differs from other organizations, public or private. And the Foreign Service, which is primarily responsible for setting the style and character of the State Department, is a rather unusual professional group. Taken together, the State Department and the Foreign Service have impeded any effort to treat the planning function seriously.

Attitudes toward planning in foreign affairs are not autonomous; they are part of a wider intellectual frame of reference encompassing prevailing beliefs about the nature of foreign policy and international affairs. These beliefs are implicit to some extent in notions of the proper way to make foreign policy and to run the State Department. Any system of beliefs is also, however, separate from attempts to incorporate it in particular programs or institutions. We must try to understand these beliefs, for they provide both general guidance and psychological security for those who accept their legitimacy. In the next two sections of this chapter, we will discuss the policymaking process and the State Department as a bureaucracy. We will discuss in succeeding sections various aspects of planning in foreign affairs, including an extensive comment on the way in which the Policy Planning Council functioned and the prevailing beliefs of many of its members. We shall conclude with proposals for a new long-range planning staff.

This analysis has been written in a time of great ferment within the foreign policy establishment. The policies, the assumptions on which they are based, and the institutions that create and implement them are all under sharp attack. This essay is inevitably part of that attack, but only in a limited fashion. The failures of planning in the past, and the potential utility of planning in (and for) the future, provide an important perspective on all the issues that are currently being debated. It is not a complete perspective, for there are problems and dilemmas in foreign policy that are only indirectly related to what planning staffs can or cannot do. The analysis of the policymaking process and the State Department in the next two sections is narrowly focused, for it is our prime purpose to understand planning, and other issues, in this context, only secondarily. These qualifications are not designed to undermine the relevance of the comments that follow, but rather to stress that they form only one part of a wider picture.

THE POLICYMAKING PROCESS IN FOREIGN AFFAIRS

The virtues of pluralism are no longer in fashion. A policymaking system that was once praised for creating a consensus, if only around an inevitably imperfect policy, now finds itself condemned for sacrificing content for the mere sake of procedural agreement. When consensus is wide and policies appear to be successful, the process of extracting agreement appears virtually miraculous, or at least an illustration of what politics is all about. When consensus is destroyed by persistent failure, the process that can no longer produce it appears ludicrous and acceptable only to the hack politician who wants only what he can get, and does not try to get what he wants (or ought to want).

The standard interpretation of the way in which noncrisis foreign policy decisions have been made emerged in the 1950s. It begins with the contention that power is diffused within the system between a large number of autonomous and competing groups. The process is essentially insulated from public opinion, since the opinion of the mass on foreign policy issues is apathetic, disinterested, and decidedly unprofound. In fact, the *direct* impact of mass opinion is felt only when one group or another feels that it is about to lose on a crucial decision and leaks inside information in an effort to redress the balance, or when the elite is so divided over ends and means that it cannot isolate outside opinion as irrelevant or uninformed. And, of course, a long-term disaster, in which costs begin to pile up in the form of casualty lists or increased taxes, may also force the mass out of its apathy. But most probably the short-term outcome is increased (and virtually primitive) support for the government in power and increased hatred for dissenters.[1]

Normally, however, the intense struggle between the various elite groups goes on far from public view; what the public, and frequently Congress, get to see is the final product of a series of bureaucratic bargains. Conflict is intense but restrained, for like the Great Powers in the classical balance of power systems, the competitors strive for gains against each other, but do not attempt to destroy each other. A systemic interest or a "strain toward agreement" keeps the conflict from getting out of hand. In addition, today's enemy may be tomorrow's ally, an observation that induces a degree of prudence from all concerned.

The test of the process is the policies it produces. The package deals that normally emerge are so difficult to negotiate, because there are so many interests to satisfy, that procedural agreement tends to become the criterion of acceptable policy: what is good is measured by what is acceptable to the players. Agreement is easiest on policies that vary only slightly from existing policies. The system is thus characterized by, in what has virtually become a cliché of analysis, incremental and marginal adjustments. Moreover, the difficulty of reaching agreement, and the dangers of unraveling it, create a situation in which many issues are not faced (until a consensus emerges via an "invisible hand," or until a crisis compels a decision), in which policies persist simply because renegotiating them would be costly, in which leadership is nonexistent and responsibility indeterminate, and in which "policy" may be nothing more than a bland statement incorporating all views—consistent or not—until "the dust settles."[2]

[1] On this issue, see Robert L. Rothstein, "Domestic Politics and Peacemaking," *The Annals* 392 (November 1970): 62-75. One critical factor in this situation is the length of the crisis: if it persists, the tendency of the mass to turn to the administration and against dissenters may slowly alter. In this situation dissenting elites have a possibility of imposing their views or having them commandeered (which is more likely).

[2] The classic analysis and defense of this position can be found in the works of Charles E. Lindblom. See the first part of David Braybrooke and Charles E. Lind-

The redeeming virtue of a system so riddled with vices is (or was) simply that it produced policies that were at least minimally satisfactory to all the competitors. It is tempting to deride an emphasis on creating consensus, with all its pluralist undertones, but it is significant that a system with so many competing centers of power does have great potential for both stalemate and chaos. The tendency to take what worked yesterday as a guide for today also presumably lessened the chances of error—biases and misperceptions, other things being equal, cancelled each other out. This is not to be treated lightly in an area dominated by uncertainty, risk, and imperfect knowledge. Producing acceptable policies, whatever the attendant imperfections, is frequently preferable to the quest for perfect policies or a prolonged struggle over parochial policies.

Short of discovering a perfect system, commitment to any policy-making system has some "opportunity costs" attached to it. Many criticisms directed at the incremental model are beside the point, for they are directed at evils that are unfortunate but inescapable costs of extracting agreement. No system that has so many centers of power and lacks central direction or an overall plan can run entirely without frictions. Other criticisms, however, are directed not so much at the deficiencies of the process but at its underlying assumptions, and these criticisms have become increasingly cogent as the environment (both domestic and international) of policymaking has been transformed.

Marginal change is acceptable only to the extent that existing policies yield satisfactory results.[3] If there is sharp disagreement or dissent about prevailing policies, a system that can only alter them in minor ways is bound to be attacked. Agreement on policy is usually widest when the problem being negotiated closely resembles other problems and has a

---

blom, *A Strategy of Decision: Policy Evaluation as a Social Process* (New York: The Free Press, 1963). Perhaps the finest case study in this tradition is Warner R. Schilling's analysis of the 1950 defense budget in Warner R. Schilling, Paul Y. Hammond, and Glenn H. Snyder, *Strategy, Politics, and Defense Budgets* (New York: Columbia University Press, 1962). This study clearly indicates all defects intrinsic to this policymaking system, but also emphasizes the greater defects of any likely alternative.

[3] Do many incremental changes add up to substantial change? In the past, a gradualist faith—akin to believing in the "invisible hand" or in the idea of progress—took this possibility for granted. The question is complex and empirical and not metaphysical. One key question is: In what environment must incrementalism function? Clearly, substantial change via an accumulation of small changes is most likely in stable periods. Substantial change is not certain even then, however, for one suspects that the lack of central direction in the system makes it difficult to sustain enough consistent small changes to produce a large result.

long history of successful compromises behind it. When new problems emerge, or when the political community begins to question its goals—which previously emerged within the process, and not as a guide to it—incrementalism has no way of providing any answers except the old one. On what can we get agreement? The possibility of finessing disagreement by buying off malcontents exists only so long as resources are very plentiful and the malcontents are not ideologues unwilling to be bought off.[4]

In short, incrementalism was and is an adequate approach to policy-making only in periods of great stability, which is to say when there is wide consensus on nonideological goals, continuity in problems, and plenty of money to paper over the cracks. In unstable times, the lack of leadership of incrementalism in the face of new problems leads to drift and inertia, and its reluctance to contemplate the long run ensures that problems will be dealt with only when they become crises. And the President, or whoever wants to try something unprecedented, can do so only by exaggerating the threats and overselling the remedies.[5] It is a system of policymaking that has always lived on borrowed time, on the faith that today's compromise can somehow avert tomorrow's crisis. And like other faiths, it confronts secular challenges that strain its power to respond.

Crisis decisions are obviously not made in an incremental fashion. But are we to presume that all other foreign policy decisions are incremental? In domestic politics, the apparent pervasiveness of incremental decisions is taken for granted. This reflects the fact that most domestic issues have a long history of precedents and, in addition, must be steered through the appropriations process at one point or another. These factors rein-force the tendency to make limited and marginal decisions, for the battle lines have already hardened, the range of expected, tangible reward is set, the time period is known, and the possibility of agreement is facilitated by the ease of measuring and comparing costs. Yet it should be noted that fundamental decisions have been made from time to time on both new and old problems, when they are salient but not in a state of mani-

[4] For criticisms of incrementalism, see Yehezkel Dror, "Muddling through—Science or Inertia?" *Public Administration Review* 24 (September 1964): 153-157; Amitai Etzioni, "Mixed-Scanning: A 'Third' Approach to Decision-Making," *Public Administration Review* 27 (December 1967): 385-392; Theodore J. Lowi, *The End of Liberalism: Ideology, Policy and the Crisis of Public Authority* (New York: W. W. Norton, 1968). For criticisms with special reference to foreign policy, see Stanley Hoffmann, *Gulliver's Troubles, Or the Setting of American Foreign Policy* (New York: McGraw-Hill, 1968), especially p. 293 ff.

[5] On the President's difficulties, see Lowi, *The End of Liberalism,* p. 182 ff.

fest crisis, and constitute more than a marginal adjustment of the last decision. In some cases, these may simply be the result of a change in the political climate, an accumulation of perceptions that a new departure is both legitimate and necessary. The early civil rights decisions and the current effort to control pollution may be cases in point. The original decision may be altered and adjusted incrementally, but it remains true that it was of fundamental significance.[6] Nonetheless, fundamental decisions and crisis decisions have hardly been frequent; in a descriptive sense, it does not appear that the distortions implicit in the presumption that normal politics involved marginal adjustments of ongoing policies were excessive.[7] But this says nothing about whether we had to be, or ought to have been, satisfied with what we settled for.

Is incrementalism equally pervasive in foreign policy? Domestic policy and foreign policy have usually been treated as separate realms. As an analytical convenience this may be justified. It is, however, and probably always has been, even in the heyday of "cabinet diplomacy," somewhat arbitrary, since foreign policy can never be wholly autonomous. Foreign policy institutions are enmeshed in the domestic political system. Appropriations and support must be sought from Congress, public opinion has to be pacified, the other bureaucracies conciliated, and programs and policies constructed and presented according to how the system functions. The distinction then between foreign and domestic policies is a matter of degree. For other countries, this generalization might have to be qualified. It is clear that foreign policy can become an autonomous dimension for Small Powers forced to seek security in the face of a direct Great Power threat or for Great Powers who feel fundamentally insecure about the possibility of maintaining their own status. But neither of these cases is relevant to our concerns.

The notion that foreign policy is the superior realm of politics owes more to the continued dominance of slogans like the *primat der Aussenpolitik* or to an ideologically derived perception of a monolithic external threat than it does to any examination of how the American system normally functions. This should not be interpreted as an argument that foreign policy and domestic policy are to be treated alike. There are

[6] Etzioni, "Mixed-Scanning," stresses the notion that an incremental system needs (and has) fundamental decisions that give direction to its incremental decisions.
[7] Even fundamental decisions could rapidly become normalized if the programs by which they were to be implemented were difficult to devise or, once devised, got locked in the bureaucracy. Thus, the decision to make a major attack on the problems of pollution has been stalled not only by the pressures of outside interest groups and the internal struggles within the bureaucracy but also by disagreements about what can and should be done now and at whose cost.

degrees of difference that prevail on many issues. Usually public opinion has a smaller direct impact on foreign policy decisions, and the Executive and the policy elites tend to have greater freedom than they normally have in domestic politics. The significance of these differences, however, in establishing a sharp dichotomy between domestic and foreign policy, has frequently been overestimated.

What is usually overlooked is that public apathy on foreign policy issues, and the greater degree of executive freedom that this permits, are directly related to the wide consensus on foreign policy goals and the ability of different administrations (until Vietnam) to keep the felt costs of foreign policy quite small. Thus, there are two points to keep in mind. First, whatever differences there are between foreign and domestic policy are not intrinsic but are related to the salience of particular foreign policy issues. Foreign policy has *seemed* different, but only because the prevailing consensus has muted the conflict between different groups or displaced it to the corridors of the executive bureaucracy. Second, even when the procedural differences that appear to distinguish many foreign policy issues—Executive dominance, fewer pressure group demands, and an apathetic public—do appear, they have not, in general, led to different *kinds* of policies. For example, the effect of Executive dominance has been diluted by internal bureaucratic conflicts that have ensured that the resulting policies will still reflect compromises among different interest groups. Such policies also tend to differ only marginally from case to case. The locale may alter and the players may change, but the rules are the same and the results are very similar.

Perhaps this overlooks an important dimension of foreign policy: the degree to which foreign policy is affected by its direction toward an environment in which predictability and control are difficult to achieve. As a result, statesmen would be compelled to be especially prudent and reluctant to take the risk of initiating action. There is some truth to this, particularly in revolutionary periods, but it does not invalidate the notion that foreign policy is similar in many ways to domestic policy. The insecurity and uncertainty of decision-making in the external world merely reinforces the tendency to make minimal decisions and to keep the boat from rocking.[8] In any case, the number of occasions in which a

[8] One could phrase this point according to the differences between knowing the system in domestic and in foreign policy. In domestic politics, the practitioner has lived with the system, knows it intimately, and can respond to its signals quickly and accurately—*ceteris paribus*. In foreign affairs, the practitioner must be familiar with both the domestic and the international systems. The latter is more difficult to understand than the domestic system because it is a more artificial and amorphous construct (since its form is so dependent on what the observer chooses to empha-

statesman is required to make decisions that appear to involve survival or even fundamental issues is not large; on such occasions his behavior may not always be incremental, but neither is the domestic policymaker's behavior. Some decisions in domestic policy, involving large expenditures on new and massive problems, are as irreversible and unpredictable as what occurs in international politics.

The argument that foreign policy and domestic policy are more similar than different can, perhaps, be carried too far. Although procedural differences do not appear to lead to different kinds of policies, it is also true that foreign policy has a special mystique attached to it. The notion that politics is *supposed* to stop at the water's edge sums it up well: there is a feeling that foreign policy should be different, that we should present a united front to the world, that issues involving questions of war and survival deserve something better than partisan backbiting. Yet, insofar as politics *does* stop at the water's edge, it does so not (or not usually) because of the aura that surrounds foreign policy but because there is a wide consensus about the actions we are about to take. When the consensus disintegrates, foreign policy can be as partisan and parochial as tax or tariff policy.

Are there any compelling conclusions that emerge from these considerations about the relationship between domestic and foreign policy? Perhaps the most obvious point is that any distinction between the two types of policy must be measured in degree and not in kind. Foreign policy *always* contains elements of domestic policy, and any issue of foreign policy may have a very large potential for becoming heavily enmeshed in domestic politics. The degree to which this is true has been masked by the tendency of foreign policy analysts, particularly those schooled in the Realist tradition, to act *as if* foreign policy was (and by right ought to be) an entirely separate realm, and by the domestic consensus on foreign policy goals, which made a transitory agreement on means and ends seem permanent and natural.

There are, as we have noted, some persisting differences between foreign and domestic policy, but they do not invalidate the point that the resulting policies in both cases are very similar: they have the same virtues and the same maladies. Thus it is true that foreign policy issues

---

size or see), and because it is more difficult to either control events or understand their dynamics. Many major misperceptions occur in international relations because it is difficult for operators in one system to understand the ground rules for operators in another system (which is, by definition, part of the first operator's international system). The result is intersystem conflict.

have tended to be disputed in a narrow arena (within the executive bureaucracies), there is less pressure from public opinion and external groups, the environment is more uncertain, and, finally, foreign policy is simply perceived as different. Though these factors affect the style and the locale of foreign policymaking, they also reinforce the degree to which foreign policymaking is influenced by prudence, habit, and tradition—which is to say, reinforcement of its incremental tendencies. As a result, foreign and domestic policies tend to have the same virtues and the same vices, even though they emerge from processes that usually differ—although more in style and tone than in substance. There is no single right relationship between foreign and domestic policies; there are only relationships that exist at historical moments. Thus, there have been periods, and they may return again, when it was accurate to describe foreign policy as an autonomous and superior realm. In our time, all the signs are not perfectly clear, but it does seem beyond dispute that domestic factors are exercising an increasing influence on the style and content of foreign policy, not only because foreign policy is becoming domesticated (that is, embroiled in the partisan play of domestic politics), but also because the issues that dominate foreign policy are no longer solely the traditional issues of war and security. Economic and social issues that once fell primarily within the domain of domestic politics have now become internationalized: they can no longer be handled in isolation by individual states, no matter how powerful, for the international system has become too interdependent—at least on these kinds of issues—to make autonomous decision-making very reasonable. This hardly means that the security issue has disappeared or been transcended, but simply that an additional range of concerns has become a legitimate international issue.

These developments are significant in understanding the utility of planning. The arguments against planning in foreign affairs were unclear when they centered on the mysteries and metaphysics of the security issue; these arguments make no sense in an international environment in which such issues as the stability of the monetary system, the control of pollution, the limitation of population growth, and the effects of an international flow of ideas and fashions are salient.

The costs of describing and analyzing both foreign policy and domestic policy in terms of only two kinds of decisions—crisis decisions and the normal incremental decisions—should be clear. The use of only two kinds of decisions has sharply foreshortened perspectives and has provided an intellectual and practical justification for ignoring long-range consequences. The planning function has either been ignored or limited to providing additional comment on today's problems. Crises, after all, can barely be planned for at all, except in the marginal sense that "contingency planning" may set the mind to thinking in relevant directions (academics would say it has a "heuristic function"). And planning is simply irrelevant to incremental decisions that rest on nothing more than a consensus on marginal adaptations of previous decisions.[9]

The future has no constituency pushing its claims in a bureaucratic system committed to the notion that the future will be another form of the present. A perception of unpredictability leads operators to insist that planning is irrelevant. It is also a protective reaction against the fear that any attempt to plan and to exercise control over the future will undermine the operator's control of the policymaking process. The attempt to determine present choices in the light of an interpretation of reasonable long-range goals is inherently destabilizing for men committed to procedural consensus. The notion that the future need not be another form of the present raises considerations that cannot easily be weighed in a bargaining process and also bestows influence on those whose skills are primarily substantive.

So long as we continue to discuss the policymaking system as only two kinds of decisions, neither of which reflects any concern for the long run, the impression is bound to persist that the only way in which we can progress is by revolution or wholesale replacement of a generation of bureaucrats. Faith in the ability of the system and its operators to solve (or even improve) pressing problems has dissipated markedly. Perhaps most significantly, confidence in the effectiveness of remedial measures—which formed so essential a part of the incremental canon—has sharply declined: the problems appear so vast, and the conventional response so inadequate, that only revolution or apathy seem justified. In addition, conflict over goals and purposes has become endemic. In the past, when a wide consensus on goals prevailed, conflict centered primarily on the choice of means; as such, it appeared to concern only the bureaucratic institutions that struggled for operational control. The question of *who* had a right to participate in the struggle was determined by gross calculations of power. It was not a system that gave the weak (be they domestic minority groups or dissenters from the Council on Foreign Relations' interpretation of the Communist threat) much opportunity to

[9] It is not clear that planning or research could perform useful (and nonpropagandistic) services for these kinds of decisions: the actual decision is made on the basis of calculations of relative bargaining strength, which makes analysis of the problem irrelevant. The problems are also, by definition, unique, which suggests that whatever information could be gathered would be obsolete before it could be passed on to the policymaker.

be heard or consulted. But now the disarray within and between the elites themselves has given new voices and new groups a chance to compete for public support and a chance to be listened to when they question the legitimacy of the system.

It no longer makes sense to think about the political system as incremental decisions occasionally interrupted by crises. Faith in the corrective capacities of crisis decisions—when the system can finally be compelled to respond adequately—is hardly sufficient. Neither reason nor record maintains that the results of "crisis management" are always salubrious. Crisis management is not the only way in which we can achieve change, unless we stumble into it. This curious faith in the virtues of crisis reached its apogee, or perhaps its nadir, with the once fashionable notion that governments would agree to disarm only after experiencing a small nuclear war. The self-correcting capacities of incremental decisions per se also will not be likely to provide a sufficient response to our current difficulties: the system is too prone to drift erratically in response to transient political forces and thus is incapable of devising programs and policies of acceptable scope and depth. A simple breakdown between incremental policies and crisis policies is, therefore, both inaccurate and inadequate: inaccurate because it ignores some important forms of policymaking, and inadequate because it is a futile way to deal with the problems (both security and nonsecurity) that currently dominate the international system.

The most profound obstacle blocking any serious attempt to reform this state of affairs is intellectual; those who run the system, and those who subsist by interpreting it, continue to think in terms appropriate to the 1950s. Unfortunately, however, traditional patterns of thought, especially among operators who know nothing else, change with marked slowness, especially if external disasters do not accelerate change, and if alternative patterns of thought have not been discussed and analyzed. We can take a preliminary step toward fulfilling the latter condition by classifying policies less simplistically.

It is wrong to condemn incremental decisions without qualification. Incremental decisions perform a useful function, even in a system in need of major adjustments. Etzioni's distinction between fundamental decisions, which set general directions in an area, and incremental decisions, which work out the details of fundamental decisions, is an improvement on the traditional formula.[10] Etzioni attempts to eliminate or control the aimlessness or randomness of incrementalism. The notion of fundamental

[10] See Etzioni, "Mixed-Scanning."

decisions, however, is perhaps too ambiguous to be completely satisfactory. Crisis decisions can clearly be fundamental: the Marshall Plan was developed as a quick response to a rapidly deteriorating Europe. Decisions made in times of crises do not always have the deliberateness and consciousness of the Marshall Plan: the expansion of the defense budget in response to the Korean War, which set the level of military spending for years to come, was initially conceived as a short-term response to the likelihood of general war.

Fundamental decisions can also occur without the immediate pressures of a full-blown crisis. The deliberate decision to begin bombing North Vietnam in 1965 may be an illustration. The Alliance for Progress is another example. Also, some incremental decisions are fundamental in intent; they are decisions that begin changing a policy by small de-escalations or small changes in direction. These incremental decisions are, in a sense, the fundamental decisions of men steeped in the lore of consensus politics, such as Johnson's decision to stop bombing in 1968. These quiet, disguised, even surreptitious decisions are incremental in style, but fundamental in purpose. They differ from other fundamental decisions not only in style but also in that they must be deliberate decisions to start a new tack. Otherwise, such decisions could easily be reversed or subverted by the normal play of the game.

We have mentioned crisis decisions (some of which may turn out to be fundamental), fundamental decisions, incremental decisions that are designed to be fundamental, and incremental decisions that should be, and occasionally are, designed to work out the details of earlier fundamental decisions. Perhaps we also ought to add the familiar category of non-decisions, which are left in abeyance either because no consensus is possible or because they are of immediate interest only to those who do not have power enough to get into the game.

Neglecting the necessity for, and significance of, different kinds of fundamental decisions explains many failures of the policymaking system. One might argue that the absence of a basic policy toward arms control and disarmament created a situation in which weapons were developed and deployed because it was technically feasible to do so, that failure to make a fundamental decision about the purpose of economic aid led to operating policies that were inconsistent and unproductive, or that policies toward NATO and Europe rigidified because no group existed to consider the long-range significance of short-range commitments. Fundamental decisions then are desirable, but are not often made because they must be made outside both the normal incremental process and the pressures of occasional crises. Not all fundamental decisions are equal, in the sense that they can be improved by the existence of a capable long-range planning staff. Fundamental decisions within the context of the incremental system are at the mercy of the policymaker's notion of tactical feasibility, although the planner may affect the original intention to change direction. Only a deliberate effort to think through basic policies and to treat seriously the possibility of influencing the kind of future we want can fully benefit from the creation of a genuine long-range planning staff.

As long as the belief persists that policies are made either incrementally or during a crisis, the view that assignment to a planning staff is a reward for good behavior, and a paid vacation from the real action, is nearly correct. Planning simply goes against everything we have been taught about the way in which foreign policy has been—and by necessity must be—made. And "planning" in foreign affairs has rarely been more than an exercise in choosing or refining the means to unquestioned ends. We see the result not only in the failure to question our purposes in Vietnam but also in less dramatic issues like the international monetary crisis and the development of generations of weapons systems solely because they were "technically sweet." We can make one small but significant contribution to correcting this state of affairs by analyzing our policymaking system less simplistically: we shall have a better understanding of how we make policy and of the contribution that planning can (and cannot) make to policymaking.

THE STATE DEPARTMENT AND THE FOREIGN SERVICE: PROFESSIONALS IN QUEST OF A PROFESSION

The State Department is a large organization dominated by a professional group with unique problems and perspectives. Only the Mafia seems to get a worse press, although for the opposite reason: the Mafia seems to work too well, whereas there are persistent doubts that the State Department works at all. It is difficult to find evidence that refutes either point of view.

Neither the State Department nor the Foreign Service has made much effort to respond to criticism. They have instead chosen, in one of Lyndon Johnson's favorite metaphors, to "hunker down," to turn inward, and to rebut criticism by insisting that the outsider can never understand (and thus justly criticize) the problems that confront the practitioner. Descriptions of the ineptitude of the State Department abound, and they have become a substitute for analysis, rather than a preface to it. It may be that the State Department is one of the few institutions in Washington that has largely escaped the academic net. Memoirs and exposés appear with regularity, and administrative studies of how the Department functions appear intermittently (following the cyclical reappearance of reorganization commissions), but attempts to analyze *why* the Department and the Foreign Service behave as they do are rare. It is impossible to comprehend the Department's attitude toward planning without first understanding the reasons for its responses to the universe in which it operates. Perhaps the argument that follows is somewhat unconventional: it emphasizes the significance of an inadequate professional doctrine, and the gap between what the Foreign Service does and what it is trained to do, rather than the excessive size of the Foreign Service, the lack of centralized control by the State Department, or the imperialism of other bureaucracies. Nevertheless, explaining why the State Department acts in a particular way may carry more explanatory power than merely criticizing symptoms or historical accidents.

The State Department is somewhat similar to what administrative specialists call public bureaucracies. For example, its goals (in theory) are externally determined and thus tend to be amorphous or ambiguous.[11] Moreover, the State Department does not have a product that can be tested in the marketplace. The normal tests of efficiency and effectiveness, by which private bureaucracies are evaluated, are therefore inapplicable.[12]

Beyond a certain point, the analogy between the State Department and other public bureaucracies begins to conceal more than it reveals. An organization that finds it difficult or impossible to submit to the market test in an economic sense must go into the political marketplace to solicit support: it succeeds or fails to the extent that it effectively manipulates its relationship with other agencies, the legislature, and its own clientele.[13] The State Department does not have a group of domestic clients that it serves and, in turn, can call on as a resource in its struggles with rival bureaucracies or the Congress.[14] This is one reason why the State Department plays the bureaucratic game so badly. A more critical reason

[11] See Robert L. Peabody and Francis E. Rourke, "Public Bureaucracies," in James G. March, ed., *Handbook of Organizations* (Chicago: Rand McNally, 1965), pp. 802-837.
[12] See Anthony Downs, *Inside Bureaucracy* (Boston: Little, Brown, 1967), p. 30.
[13] Peabody and Rourke, "Public Bureaucracies," p. 817 f.
[14] Downs suggests that "within a democratic society, bureaus that serve the electorate directly are less likely to ossify than those that do not. Excessive rigidity in such bureaus as the State Department, AID, and the military services, therefore, may persist for extensive periods." *Inside Bureaucracy,* p. 164.

is that the Department, and especially the Foreign Service, does not feel that it ought to be (or has to be) game-playing at all; different from other public bureaucracies that lack tangible evidence of real achievement, the State Department feels that its authority should come from its professional skills and not from its political support.

The State Department must compete for support, however reluctantly, in domestic affairs. But it must also function in an international environment that appears fundamentally unpredictable and uncontrollable. The uncertainty of the external environment imposes substantial pressures on any group that is assigned responsibility for manipulating this environment in the national interest. How can we know that the actions of the State Department have been successful or unsuccessful, right or wrong? In the short range, there is no satisfactory answer to this question. How then can the State Department survive against its critics? Philip Selznick provides the classic defense:

> the basic answer society has evolved for the protection of institutional integrity is professionalism. . . . In the case of organizations that initiate ideas, where creativity and independence are at a premium, the role of internal and external professional associations can be crucial, buttressing the independence of key personnel. If a man is to take risks, he needs social supports.[15]

Professionalization institutionalizes and legitimizes the practitioner's behavior, most critically in that he is permitted to maintain that only other professionals have the right or ability to judge his actions.

Does the Foreign Service have all the attributes of a profession? It has a code of ethics, a style of behavior, a sense of detachment toward its subject matter, and a system of internally controlled rewards and recognitions. It is, however, unclear whether the Foreign Service has an accepted body of esoteric knowledge, characterized by "a common language, which is understood only partially by outsiders."[16] The presence or absence of this characteristic is ultimately decisive, for without it we would have professionals, but not a profession.

The Foreign Service officer possesses, or believes he possesses, professional knowledge and skills. What is at issue is the quality of that knowledge and skill: Is it sufficiently integrated, coherent, and esoteric to be

[15] Philip Selznick, *Leadership in Administration* (New York: Harper and Row, 1957), pp. 132-133.
[16] William J. Goode, "Community within a Community: The Professions," *The American Sociological Review* 22 (April 1957): 194. The other characteristics mentioned earlier in the paragraph are fairly standard in discussions of professionalization.

treated as a professional body of knowledge? The knowledge and skills of the Foreign Service officer are unique in one sense. As Smith Simpson has noted, "unlike any other profession, however, that of foreign affairs is deemed by the Department to require no preparation, save of the most superficial sort."[17]

The only justification for this state of affairs is that necessary skills can and must be acquired on the job. Acquiring skills on the job explains the belief that advanced and specialized training is unnecessary or irrelevant, and that the best preparation comes "from the general education, background, previous experience, temperamental fitness, and intellectual qualifications of the applicant."[18] Ellis Briggs, also experienced in these problems, summarizes the traditional attitude quite well: "Granted that by its nature diplomacy is an imprecise business . . . there is nevertheless a feel for and a familiarity with it, acquired by skilled operation of the machine of foreign affairs and in no other fashion."[19]

Another aspect is that academic training is unnecessary. The academic deliberately attempts to establish categories of recurring actions. The practitioner believes that he himself does not categorize—although he generalizes his experiences as much as the academic does, but less consciously and more crudely. Briggs again exemplifies the conventional wisdom when he asserts that "no two situations are alike" and "the only thing that is predictable about diplomacy is its unpredictability."[20]

What preparation is useful for a practitioner compelled to operate in so unpredictable a universe? Specialized or theoretical knowledge is not the answer, for each problem is unique and unclassifiable. Even general knowledge may not be intellectually useful. What remains might be called "procedural style." Kennan illustrates the point beautifully when he notes, in an address to the Foreign Service Association, that:

Any of us who has had so much as a single year in this work has learned, I am sure, the first great lesson it has to teach: and that is, that what is important in the relations between governments is not just, or even predominantly, the "what" but rather the "how"—the approach, the posture, the manner, the style of action.[21]

[17] Smith Simpson, *Anatomy of the State Department* (Boston: Houghton Mifflin, 1967), p. 10.

[18] Henry Serrano Villard, *Affairs at State* (New York: Thomas Y. Crowell, 1965), p. 145.

[19] Ellis Briggs, *Farewell to Foggy Bottom* (New York: David McKay, 1964), p. 45.

[20] *Ibid.*, p. 40. See also Franklin A. Lindsay, "Program Planning: The Missing Element," *Foreign Affairs* 39 (January 1961): 279-290.

[21] George F. Kennan, "Diplomacy as a Profession," *Foreign Service Journal* 38 (May 1961): 23. An experienced journalist who has covered the State Department

The stress on "how," rather than "what" or "why," provides much of the explanation for the personal qualities that the Foreign Service emphasizes and rewards. Characteristics that facilitate accommodation rank high: one study lists tact, subtlety, sophistication, and sensitivity, all of which presumably can be gained only from experience.[22] Moreover, the bias passed on in "on the job" training is clearly toward passivity and against activism. Anticipating problems is impossible in an unpredictable world, but it would also be unwise even if conceivable—*pas trop de zèle,* as Talleyrand noted. And Briggs is quick to agree: "the crusading spirit does not inhabit my locker."[23] Precedents provide a compendium of the "traditional wisdom"; they are related to specific cases by an analytical style that is intuitive and impressionistic.[24]

The finished product is the "great generalist," the man who can be thrown into every situation and counted on to emerge with an acceptable settlement. The heroic proportions this mythical figure assumes in some of the "old boy" memoirs are almost ludicrous. Villard, for example, declares that "generalists are fast disappearing from the scene, and with them are going the assets of perceptiveness, sound judgment, panoramic understanding, and intuition tempered in the fires of practical experience."[25]

The superiority of the generalist over the specialist is taken for granted. This is perhaps best exemplified in poet-diplomat Alexis Saint-Léger's comment on two French statesmen: "Poincaré knows everything and understands nothing; Briand knows nothing and understands everything." Unfortunately, in the case of the Foreign Service Officer, that understanding may be nothing more profound than a recitation of conventional pieties.

What constitutes an adequate body of professional knowledge? Two conditions have to be satisfied. First, the body of professional knowledge has to be technical or esoteric enough to impress outsiders and to justify the claim that only a member of the profession can understand and

for many years attributes this saying to senior FSOs: "After all, what needs to be done is usually fairly obvious common sense. [Especially if it just involves doing the same thing again and again.] The crux is *how,* and *when* to do it." (Italics in original.) See John P. Leacacos, "Kissinger's Apparat," *Foreign Policy,* no. 5 (Winter 1971-72), p. 5.

[22] John Ensor Harr, *The Professional Diplomat* (Princeton, N.J.: Princeton University Press, 1969), p. 44.

[23] Briggs, *Farewell to Foggy Bottom,* p. 1.

[24] See Regis Walther, *Orientation and Behavioral Styles of Foreign Service Officers* (New York: Carnegie Endowment for International Peace, 1965), p. 16.

[25] Villard, *Affairs at State,* p. 35.

employ it. Second, it must have a record of success in application that is clear and irrefutable. The procedural skills of the Foreign Service "generalist" cannot fulfill either condition. Worse yet, it is not clear that the knowledge and skills that the Foreign Service claims are its own have much to do with how Foreign Service Officers spend their time.

If the Foreign Service stressed substantive skills, it might be able to sustain a claim to a special body of knowledge. To do so, however, would both destroy its image of itself and grant wide authority over vast areas of foreign affairs to outside experts. The Foreign Service has obscured the issue by insisting that training as a generalist is absolutely necessary for men who are going to become policymakers at the top of the State Department hierarchy, and by insisting that the real experts in a field are the desk officers or embassy officials of the Foreign Service.[26]

The skills of the generalist-negotiator and the skills of the observer do not necessarily correspond. FSOs trained as all-purpose negotiators might be very bad observers and reporters of events, and vice versa. There is some overlap, but it is also clear that the two skills rest on different kinds of aptitudes and training. The negotiator must develop an intuitive and highly personal ability to recognize opportunities for bringing opponents together. The observer and the reporter, conversely, must develop intellectual and analytical skills that are not widely different from those of the social scientist—the skills are merely applied to more immediate events.

This distinction would be irrelevant if the normal FSO spent a substantial part of his career involved in negotiations: his training and his work would be in symmetry. The great majority of FSOs, however, spend most of their careers observing, reporting, moving about, and, as one friendly critic notes, "keeping their noses clean." The first two tasks are done badly because the FSO is not trained to perform them systematically. What he needs is not "on the job" training by osmosis, but a thorough attempt to instill analytical principles that would make his observations and reports less amateurish.[27]

---

[26] See Simpson, *Anatomy of the State Department,* p. 44. The same point was made to me several times in a number of interviews. The State Department shares its bias with, or perhaps one should say inherited it from, the Foreign Office in London. A recent report saw no reason to alter the traditional British view: "we do not believe that the Diplomatic Service should be made up of experts. Its members should remain generalists . . . the abler men in the Service should be as nearly interchangeable as possible and should each have had the widest possible variety of experience by the time they reach the top." *Report of the Review Committee on Overseas Representation, 1968-1969,* Chairman, Sir Val Duncan, Cmnd. 4107, July 1969.

[27] The quoted phrase is from *ibid.,* p. 13. That observing and reporting involve more than just passing "the facts" along does not always occur to the practitioner.

One other factor makes the necessity of reeducating the Foreign Service imperative. Over the past two decades there has been a radical revision of the ratio of FSOs stationed at home and abroad. The following table illustrates the point in a striking fashion:[28]

Deployment of Foreign Service Officers

Year	At Home	Abroad
1948	185	1,147
1969	1,700	1,500

These figures signify more than a vast increase in the number of FSOs. They also mean that the majority of FSOs at any moment are no longer involved in any representational activities: they are instead occupying positions within the State Department that *should* require analytical and interpretive skills of the first order. It is possible to argue, of course, that the FSOs should not hold these positions, and that they should be trained only for the classic diplomatic functions. They *do* hold these positions, however, and there is little likelihood that they will be compelled to give them up (where would they go?), or that they will be trained to carry them out well.

The contention that the skills of the generalist are preeminent also rests on an image of the international system that is obsolete. It was possible to ignore the specialist and the trained observer before the rise of Hitler and Stalin, although it was unwise even then, because the dominant Great Powers sought the same kind of goals, used the same means, and more or less agreed on the principles by which the system was to be run. The classic definition of the diplomat as "eternally between," negotiating differences according to traditional formulas, seemed appropriate. Nuclear weapons, the rise of non-Western and nonviable states, the problems of economic development and economic integration, and the intrusion of domestic factors into foreign policy have increased the significance of the specialist and decreased the value of the expert in negotiation. It is no longer possible to send someone trained merely as a diplomat to the

He could profit from reading Darwin, who is usually cited for "letting the facts speak for themselves." Darwin himself knew better, and wrote that "no one could be a good observer unless he was an active theorizer." And, "How odd it is that anyone should not see that all observation must be for or against some view if it is to be of any service." Quoted in Arthur Koestler, *The Act of Creation* (New York: Dell, 1964), p. 135.

[28] The chart is borrowed from John Franklin Campbell, " 'What Is to Be Done?'—Gigantism in Washington," *Foreign Affairs* 49 (October 1970): 93.

highly complex international negotiations of the current era: he must first become a competent specialist.

The claim that the Foreign Service already has the best experts is a variation on the preceding theme. It makes sense only in the narrow context that the State Department alone may possess the latest information about a specific problem—which hardly endows its experts with superior judgment. A perception of the *kind* of expertise is relevant. Thus State's experts are better not because they know more or are more intelligent but because they are superior operators, expert in the extraction of agreement. The great hero for the FSO is the successful trouble-shooter who can be sent anywhere and counted upon to paper over the cracks for a while—and that, as the argument goes, is the most that can be expected in an unpredictable world. This pattern of response perhaps accounts for the Department's tendency to assume that the way to break a stalemate or unravel a dilemma is to send a new negotiator. There is no questioning of assumptions, no attempt to speculate on whether the basic approach needs to be altered. That would be impossible, as well as dangerous, for a generalist.[29]

One of the major problems that most modern organizations face results from the conflict between authority and ability (or hierarchy and specialization).[30] Increasingly complex problems and pressures demand increasingly specialized responses. Men rise, however, in the chain of command not because of their narrow, technical expertise but because they presumably possess the wider capacities necessary to direct a large organization. The inevitable result is a paradox: the higher the level of authority, the lower the level of knowledge. The State Department attempts to obscure this issue by insisting that the knowledge of the generalist is sufficient, for his task does not require specialized knowledge.[31] The conflict between the two patterns of authority is also

[29] We are not the only country that suffers from excessive reliance on generalists. Thus John P. Lewis, writing about his experiences in India, attacks the generalists in the Indian Civil Service for impeding economic and social development. He notes that they are overly cautious, more concerned about avoiding mistakes than achieving goals, without passion for their work, and willing to rely on group action—which gets nothing done—so long as they manage to avoid responsibility for whatever happens. It all sounds sadly familiar. His comments are quoted in Albert Waterston, *Development Planning: Lessons of Experience* (Baltimore: Johns Hopkins Press, 1965), pp. 258-259.

[30] See especially Victor A. Thompson, *Modern Organization* (New York: Alfred A. Knopf, 1961).

[31] We are not arguing that generalists are useless or irrelevant. There must be men available to fill the major policy roles who can make sensible decisions on varying issues and over a wider range than the specialist. The number of such roles, however, is small, and it is absurd to train large numbers of FSOs for a job they are

mitigated in the State Department by the prevailing consensus between its experts and its generalists: the role of the expert is always entirely secondary to the role of the generalist.[32] Nevertheless, the more important a problem becomes, and the higher in the hierarchy it goes, the less likely it is that expert knowledge will be applicable.[33] This may explain why so much official thinking appears to occur within the framework of out-of-date analogies with the past. The only substantive knowledge that the upper reaches of the hierarchy tends to have is extrapolated from its experience in the field twenty or thirty years ago.

The Foreign Service emerges as a profession with an extraordinarily insecure expertise. Its members are trained to be generalists, skilled at facilitating the process of accommodation, but few of them ever negotiate anything (beyond their own careers), and when they do, they find themselves increasingly irrelevant because all problems have become so complex that the negotiator must also be a specialist. In addition, their skills and knowledge are hardly so esoteric that only other professionals can interpret them. The demand for judgment by peers alone, which lies at the heart of professionalization, is especially irrelevant: without an adequate professional doctrine, judgment by peers merely protects and obscures incompetence. Moreover, the tendency to see themselves as just intermediaries increases the possibility that one of the greatest dangers of professionalization, an obsession with means and an indifference to ends, may come to dominate the virtues of professionalization. This also reinforces the conservatism of the policy process, for another voice that might raise questions about purpose and direction remains silent. Finally, the Foreign Service has no record of success with

---

unlikely to hold. Most jobs for which the generalist is presumably being trained have been going to outsiders—lawyers, academics, and journalists—who appear to do as well, or as badly, as the FSO, and without the latter's training. Finally, one might question the wisdom of trying to train a corps of all-purpose decision-makers—if that is what we want to do—by shifting them about so that they learn a little about many things. Perhaps there is no formal way to train such a group, for the skills may not be transmittable. The skills may be highly individualized, and they may also be revealed just as efficaciously in specialized activities as they would be in whatever one expects generalists to do. Indeed, it may be wiser to train a person initially as a specialist, for the best test of the wise generalist may be the ability to relate a specific body of knowledge to the wider concerns of a particular area or time.

[32] For comments on how conflict between hierarchical and specialized positions can be mitigated, see Robert Presthus, *The Organizational Society* (New York: Random House, 1962), pp. 56-58.

[33] Interesting remarks on this phenomenon about Vietnam appear in James C. Thomson, Jr., "Why Vietnam? An Insider Looks Back for Answers," *The Washington Post,* April 14, 1968.

which to deflect criticism—although they do have the reasonable retort that they have been ignored too frequently to be responsible for all our foreign policy failures.

The difficulties of sustaining a claim to real professional status are severe. The Foreign Service might have reacted by attempting to reconsider its role and purpose in the contemporary world. They have instead chosen to reassert the supremacy of a role that is increasingly irrelevant to the major problems of foreign policy. They have attempted to retain amateur standing in a specialized world, rather than pay the price of true professionalization. Any other response would have created enormous morale problems in the Foreign Service, for the image of an elite corps of generalists would have had to be radically revised. In some ways they have made a virtue of necessity; only the insistence on the necessity of a corps of generalists has enabled the Foreign Service to claim any role in the conduct of foreign relations.

It is always more difficult to explain how a particular view arose than how it manages to persist. The problem of origins tends to be too circular to allow a separation into cause and effect. The pattern of response and reaction by the State Department probably arose from the reluctance of the senior Foreign Service Officers to admit, in the years immediately after World War II, that their interpretation of the external world was essentially parochial and reactionary, and also arose from the relative ease with which they could sustain that view at the height of the Cold War. The absence of alternative groups of experts, and the dominance of a conservative ethos like Political Realism, hindered any effective challenge to prevailing views.

Continual challenges to the effectiveness and wisdom of the Foreign Service have caused it to turn inward. No one can read the memoirs of former members of the Foreign Service without being repelled by the constant assertion of superiority and the persistent contempt for outsiders—be they politicians, academics, journalists or mere "bleeding hearts"—who meddle in the realm of world politics. Villard, for example, complains bitterly that

> entrance standards have been lowered in the name of recruitment, its top posts bartered away for political purposes, its career men ignored . . . the advice of its experts has been disregarded by the White House, its best thought contradicted by politicians for the sake of domestic politics.[34]

---

[34] Villard, *Affairs at State*, p. 12. See also Briggs's comment that nonprofessional ambassadorial appointments are always for the good of the nominee or his party, but "[p]rofessional appointments are made for the good of the country." Briggs,

And he concludes many pages later with the complaint that "the Foreign Service no longer prides itself on being an elite corps; it seems to pride itself on *not* being elite."[35] Mr. Villard's anger was directed at efforts, from the Wriston report onwards, to broaden the base of the Foreign Service not only in its presumed professional skills but also in the kind of people it recruited.

The notion that the Foreign Service is an elite corps is one of Washington's most cultivated myths. The only sense in which it is (or has been) true concerns the ethnic and educational background of most of its membership. It is not true in an intellectual sense, for the Foreign Service is not only anti-intellectual in operating style but also recruits according to standards that are only minimally intellectual.[36] The threat from external critics also has placed a premium on controlling internal dissent: overt disagreement with the prevailing policy line provides too much potential ammunition for critics to be countenanced. Thus all the normal organizational tactics to control dissidents are employed: recruitment, training, on the job socialization, reward systems, and even patterns of dispensing authoritative information are structured to maintain internal unity against outsiders, and to bolster morale by insisting that an elite with unique skills is bound to be misunderstood by politicians and other provincials.[37] The last point perhaps accounts for the many memoirs that

---

Farewell to Foggy Bottom, p. 48. The notion that professional appointments have also been made on the basis of personal favoritism apparently escapes Briggs, as does the realization that many nonprofessional ambassadors have performed far more capably than their Foreign Service counterparts.

[35] Villard, *Affairs at State,* p. 156.

[36] The Foreign Service would respond that its members are selected through very rigorous testing. It should be noted, however, that the competitors in the entrance exam are matched only against the group with whom they are taking the test. Thus the Foreign Service may indeed be taking *some* (n.b., not all, for many who place high on the intelligence test subsequently fail the oral interview) people who place highest on an exam, but that says nothing about how bright they are. If the crop of candidates taking the exam is uniformly mediocre, those who do well may only be the proverbial one-eyed men in the kingdom of the blind.

I asked the State Department for permission to test the foregoing argument. Predictably, it was denied. The evidence I do have is from a strikingly limited sample: in nine years of teaching at Columbia and Johns Hopkins, I have never had a first-rate student indicate a desire to join the Foreign Service. Those who were interested tended to be reasonably good students with grades just below the threshold required to get into a good law school or graduate school.

I admit the fact that I am drawing on a very poor sample. The Foreign Service should not object, for I am relying on a combination of personal experience and intuition.

[37] The manner in which organizations control dissent and lessen the impact of conflict is discussed in James G. March and Herbert A. Simon, *Organizations* (New York: John Wiley and Sons, 1958), p. 125 ff.

are filled with pseudo-aristocratic pathos for those who must expend their skills without recognition by the society they protect—in spite of, and not because of that society.[38] The image is of a little band of outsiders, armored in the traditional wisdom, alien to American society yet reflecting its very best qualities, persevering out of service and dedication to protecting the national interest—the archetypal myth of the feudal knight in a mass society.

Besides the normal tactics large bureaucracies employ to control deviants, the State Department developed an interpersonal style in its internal relations that was designed to avoid the risks of dissent. A well-known study by Professor Argyris of Yale thus notes that

> the *living system* of the State Department in general, and of the Foreign Service in particular, is so constructed that it predisposes the State Department to managerial ineffectiveness. It contains norms that inhibit open confrontation of difficult issues and penalize people who take risks . . . [it] rewards certain types of interpersonal styles, helps to create a perception of the Foreign Service as being a rather closed club, induces a degree of blindness on the part of the members concerning their impact on each other and "outsiders," and generates an intricate network of organizational defenses that makes the members believe that changing it may be very difficult if not impossible.[39]

This interpersonal style—prudent, cautious, self-satisfied, intolerant of other views, rigid in its own—merely reinforces personality characteristics that emerge from an external operating style that is anti-intellectual and anti-activist. The result is a "curator mentality," the desire to pass on to successors policies that have been unaltered, unchallenged, and unsullied.

THE STATE DEPARTMENT IN A CHANGING WORLD;
OR, HOW TO GUARANTEE IRRELEVANCE

Organizational logic is intrinsically conservative: it leans toward tradition, consistency, collectively defined ends, and the wisdom of history.[40] New problems are threatening for they reveal the limitations of standard

[38] George Kennan's memoirs are filled with this sense of separation from the mainstream of American society. The point is brought out well in an interesting review by George Kateb, "George F. Kennan: The Heart of a Diplomat," *Commentary* 457 (January 1968): 21-26.

[39] Chris Argyris, *Some Causes of Organizational Ineffectiveness within the Department of State* (Washington, D.C.: Department of State, 1967), p. 1 (italics in original). Argyris defines the "living system" as representing "how things are, not merely how they are supposed to be." (p. 2)

[40] See Presthus, *The Organizational Society,* p. 291.

procedures. New problems also demand innovation, and innovation is dangerous. Innovation is dangerous because it cannot be controlled and because it substantially increases the possibility of visible error. New problems and the necessity of new techniques are unsettling for a professional group compelled to operate with a doctrine that implicitly asserts that no problems in foreign affairs are new enough to eliminate the need for the all-purpose generalist. But some problems are new; that is, they involve entirely new dimensions or new interactions and cannot be easily integrated within a doctrine that takes its standards from the operation of the European state system (ca. 1875). The Foreign Service has responded characteristically by either ignoring these problems or insisting that they are not really political—they are, in effect, another's business. Thus, the political significance of military and economic aid, the implications of strategies designed to deter or fight various wars, the impact on international stability of a nonviable and poverty-struck underdeveloped world, and the significance of the breakdown of the distinction between domestic and foreign policy in some western states have all been analyzed elsewhere (usually in the Pentagon). It is difficult to see what generalists could contribute to a discussion of these issues. Yet they are critical issues that have not been *taken* from the State Department, but have been given away in the hope that they will disappear.[41]

A rapidly changing environment, urgent problems that defy conventional solutions, and an organization under stress from criticism by important sources of support would appear to have a large vested interest in fostering innovation. However, despite the fact that the external situation has been so favorable, both the State Department and the Foreign Service have lacked the motivation to take advantage of it. Their norms do not favor change, they are dominated by a professional ideology that punishes dissenters, intra-organizational conflict (that may increase the probability of innovative proposals) is deliberately muted, and the internal operating environment is dominated by men schooled in the same tradition.[42] The last point may be particularly important, since there is

[41] The contention that all would be well in foreign affairs if everything could be centrally controlled by the State Department has always missed an essential point: the Foreign Service has never wanted to have anything to do with many issues that AID, ACDA, the Pentagon, and the White House (among others) have made their own.
[42] On factors that favor or impede innovation in an organization, see Lawrence B. Mohr, "Determinants of Innovation in Organizations," *American Political Science Review* 63 (March 1969): 111-126; Presthus, *The Organizational Society*, p. 293; James Q. Wilson, "Innovation in Organization: Notes toward a Theory," in James D. Thompson, ed., *Approaches to Organizational Design* (Pittsburgh: University of Pittsburgh Press, 1966), pp. 195-218.
Some of the difficulties of innovating within the State Department are revealed in

empirical evidence indicating that conversations with trustworthy sources in one's environment are more likely to influence behavior than is any other kind of communication.[43]

This does not mean that innovative proposals do not ever emerge within the Department. They do, as the recent movement by younger members of the Foreign Service to institute major reforms attests. Members who are most committed to the organization's goals and norms may also be the most severely critical, because they care enough to respond to threats and dangers. It is very unlikely, however, that they will do more than criticize the means by which the organization carries out its tasks: the ends remain sacrosanct.[44] Any large organization may have many proposals for innovation appearing from within, but little likelihood that they will be accepted because of all the possible centers of resistance.

That a Department committed, trained, and organized in this fashion would find planning for the future congenial is improbable. The "long range" has been defined in terms of the next Presidential election: anything else would be unrealistic. Since the next election may force a change of the guard (not necessarily a change in policy), the payoff for worrying about anything more extended is nil. It is also true that environments that do not appear to be susceptible to control (or "planned influence") are not likely to induce much concern with the quality of the knowledge that practitioners employ or with the planning exercises they do or do not undertake.[45]

---

a recent case study by Frederick C. Mosher and John E. Harr, *Programming Systems and Foreign Affairs Leadership* (New York: Oxford University Press, 1970). The authors relate the effort to install a country-oriented (rather than agency-oriented like the PPBS system) programming system in the Department, the resistance it met both within the Department and from other agencies, and its ultimate failure. Their analysis is interesting, if unsurprising, but it could have been improved if they had attempted to reveal what their programming system could do. One has to take on faith their assumption that it was both useful and superior to other alternatives.

[43] See Carl Hovland and Walter Weiss, "The Influence of Source Credibility on Communication Effectiveness," *Public Opinion Quarterly* 15 (1951): 635-650. This factor indicates that the presence of what Chadwick Alger has called "external bureaucrats" (outsiders serving for some period of time as insiders) may indeed be useful in making the bureaucracy more adaptive and innovative, and less rigid and orthodox. This presumes, however, that the outsiders have something different to offer than the insiders. See Chadwick F. Alger, "The External Bureaucracy in U.S. Foreign Affairs," *Administrative Science Quarterly* 7 (June 1962): 50-78.

[44] See Bernard Berelson and Gary A. Steiner, *Human Behavior: An Inventory of Scientific Findings* (New York: Harcourt, Brace and World, 1964), p. 379.

[45] On the relationship between the nature of the operating environment and the kinds of intelligence an organization seeks, see Harold L. Wilensky, *Organizational*

As a result of its commitment to preserving inherited policies, and its tendency "to nibble around the edge of problems" when they arise, the State Department reinforces the incrementalism of the larger political system within which it operates.[46] The State Department has little choice in the matter, because it lacks substantive knowledge that would provide a basis for criticizing, evaluating, and altering ongoing policies. It thinks about the content of policy only when emerging problems have already made that content problematic. Meanwhile, until a major crisis arises, all its tendencies are incremental: policies differ only marginally from previous policies and tend to be negotiated slowly and painfully with other centers of power (White House, Congress, Pentagon, CIA). The State Department bureaucracy may even be more incremental than most large bureaucracies because its decisional process is secret (and not exposed to subversive influences) and because its ambiguous professional competence puts a premium on detecting continuities everywhere.[47]

Numerous studies have begun to appear that offer suggestions for reforming both the Foreign Service and the State Department. Two recent articles by members of the Foreign Service have stressed the indisputable fact that the Foreign Service has grown too large, and that there are too many senior FSOs for too few senior positions.[48] As a result, there is growing disaffection both by junior officers who are blocked from responsible positions and by senior officers forced to accept make-work jobs (presumably below their capabilities). While all this is undoubtedly true, the tendency to blame the problems of the Foreign Service primarily on size is unconvincing. There is no compelling evidence that small groups of untrained mediocrities will perform markedly better than large groups of untrained mediocrities.

More impressive is the recent, 600-page State Department study entitled "Diplomacy for the Seventies."[49] The main conclusion is that the era of "talented generalists" is over and that their successors will be a "new breed of diplomat-managers." The Kennedy administration advocated much the same thing several years ago when it formulated a

Intelligence: Knowledge and Policy in Government and Industry (New York: Basic Books, 1967).

[46] The quoted phrase is from Simpson, *Anatomy of the State Department,* p. 129.
[47] On the differences between incrementalism in a bureaucracy and elsewhere, see Francis E. Rourke, *Bureaucracy, Politics, and Public Policy* (Boston: Little, Brown, 1969), p. 103 f.
[48] See Campbell, " 'What Is to Be Done?' " and Richard Holbrooke, "The Machine That Fails," *Foreign Policy,* no. 1 (Winter 1970-71), pp. 65-77.
[49] My information comes from a story in *The New York Times,* December 9, 1970.

proposal for a "new diplomacy" that would be more activist, managerial, and executive than the "old diplomacy."[50] This is also very similar to the persistent demand that the State Department should take charge in foreign affairs, although no one has been clear about how this could be done—or why.

Training the new FSOs in modern management techniques may not, however, be the panacea that the authors of the report believe it will be. Much depends on the role that one believes the Foreign Service ought to be playing in the years ahead. Thus if the FSOs are to be removed from both their traditional role of observing events from abroad and their new role of analyzing developments from Washington, training them to monitor and run programs abroad (in agriculture, labor, commerce, and science) may be worthwhile. This might be a wise development for it would end the pretense that the Foreign Service had to contribute to the making of foreign policy (as distinct from its implementation). But if we are concerned with developing a staff that is able to make substantive contributions to policymaking, this is not the way to do it.

The international environment in the next several decades is likely to become increasingly complex, fragmented, and multilayered. This makes the need for a competent Foreign Service even more compelling than it has been in the past. The notion that effective policy can be made in Washington and simply passed on for implementation in local areas is likely to become more and more suspect and inadequate. The need for accurate, timely, and detailed local knowledge is bound to increase; without it, centrally determined policy will always be obsolescent. Thus a more effective flow of information between the field and Washington will become imperative, for we will no longer be able to rely on the simple rules of thumb that guided the policy process during the Cold War years.

I do not mean that policy can or should be made in the field. The contribution that the field can make to policymaking should increase, however, and the degree of flexibility that the field has in implementing and explaining policy probably also ought to be enhanced. A planning staff, properly used, can be an important mediator and analyst in the inevitable conflicts. The argument that the field has something important to contribute to the policy process in Washington rests not only on a judgment about the international environment but also on the assump-

[50] The report also advocates various measures to reduce conformity and enhance the possibility of innovation. This is entirely admirable in intent, but it is not clear that much improvement will result merely from turning today's FSO into a managerial type.

tion that the agents in the field—the Foreign Service, in particular—are part of an elite service.

The observer would hazard the opinion that reforms now being discussed will improve the State Department, but not in the right direction. It seems imperative to create and maintain a Foreign Service that is capable of effective observation, reporting, and analysis of foreign affairs, for these are indispensable tasks if the government is to act wisely. Thus, both the managerial and ceremonial roles of the Foreign Service ought to be deemphasized, and an increased emphasis ought to be placed on the intellectual role of the FSO. This implies that recruitment procedures should be altered, and that the image of proper training for an FSO should be radically revised. It means that the anti-intellectual bias of the Foreign Service will have to be eliminated: it may even mean candidates should be required to have several years of graduate training before joining the Foreign Service. The FSOs must be taught more than the chessboard theory of diplomacy. Moreover, some effort to improve their knowledge of the domestic political system, and to qualify their belief that every intrusion of domestic affairs into foreign policy is illegitimate, might be very salutary. Until these reforms are initiated (and supported by the President and his Secretary of State), perhaps it is best to implement these managerial reforms into the Department, and to bypass the Department as often as possible on serious matters of policy. Since the position of the State Department is already known on most issues, nothing much would be lost.

John Franklin Campbell's *The Foreign Affairs Fudge Factory* appeared shortly before this text was completed.[51] Nevertheless, it is worth a comment for it exemplifies the attitudes of the Foreign Service that I have been criticizing. In addition, the favorable public reception that the book received illustrates the profound difficulties that confront anyone intent on a fundamental reorganization of the Foreign Service and the State Department.

Campbell begins by attacking very familiar evils: the growth of the foreign affairs bureaucracy outside the State Department (especially in the White House, the Pentagon, the CIA, and the USIA and the naïve and delusive interventionism that characterized its policymaking during the Kennedy and Johnson presidencies. No doubt, these developments can be legitimately criticized, and Campbell can be faulted only for his superficiality. The real fault, however, in Campbell's analysis lies not so much in what he criticizes as in the alternative that he offers. His tactic

[51] New York: Basic Books, 1971.

throughout his book is to contrast the weaknesses and failures of the "New Diplomacy" with some hypothetical virtues of the "Old Diplomacy": all would be well, he argues (or, rather, asserts, for Campbell apparently feels the virtues of the "Old Diplomacy" are so self-evident that they need not be demonstrated), if only foreign policy once again could be left in the sole custody of "professionals" trained to understand its intricacies.

At one point, Campbell admits that the Foreign Service President Kennedy inherited was "schooled in caution and shorn of expertise."[52] Yet, strangely enough, he wants it to be given more responsibility for the direction of foreign affairs. The sleight of hand by which Campbell manages to justify this curious argument is obvious: he contrasts the failures of the "New Diplomacy" not with what the existing Foreign Service could do but with an image of what the Foreign Service *might* do if it were truly the elite service its members believe it to be. Thus the faults of the Foreign Service, in Campbell's estimation, are always another's doing, whether it be Senator Joseph McCarthy, the authors of the Wriston report that allowed outsiders into the Foreign Service, or high officials who choose to make foreign policy without consulting the State Department.

That the Foreign Service, *even in its own interpretation of what it might or should be,* is a less than perfect instrument has not occurred to Campbell. That it might be badly selected and trained, that it might not be elite at all, is a judgment that can be made only if we begin by asking what the Foreign Service does and what constitutes the cutting edge of its professional expertise. We have attempted to do that in the preceding pages. We cannot begin to understand the real problems of the Foreign Service by emphasizing an oversimplified dichotomy between the "New" and the "Old" Diplomacy—our alternatives are not limited to a choice between the naïve enthusiasms of the Rostows, Hilsmans, and Taylors, and the persistent negativism of the experienced Foreign Service Officer who is unwilling to risk anything not sanctioned by precedent. (It is instructive to note that almost all the successes and virtues that Campbell attributes to the Foreign Service are negative: they involve preventing the government from doing something that might get it into trouble. This is not a trivial virtue, and it is much in fashion at the moment, as is any stance that appears to offer the prospect of keeping us out of more Vietnams. Nevertheless, it is far from clear that this is a sufficient basis for a Foreign Service that is truly elite and truly professional.)

[52] *Ibid.,* p. 97.

Since Campbell assumes without question that the Foreign Service is omni-competent, and its disabilities entirely imposed from without, his suggestions for reform miss the heart of the problem. He wants to cut the Foreign Service in size (which essentially seems to mean throwing out the specialists "Wristonization" brought in) and centralize the control of foreign affairs in the Department of State (and, a fortiori, in the Foreign Service). I find it doubtful that this kind of reform, which merely replaces one group of incompetents with another, is what we need. No reforms make sense unless they correlate the training and the skills that the Foreign Service should possess with the tasks it must perform and the world in which it must operate. Any attempt to spell out this correlation in greater detail would take us far beyond our purpose, which is to understand the limits and possibilities of planning in foreign affairs. What should be clear, however, is that the problems of the present and the future are too complex and too specialized to be dealt with by men who continue to pride themselves solely on the possession of personal characteristics that facilitate amiability, rather than intellectual characteristics that facilitate substantive agreement. Men trained in the "Old Diplomacy" are unlikely to take the need for planning seriously, and it is clear by now that the problems we face can no longer be dealt with by ad hoc improvisations. But what kind of planning staff do we need? And what kind of planning has actually taken place? We shall deal with these questions in the ensuing sections.

POLICY PLANNING IN THE STATE DEPARTMENT

The Policy Planning Staff of the State Department was created in the spring of 1947 in response to the desires of Secretary of State Marshall. It was abolished as an independent entity in the summer of 1969, and incorporated as a planning and coordinating staff directly within the office of the Secretary of State and his three principal deputies. For a short period of time, the Policy Planning Staff had been a reasonably successful institution, not because it did much planning or merchandised any unusual ideas, but because it had the ear of the Secretary of State. And in Washington, status and success are defined by presumed influence over a paramount decision-maker.[53]

[53] My interpretation of the record of the Policy Planning Staff and the Policy Planning Council rests on both the usual published sources and on a series of interviews with about twenty-five members. The interviews were interesting and useful, and I should like to express my appreciation to them all.

My views on the record of the PPS and the PPC and on the quality of its work would not be shared by many of its members. My interpretations are entirely my own, and no one else shares responsibility for them.

The ultimate decline of the Policy Planning Staff was probably as predictable as anything can be in the American system of government. Marshall's successors never conceived the role of the PPS in the way in which he had. The Staff's early successes also inevitably antagonized the operating Bureaus of the Department, and they fought a typical bureaucratic rearguard action to limit its influence: they insisted that its policy papers must be presented to them before they were sent on to the Secretary. The combination of a less direct relationship with the Secretary of State and less autonomy in presenting an independent viewpoint undermined the status of the PPS. Under its last two directors, the reputation and influence of the Staff (by then renamed the Policy Planning Council) sunk so low that its disappearance was barely noticed.

None of this was surprising to those familiar with the way in which either the policymaking system or the State Department functioned. From the viewpoint of those who like to consider themselves as sophisticated observers of the Washington scene, the whole notion of planning in foreign affairs seemed wildly utopian. It was more surprising that the Staff had been created at all than that it failed. It was not unexpected that the PPS expended its energy on activities that had little to do with planning. Staffs survive and prosper by handling the problems of the moment: the PPS was no more immune from this "law" than any other bureaucratic entity.

Significantly, the PPS was created by a Secretary of State whose previous career had been in the military. The idea would not likely have occurred or appealed to a Secretary schooled in the normal tradition of foreign affairs. As George Kennan, the first director of the PPS, points out, Marshall wanted a planning unit "to fill, at least in part, the place of the Division of Plans and Operations to which he was accustomed in the War Department."[54] Planning had always been a reasonably honored tradition in the military, and Marshall was perhaps unaware how unusual his proposal was in the operating code of the State Department.

The functions of the Staff were defined in typically broad language. The staff was to formulate "long-term programs for the achievement of U.S. foreign policy objectives"; to involve itself in "anticipating problems which the department may encounter in the discharge of its mission"; to undertake and prepare studies on "broad politico-military problems"; "to evaluate the adequacy of current policy" and to make advisory recommendations on it; and, finally, to coordinate planning activities with-

[54] George F. Kennan, *Memoirs: 1925-1950* (Boston: Atlantic-Little, Brown, 1967), p. 313.

in the State Department.[55] What this meant was not absolutely clear. The Secretary of State, however, gave Kennan one piece of useful advice: "Avoid trivia."[56]

The small group that Kennan assembled in May, 1947, originally contained only five members. It was immediately thrust into the most pressing issue of the moment: Marshall gave Kennan orders to prepare recommendations, within two weeks, on the problem of European recovery. The important role that Kennan and the PPS played in the creation of what came to be called the Marshall Plan has been amply documented.[57] The manifest success of the PPS on this issue, the estimable reputations of its original membership, and the fact that Marshall took the advice of the PPS seriously combined to give it a working brief on all the major issues of the day. In the next two and a half years, for example, the PPS offered comments and counsel on the Berlin blockade, the future of Germany, European unification, NATO and the Western European Union, and the problems of Japan, China, and the Far East.

Dean Acheson replaced Marshall as Secretary of State in January, 1949, but Kennan continued to direct the PPS. Kennan noted, however, that "there was a perceptible change in the position and the possibilities of the Planning Staff." The problem, from Kennan's point of view, was that Acheson

> saw me only as an individual—as one, in fact, of a group of individuals whom he had around him and with whom he likes to explore ideas— people of quite heterogeneous background and outlook, to whose disparate views he listened as might a judge to the arguments of the opposing counsel. The thought of consulting the staff as an institution and conceding to it, as did General Marshall, a margin of confidence within which he was willing to respect its opinion even when that opinion did not fully coincide with his own—the thought, in particular of conceding to the staff a certain function as the ideological inspirer and coordinator of policy, bringing into coherent interrelationship the judgments and efforts of the various geographic and functional divisions of the department—all this would have been strange to him.[58]

As a result, Kennan began to feel like the "court jester," no doubt an honorable position, but less exalted than the "ideological inspirer and coordinator of policy." Neither Kennan and his colleagues nor Acheson

[55] *Ibid.,* p. 327.
[56] *Ibid.,* p. 326.
[57] In addition to Kennan's *Memoirs,* see Joseph Marion Jones, *The Fifteen Weeks* (New York: Harcourt, Brace and World, 1955).
[58] Kennan, *Memoirs,* pp. 426-427.

thought there was much virtue in attempting to plan for the future.[59] Their focus, on the contrary, was exclusively on controlling and coordinating the present.

The PPS continued to be involved in major issues throughout Acheson's tenure and continued to have some of the Secretary's interest, but Kennan's dissatisfaction mounted. It came to a head in September, 1949, when a procedural argument arose over how the PPS's papers were to be handled. They had previously gone directly to the Secretary of State, which meant that he had before him a clear statement of the views of the PPS. In September, however,

> a staff paper ready for presentation to the Secretary . . . was first laid, at Mr. Webb's expressed wish, before the body of senior officials—Assistant Secretaries and others—who attended the Under-Secretary's regular morning meetings. Several of these gentlemen expressed disagreement with one or the other of its features . . . whereupon the paper was returned to me with Mr. Webb's request that I reconcile these differences by discussion with the respective gentlemen and rewrite the paper before submitting it to the Secretary of State.
>
> It was perfectly clear what was involved in this procedure: the staff was to be deprived of direct access to the Secretary of State in the presentation of its views; from now on, staff papers would be subject to the veto of any of the chiefs of the operational divisions of the department.

Some of Kennan's staff were in favor of accepting the new procedure. Kennan was not, for he insisted that the

> whole *raison d'être* of this staff was in its ability to render an independent judgment . . . If the senior officials do not wish such an independent judgment, or do not have confidence in us to prepare one which would be useful, then I question whether the staff should exist at all.[60]

But it became clear that the senior operating officials had no desire to have an independent staff with direct access to the Secretary criticizing

[59] The well-known NSC-68 study began in the PPS, but neither Kennan nor Charles Bohlen thought it especially useful: "Although Bohlen accepted as necessary an attempt, such as the study group effort, to define the problem and outline a response to it, such planning, he apparently thought, could not legitimately rest on any particular prediction about future Soviet behavior, for any prediction would be too arbitrary . . . [Kennan] . . . went on to conclude that formal policy planning of this character is necessarily too simplified to be useful." Paul Y. Hammond, "NSC-68: Prologue to Rearmament," in *Strategy, Politics and Defense Budgets,* pp. 310-311. They both believed in the "esoteric skill" of diplomacy, rather than in general statements of policy (pp. 315-317).
[60] Kennan, *Memoirs,* pp. 465-466.

or kibitzing their ventures. The Secretary of State, for whatever reason, did not choose to support Kennan. Consequently, Kennan resigned, and was replaced as director by Paul Nitze.

Shortly thereafter, Kennan recorded his evaluation of the PPS during his tenure. He noted that it has

> simply been a failure, like all previous attempts to bring order and foresight into the designing of foreign policy by special institutional arrangements within the department. Aside from personal short-comings, the reason for this seems to lie largely in the impossibility of having the planning function performed outside of the line of command . . . But when it comes to any formalized staff effort, anything that has to be put down in writing and is designed to serve as a major guide for action, the operating units—the geographic and functional units—will not take interference from any unit outside the line of command. They insist on an effective voice in policy determination; if one of them cannot make its voice alone valid, it insists on the right to water down any recommendation going to the Secretary to a point where it may be meaningless but at least not counter to its own views. If an unwelcome recommendation does find the Secretary's approval, they will perhaps give it a perfunctory recognition, but they will pursue basically their own policies anyway, secure in the knowledge that no one can really survey their entire volume of work; that the issues which agitate the present will soon be outdated, and that the people who are trying to force their hand will soon be gone.[61]

The PPS never again attained the status and influence that it had under Kennan (especially during Marshall's tenure). It continued to work on important problems, and the next three directors (Nitze, Robert Bowie, and Gerard Smith) all enjoyed the confidence of the Secretary of State (which was not true, according to most reports, of the last two directors, Walt Rostow and Henry Owen).[62] As the years passed, however, the PPS was increasingly dominated by the operator's ethos. Its members tended to become—or tried to become—free-lance operators, always (in typical bureaucratic style) seeking to be actively involved in the most immediate issues. Planning, prediction, and a concern for the significance of long-range developments were honored rhetorically and ignored in practice.

The papers prepared by the members of the PPS are classified. It is thus

[61] *Ibid.,* p. 467.

[62] On the relatively high status of the staff during the Marshall and Acheson years, see also Dean Acheson, *Present at the Creation: My Years in the State Department* (New York: W. W. Norton, 1969), pp. 214-215; Townsend Hoopes also compares the staff in 1965 unfavorably with the Kennan and Nitze staffs. See *The Limits of Intervention* (New York: David McKay, 1969), p. 1.

impossible to submit any of them to extensive analysis.[63] That is not, however, so disabling as it might appear. There was never a simple PPS "line" on particular issues, and the members frequently were in disagreement.[64] What they said was not so important, from the point of view of this essay, as what they were talking about. And what they were discussing was what everyone else, especially *The New York Times,* was talking about. In the Nitze years, for example, the staff worked on such current matters as the major National Security Council studies of military preparedness, Iranian oil and the problem of Mossadegh, and the Korean negotiations. In this period, the papers that were to be discussed in the National Security Council also usually originated in the PPS (and were sent on without the approval of the Secretary of State). During the Dulles years, under Bowie and Smith, the staff worked on most of the major current issues: the aid program and the ways and means of organizing it, the offshore islands problem, Berlin, the Mideast crises, disarmament and arms control proposals (the test ban), the significance of the MRBM and the onset of the missile age, and the possibilities of a multilateral nuclear force for Europe.

The Policy Planning Staff was bureaucratically upgraded in 1961; it became the Policy Planning Council (PPC). The director now had the rank of an Assistant Secretary of State. This was done apparently to indicate the significance that the Kennedy administration attached not only to planning but also to its potential role in policymaking in the Department of State. The new director was George McGhee, but he departed before the year was over. He was succeeded by Walt Rostow (1961-1966) and then by Henry Owen (1966-1968).

Rostow's Council also worked on many urgent problems of the moment, such as the MLF, the role of tactical nuclear weapons, and the problems and prospects of reaching an international commodities agreement. Rostow, however, also attempted some minor innovations. On the one hand, he encouraged some studies on a few obvious but longer-range (definition: they were not concrete issues already on the Secretary's desk) problems, such as regional cooperation in Asia and an AID agricultural fund. On the other hand, he set the Council to work on prepar-

[63] Edited versions of some papers occasionally appeared in journals. In addition, some staff members were not reluctant to let outsiders read their analyses (although, of course, without permission to quote).
[64] This was a leitmotif of my interviews: without fail, I was told that there was as much disagreement about Vietnam and the ABM-MIRV dispute within the PPC as there was in the outside world.

ing National Policy Papers, which were to summarize current problems with, and current policies toward, particular countries. This was, predictably, a disastrous enterprise: it was discussed with embarrassment by all concerned. The few studies that were completed were enormously time-consuming, empty in content, and obsolescent, if not obsolete, by completion.

Owen's Council also attempted to combine a study of immediate issues with attention to the problems of the near future. The issues involved in the nonproliferation treaty and the evolution of the strategic balance between the United States and the Soviet Union were extensively analyzed. So, too, were issues like technical aid, malnutrition, and the possibilities of creating a public corporation to foster investment in the underdeveloped nations.

Did the upgrading of the PPS and its subsequent concern with longer-range issues indicate that it had truly achieved a new status under the Kennedy and Johnson administrations? The new PPC had time to study issues that were not of top priority only because its influence had sunk to zero. The reason was not difficult to discover: Dean Rusk was not convinced that Rostow and Owen were worth consulting or that a body like the PPC had anything of significance to contribute to his policymaking.[65] Rusk's negative attitude toward planning might have prevailed whatever the circumstances. Yet, in defense of his attitude, the quality of the work emerging from the PPC—even on its own terms, as a comment on current problems—had fallen off markedly. Rusk, for example, might have concluded that the distortions and oversimplifications intrinsic to Rostow's notion of "stages of economic development" were characteristics of his intellectual efforts. Rostow's sophomoric fascination with various doctrines of counterinsurgency warfare, which began to appear less appealing as the Vietnam War dragged on, may have confirmed this judgment. Rumors that Rostow had (or wanted) a direct line to the White House may also have influenced Rusk's attitude: true or not, this was not likely to lead to a relationship of mutual trust. As for Owen, his stock had declined sharply after a desperate and misconceived effort to achieve agreement on the MLF (a multilateral nuclear force) had to be quietly shelved at the order of the President. (Rusk himself was

[65] These considerations also appeared frequently in my interviews. Some confirmation can be found in Chester L. Cooper's comment on the PPC's influence on the Vietnam question: "These folk saw so few important communications on Vietnam that their assistance to policymakers was minimal." *The Lost Crusade—America in Vietnam* (New York: Dodd, Mead, 1970), p. 415.

apparently not enthusiastic about some of Owen's other papers: he reportedly sent at least one back with the comment that it was not challenging enough.)[66]

Some reasons for the failures of the PPS and the PPC are already apparent: no planning unit forced to operate within the normal context of the American policymaking system, or within the confines of the State Department, could ever be wholly successful. There are, however, other factors that also impede the possibility of effective planning. Two in particular stand out. The first concerns the manner in which the planners and the operators ought to relate to each other. The standard argument, much favored by Kennan and others, is that the planners and the operators cannot be separated from each other: independent planning staffs are thus bound to fail. Stanley Hoffmann has also argued that the critical error in our approach to planning "is having the division between planners and performers at all . . . [it] divorces inspiration and management and as a result helps to sterilize both."[67] We shall raise some questions about the accuracy of this judgment. The second factor concerns the relationship between prevailing beliefs about the nature of international politics and the likelihood that either planners or operators will take the planning function seriously. This has much to do with Kennan's argument that the dilemmas of planning can be resolved only if the Secretary of State "will thresh out a basic theoretical background of his policy."[68]

Before turning to these issues, it may be useful to look more closely at the men who served on the PPS and the PPC and at how they regarded their duties.

THE POLICY PLANNERS: A PROFILE

It has always seemed paradoxical that policy planning has been held in low esteem, but that an appointment to the staff of either the PPS or the PPC has carried some prestige with it. The mystery is not profound.

[66] On the last point, see John P. Leacacos, *Fires in the In-Basket—The ABC's of the State Department* (Cleveland: World Publishing Company, 1968), p. 529. According to Leacacos, Rusk also asked Owen to seek "unorthodox" ideas, even those that were "not considered immediately feasible." (p. 528) Perhaps this was Rusk's idea of a joke, or perhaps, considering his indifference to long-range planning, he was merely trying to get the PPC off his back. When the fresh and unorthodox ideas turned out to be warmed-over commonplaces from the previous decade, one can sympathize with Rusk's attitude.

[67] Hoffmann, *Gulliver's Troubles*, p. 319.

[68] Kennan, *Memoirs*, p. 467.

Selection, especially for FSOs, has usually indicated approval of past performance and an implicit promise of future promotion.

Who were the men selected to be planners? If they were chosen from the diplomatic corps, they had usually attained the rank of Counsel or First Secretary at an important embassy. A few were appointed from even higher ranking positions (for example, chief or assistant chief of a bureau or special assistant to the Secretary of State), though infrequently; even less frequently, a few officers below the rank of Counsel were given appointments (and then subsequently promoted to the rank of Counsel after leaving the staff). The rank factor, of course, tended to determine the age factor: fully two-thirds of the total membership were between forty and fifty years old when appointed. Well over half went to what are normally described as "prestige schools"; about the same percentage had graduate training of some sort, although, one might add, the two groups were not identical. Almost all the FSOs who served on the staff moved upward, usually to a high ranking position in one of the bureaus.

The case of Jacob Beam may provide the norm. He joined the PPS after being Counsel of the Embassy in Moscow, and then became director of the Office of Eastern European Affairs. Outerbridge Horsey is another case. He went from Counsel in Rome to the PPS, and then became Deputy Director of the Office of British Commonwealth and Northern European Affairs. Max Bishop was Counsel of the Embassy in Tokyo, spent a short period on the PPS, and became Chief of the Division of Near Eastern and Asian Affairs. George Jones was Counsel in London, joined the PPS for a term, and then became Director of the Office of Near Eastern Affairs. These were not unusual cases. Appointment to the planning staff was not a sign of disapproval. These men were apparently chosen because they had been successful operators, and not because they had revealed any aptitude for planning—which would have been difficult to do.

Kennan's original staff had been selected rather quickly and under extreme time pressures—this meant that the sheer question of availability tended to determine choice in several cases. As time passed, however, and choices could be made in a more regular fashion, a pattern in recruitment could be detected. Kennan chose some men because of the specific expertise they possessed, but he chose others because he (or others) thought they were "wise men" or "great generalists" capable of offering the Secretary the benefits of their experience and judgment. But as the staff grew larger, it also grew more specialized: experience, particularly experience in the pre-war or war-time Foreign Service, was not a solvent for the problems that began to emerge in the 1950s and the 1960s.

What this meant is that the percentage of FSOs on the staff began to decline. In the total membership from 1947 to 1968, about 40 per cent were FSOs.[69] Part of that 40 per cent came by lateral appointment, especially those who were regional or economic specialists. In addition, a number of specialists were appointed from outside the Department of State as the need arose and an internal choice could not be made. In the final count, at least two-thirds of the total membership of the PPS and the PPC could be classified as specialists (some of whom were FSOs but usually via Wristonization or some such process). As a result, in the abstract, it would seem safe to presume that the conservative impact of the training and ethos of the normal FSO would be considerably diluted. In reality, as we shall see, it did not work that way: most of the specialists and other outside appointments were chosen because they shared the same biases as the rest of the State Department, and not because they showed any likelihood of challenging the conventional wisdom.

It would be unfair, perhaps absurd, to expect operators to be aware or concerned about the realm of the theorist. The Policy Planning Staff, however, was in an entirely different situation. Relieved of operating responsibilities and legitimately concerned with anticipating future problems, a staff with a majority of specialists and outsiders had every opportunity to seek the best advice it could find, to ponder critics, to raise irritating questions, and to become the constituency for the future that the Department so obviously needed. But it never occurred to the directors of the PPS and the PPC that any of these tasks had much to do with the real functions of a planning staff in foreign affairs. In fact, raising these issues and not understanding why they were irrelevant indicated that the questioner was naïve.

Why this should be so becomes immediately clear if we understand the single principle upon which all the planners agree: success or failure for a planning staff depends not on what it does, or who is on it, or where it is placed, but on the willingness of the Secretary of State to listen to it, to consult it, and to protect it from enemies. This simple principle accounts for the irrelevance of the PPC in the Kennedy and Johnson years. Dean Rusk, either because of his low regard for the staff or because of tradi-

[69] The careers of the non-FSOs on the staff both before and after their appointments were more varied than those of the FSOs. They were drafted from journalism, other government agencies (especially the intelligence outfits), and occasionally from the universities. There was no pattern to the jobs they accepted after leaving the staff. Clearly, however, the non-FSO suffered no loss of status in joining the planners, and many went on to prestigious jobs.

tional views about how the Department should function, turned only to his geographical and functional bureaus for policy advice. Concerning advice on urgent issues, he did not see what the planners could do that the bureaus themselves could not do equally well. In contrast, when Marshall was Secretary of State, Kennan and his staff were expected to comment on major issues in order to give the Secretary an unbiased (but not necessarily decisive) view of events.[70]

Measuring the effectiveness of a planning staff solely by whether it has a powerful patron who chooses to listen to it is reasonable—so long as one does not expect it to do any planning. Influence on immediate issues as a criterion of effectiveness is hardly an unusual standard in Washington. It is questionable, however, whether it is sufficient for a planning staff. The Secretary of State is very busy and he has a short term of office. If he thinks about his planners according to what they can contribute to immediate issues, and they in turn conceive their role in the same fashion, the result may be an influential planning staff. But the paradox is that the planning staff buys influence at the cost of relinquishing the other roles it can play. The planning staff can afford neither to worry about problems that have not yet arisen nor to criticize the direction of received policies. Criticism (the much renowned "gadfly role") has the unfortunate tendency of ejecting one from the Secretary's "stream of thinking," which some Secretaries have regarded as disloyal. Finally, the quest for immediate influence forces the planner to play bureaucratic politics without the power (or the responsibility) that goes with a position in the regular hierarchy. It is not surprising that he finds it difficult to compete or that the regional bureaus regard him as a parasite.

What emerges from the interaction of these factors is a planning staff with an operator's perspective. Criticism that the staff has frequently become too involved in current issues is easily turned aside by the argument that the proper role of a planning staff has been misconceived. Robert Bowie, for example, admits that the criticism is "partly valid," but that

it reflects a misconception of what is useful, and possible in long-term planning. The purpose of a policy planning staff is not merely to produce literature, but to produce results. For better or worse, foreign policy becomes operative largely in specific decisions. . . . If insights and thinking on long-term factors are to be effective, they must be

[70] Some members of Owens's staff noted that he feared that too much criticism would lose influence for the PPC. This was an odd point to make during a period when the PPC did not appear to have any influence.

brought to bear on such decisions as they are made. It is true, however, that the Policy Planning Staff will have no special contribution to make if it becomes immersed in current activities.[71]

By what contortions, we may reasonably ask, is the dilemma to be resolved? How does one participate in current decisions and yet retain a commitment to long-range issues?[72]

Most dilemmas can be resolved by rhetorical skill and this one is no exception. It is not necessary to choose between the short run and the long run; they must be combined. The planners, according to Rostow, "must understand fully the operational environment in which a new concept must take hold if it is to be successful . . . the task is to conceive of specific objectives in particular theaters of activity and of how to move forward toward those objectives under rapidly changing operational circumstances."[73]

Is there a meaningful criterion that determines our choice of specific objectives? Rostow believes he has found it in the contention that objectives will be chosen in order to "make the nation's position on the world scene better in the future."[74] After all, who would choose objectives to make our position worse? A formula as meaningless as this has no substantive significance; it is merely another way of saying that there is no necessity of thinking seriously about the future. There is additional, indirect evidence for this negative conclusion in Rostow's enthusiasm for another familiar truism: the long run is the accumulation of what we do in the short run. This is true, for what else could it be? The implication that should be drawn from this, however, is not that the future will take care of itself, but that we must worry about the criteria that would allow us to make reasonable connections between our goals and our actions. On these matters, Rostow has nothing to offer.

A planning staff that actually planned would probably be ignored by

[71] Bowie's comments can be found in the symposium "Planning in the Department," *Foreign Service Journal* 38 (March 1961): 24.

[72] One answer is that you do not: instead you maintain that the role of the planner is to "chip away at the boundaries of United States' policy." Even within the fraternity of operators, this is a notoriously limited interpretation of what a planning unit can do. The comment was made by Gerard Smith in the symposium mentioned in footnote 71 (p. 21).

[73] W. W. Rostow, "The Planning of Foreign Policy," Department of State *Newsletter,* June 1964.

[74] W. W. Rostow, "The Planning of Foreign Policy," in E. A. J. Johnson, ed., *The Dimensions of Diplomacy* (Baltimore: Johns Hopkins Press, 1964), p. 44. Rostow thought so well of his own views on planning that he continued publishing identical versions in different places—which may prove that he had not lost complete touch with the academic world.

the Foreign Service. It would be an article of faith that the planning staff could do nothing of importance. But a group of operators camouflaged as a planning staff is an entirely different matter: they might be dangerous, especially if the Secretary of State listens to them. Thus, the Foreign Service has always preferred to have planning in its own hands. A committee of the American Foreign Service Association, for example, concluded that "planning and programming should be done principally by the operators rather than by specialized planning staffs. In organizational terms, it should be done mainly in the bureaus."[75] The British apparently share these views, for the Plowden Report (1964) noted that "the principal planners should be career officers. An experienced general service officer will be less likely to approach his task from too academic a point of view." It also warned that the "planning staff should not spend too high a proportion of their time scanning the horizons of the distant future."[76] As Lord Strang once noted, "Events are very strong." One cannot help recalling Lord Halifax's comment (unfortunately, on the eve of World War II): "I distrust anyone who foresees consequences and advocates remedies to avert them."[77]

The Foreign Service is also suspicious of specialists. The increasing number of specialists on the PPS and the PPC, however, limited the possible challenges the planning staff might make to the operators. From all reports, the regional specialists tended to be more concerned with immediate relevance and more reluctant to question purpose or method.[78] It was also true that the area specialist remained too close to his regional bureau to exert much independent influence. He may already have become identified with established policies. Perhaps more critically, his subsequent career was likely to be made in his regional bureau; raising questions about the performance of that bureau was not likely to be considered prudent. Area research, like much of the Department's research, inevitably aimed neither at breaking new ground nor at criticizing old approaches, but at improving the means to carry out unexamined ends.[79]

[75] "Toward a Modern Diplomacy," *Foreign Service Journal,* November 1968 (Part II), p. 48.

[76] *Report of the Committee on Representational Services Overseas* (Chairman: Lord Plowden), Cmnd. 2276, February 1964, p. 56.

[77] Quoted in Anthony Sampson, *Anatomy of Britain* (London: Hodder and Stoughton, 1962), p. 311.

[78] This point was made frequently in my interviews.

[79] See William R. Polk, "The Scholar and the Administrator in International Affairs," *Bulletin of the Atomic Scientists,* March 1966, p. 6. For other evidence that government reports tend to defend existing policy against outside critics, see

A planning staff that does not criticize ends, that does not seriously think ahead, and that is afraid to take issues off the "back burner" for fear of losing influence is essentially irrelevant. This means that all the impressive descriptions of what a planning staff *might* do to improve the quality of policymaking are meaningless. The planners have instead sought other roles for themselves. As one of them pointed out some years ago, "The path of least resistance is always toward worrying about what everybody else is worrying about, instead of about what nobody is but somebody should."[80] This does not mean that everything the PPS or the PPC did was useless or inferior. What it performed was in general done as well as anything else done in the State Department. But it also did not do anything original. Therefore, the Nixon administration's decision to eliminate the PPC and make it part of the Secretary of State's executive staff seems eminently reasonable. The staff that used to be the PPC can now do openly what it always did under the guise of planning: attempt to have a say in current policy by influencing the Secretary's thinking.

It is wrong, from this perspective, to criticize the quality of the "research" turned out by the PPC, which was a planning staff that neither planned nor did any research. As far as current policies go, members offered opinions and suggestions that were a synthesis of the work of others. But because of an inability or a reluctance to raise fundamental questions about policies—for reasons that we have discussed—the "other" researchers to whom they turned frequently were publicists, journalists, or policy specialists.[81] This was as it should be. Specific policy advice rests on intimate knowledge of the details of situations.[82] In this con-

Charles Frankel, "The Difference between Being In and Being Out" (paper delivered at the American Political Science Association Convention, September 1968, p. 6).

[80] George Allen Morgan, "Planning in Foreign Affairs: The State of the Art," *Foreign Affairs* 39 (January 1961): 276.

[81] This became clear in questioning members of the staff about their familiarity with theoretical work in their specialized areas. They were familiar with very little—usually pleading that they lacked time and that academic work was irrelevant anyway (a judgment that is probably right, but still based on hearsay).

Robert Packenham's interviews with officials concerned with development problems yielded much the same results: they were not aware of research findings, and the only theorist they found useful was Hans Morgenthau. See "Political Development Doctrines in the American Foreign Aid Program," *World Politics* 18 (January 1966): 234.

[82] It was striking how frequently the planners complained that academic consultants turned out to be useless because the insider had to spend most of his time briefing the outsider on the latest facts. Clearly, they wanted advice from the academic that had nothing to do with the academic's function per se.

text, the scholar or the theorist is likely to be useless; the policy planner would have to seek a different *kind* of influence *for himself* before the insights of the theorists would seem germane to him.[83] Seeking to influence the point of decision may concentrate the mind wonderfully but also turns it away from the only areas in which the planner might have a major role.

Perhaps it is worthwhile to make a special effort to avoid misunderstandings about the value of policy analysis. I am *not* arguing that it should not be done or that it may not be useful to the policymakers. I *am* arguing that policy analysis should not be confused with planning, and that a staff that spends all or most of its time on such work should not be labeled a "planning staff." Thus, the Policy Planning Council ought not to be criticized for doing policy analysis, but rather for not doing it well or imaginatively, and then mislabeling it as "planning."

The utility of policy analysis is usually taken for granted within the government—in the abstract. I was struck, however, by the number of times I received negative answers during my interviews when I asked whether a particular piece of policy research was useful. One difficulty was a matter of timing: if the research was done on a problem that was of top priority, then it was almost always obsolete by the time it was completed; if it was about a problem that was not yet significant, no one had the time or inclination to read it.

Policy analysis, whether done in or out of the government, also suffers from a tendency to remain within familiar categories. This helps to account for the fact that such analyses are far more effective in attacking existing policies than in suggesting viable alternatives: the latter, which are familiar to anyone moderately informed, have usually been rejected for what seemed to be sensible reasons.[84] Thus the publicist merely succeeds in reshuffling the same set of perceptions and assumptions, without really forcing anyone—particularly the policymakers—to rethink what he takes for granted. Moreover, most policy research concentrates

[83] See Chapter 3 for more comments on this point.
[84] As an illustration, one European expert cited two policy works by a publicist-professor that had been reviewed as "brilliant" by several journalists (and *Foreign Affairs*). The first work, following the fashion of the moment, advocated an "Atlantic" rather than a "European" or a "national" solution to Europe's problems. More recently, fashion having changed again, the analyst attacked the "Atlantic" solution and advocated a "European" solution for Europe's problems. This statement of alternatives is simplistic and superficial; the alternatives are also so obvious and familiar that they force no one out of the comfort of conventional wisdom. It is also striking how such books are written as though diplomatic constellations were formed in a vacuum and social, economic, and technological changes had nothing to do with the future of politics.

too exclusively on "high" politics and traditional categories of analysis. Consequently, it is useful only for an increasingly narrow range of issues.

The issue of who should or should not be doing policy research is of great significance. Some group in the government ought to do it, but it is problematic whether that group should be defined as "planners." Given the difficulty of separating policy research from more theoretical research in the current phase of political science, whatever guidelines we establish must be reasonably loose. We do, however, have certain benchmarks from which to proceed. The essential one is that policy research on immediate issues—the "what shall we do now" analyses—should not constitute the academic contribution to policymaking, for it is usually out-of-date and slights the kind of work the academic should really be doing. Policy research on immediate issues also should not be the *sole* contribution of a long-range planning staff. The primary concern of this staff must be with the middle- and long-range factors that will condition the environment in which specific decisions will be made; the staff must also constantly question the relevance and adequacy of the assumptions and beliefs with which policymakers operate. The planner's influence on the choice of policies should always be indirect. If he goes beyond that, he is illegitimately intruding into the realm of the operator; and if he fails to reach the level of indirect influence, policymaking can never escape the restriction of habit and tradition. The practical significance is that a new long-range staff ought to limit as sharply as possible the number of immediate policy issues it deals with: the staff should do only the minimum necessary to survive during its formative years. Other staffs can do this kind of work just as effectively—perhaps more so—without sacrificing any skills or integrity.

Kennan believed that a planning staff could never succeed in the Department of State unless the Secretary of State provided a "basic theoretical background" for his policy. After he resigned, Kennan (as well as other former members of the planning staff, and Hans Morgenthau and Reinhold Niebuhr) attempted to provide that background. The result was Realism, a body of doctrine that has never lost its power to entice. The Foreign Service has always found it admirable; the doctrine of Realism confirms all prejudices and requires very little from the true believer. But it did not, as Kennan hoped it would, provide the background that would make policy planning a significant function. Why is it that a doctrine so attractive to both theorists and practitioners nonetheless failed to lead to either a better understanding of world politics or more coherent practical actions?

POLITICAL REALISM AND POLITICAL PRACTICE

Political Realism dominated the discipline of international relations throughout the 1950s. There were occasional complaints that it went "too far," or that it did not esteem what should be properly valued, but there was little fundamental disagreement with its interpretation of what international politics was all about. Even the liberal left joined the chorus, perhaps out of guilt for opposing rearmament against Hitler in the 1930s, or perhaps for fear of being branded naïve again in the face of a new threat.

Realism is no longer in style in academic circles. It has been under continuous attack for over a decade—and the worst sort of attack, for it has been ignored as an anachronistic remnant of the discipline's early years. However, its staying power, although in a less formal and coherent fashion, has been much stronger in the practical world. This is not surprising, since there is normally a gap between when a doctrine is articulated in intellectual circles and when it is accepted by practical men—and a gap between when it is rejected by the theorists and when it is rejected by the practitioners. The inconsistencies that trouble the theorist and make him more receptive to new doctrines always appear less salient to men working on daily problems: the erosion of the woods is rarely immediately apparent to those who live amid the trees.

Whatever its current status, Realism reflects an important part of our recent intellectual heritage. The ease and pervasiveness of the dominance of Realism in the post-World War II years owes a great deal to the fact that it always seemed natural and right to the practitioners—it encapsulated what they took for granted, especially after the failures of the 1930s and during the height of the Cold War. In fact, Realism was an oddity in theoretical terms, for it was always more attractive to practitioners than to theorists; the former were delighted to find that they were really "speaking" theory, but the latter were increasingly ambivalent about a doctrine that mixed normative, descriptive, and metaphysical statements indiscriminately. Realism was the doctrine that provided the intellectual frame of reference for the foreign policy establishment for about twenty years, perhaps more. We need to understand the vision of world politics Realism made fashionable not only because it helps to explain the failures of planning but also because it shares the responsibility for many disastrous errors in judgment over the last twenty-five years.

Realism became popular in the years immediately after World War II. It was not, however, a new doctrine. The first generation of Realists (apart from Machiavelli and Hobbes) emerged in the 1930s: the writings of Nicholas Spykman, Reinhold Niebuhr, and E. H. Carr. They were either ignored or accused of unwarranted cynicism.

The different reactions that Realism engendered in the 1930s and the 1940s are only somewhat, if at all, attributable to the superior insights of postwar Realists such as Hans Morgenthau and George Kennan. The prevailing way of attempting to solve the problems of world politics in the 1930s was inadequate. The failures of the "legal-rational" approach were such that this approach was out of joint with a world that included several classic nonlegal, nonrational types. No amount of manipulation could transform Hitler into a Manchester businessman, and faith in the law-abiding world of the future could hardly survive a contemporary world of increasing tension and *sauve-qui-peut* philosophy. Nonetheless, the new approach implicit in the Realist doctrine was not immediately or widely accepted. It probably requires a disaster of major proportion before the shock of recognition occurs and a new doctrine succeeds in thoroughly routing the incumbent. Thus, World War II converted Realism from an esoteric, private critique of the behavior of the Western democracies into a popular and fully articulated interpretation of world politics.[85]

Why do we accept *any* doctrine or approach as legitimate? The answer hardly lies in methodological norms alone, for they are an insufficient response to the complexity of the world. Inevitably, an arbitrary and personal element underlies our choice. Perhaps the best we can say, which may merely be another way of concealing our ignorance, is that the doctrine we choose to adopt has the power of clarifying what puzzles us. We cannot account for our choice by reason alone, nor by experience, since we experience only through the perspective of the doctrine in question. Polanyi's emphasis on the significance of the tacit components of our knowledge and beliefs may provide the most valid interpretation:

> We grant authority over ourselves to the conceptions which we have accepted because we acknowledge them as intimations—derived from the contact we make through them with reality—of an indefinite sequence of novel future occasions, which we may hope to master by developing these conceptions further, relying on our own judgment in its continued contact with reality.[86]

[85] For an examination of the major strands of thought in the 1930s, see William T. R. Fox, "Interwar International Relations Research: The American Experience," *World Politics* 2 (October 1949): 67-79.
[86] Michael Polanyi, *Personal Knowledge* (New York: Harper Torchbooks, 1964), p. 104.

Realism, therefore, was accepted because it seemed to have grasped the natural order of things in international politics, and seemed to promise that emerging puzzles could be solved by its standards.

Realism involved commitment to a set of propositions about international politics that were essentially extrapolations from the diplomatic history of nineteenth-century Europe. They were propositions that the generation of statesmen in Europe after 1919 either had lost or misunderstood: reeducation in the "perennials" was clearly necessary. The catechism was simple. Given the opportunity, all states sought, or would seek, power, which was an essential prerequisite for the achievement of other goals. Today's enemy could be tomorrow's ally (n.b., not "friend," for, as Salisbury put it, "Great Britain has no permanent friends, only permanent interests"). The use of any means was acceptable (atomic weapons created a dilemma, resolved by silence or metaphysical despair), or at least possible, though only one or two might be appropriate at any single moment. The best operator was the man who possessed "traditional wisdom," and the man who possessed "traditional wisdom" was the best operator.

The scenario and the stage directions are very familiar. The metaphor is deliberate, for many Realists considered international politics a great drama in which wise statesmen made hard choices in a bitter but limited struggle for dominance. Their power and fallibility constrained them, but they never fell victim to illusions about the true nature of the world. It was a world in which states were involved in an unending struggle with each other (because that was the nature of states in an anarchic world); power was necessary to survive in it or to continue to fight; and all states were potential enemies (Realism requires enemies more than it needs friends), but the worst might be avoided by clever diplomacy and by virtue of the fact that all shared a similar conception of rational behavior.[87] It was a dramatic picture, and an exciting one, for it was a

---

[87] The label "rational" is usually attached to behavior *before* we act. But "rational" here implies more than the warranted adoption of means to achieve ends derived from our values. It implies, in Oakeshott's sense, that there is a "tradition of the activity" in which we are engaged, and rationality is therefore a quality of our act itself (and not something we do beforehand), a quality that Oakeshott describes as faithfulness to our knowledge of how to conduct an activity. There is an "intelligence" appropriate to the idiom of each activity and displaying it is rational. In this sense, each frame of reference has its conception of rational behavior, which cannot be understood short of comprehending the true nature of the activity; for Realism, truly rational behavior could only be illustrated by pointing to successful practitioners like Bismarck and Talleyrand. The problem is that this is a perfectly circular definition of rational behavior: it provides no way to discriminate rational from nonrational behavior—except for the much-derided notion of success. For the argu-

drama of war in which the wartime mind predominated. This made it attractive to an emerging generation of statesmen whose views had been formed as a response to the failure to stop Hitler before it was too late, and who were thus predisposed to a doctrine that would guarantee that the same errors would not be committed against Stalin.

The Realist model of world politics was also simple and elegant. An image of states as billiard balls, interacting within a specific arena and according to established rules, became increasingly prevalent. Since there were only a few immutable patterns of behavior in politics, the role of the statesman was easy to understand—and very critical. He was to judge, by experience and intuition, the amount of force necessary to provide movement in a preferred direction. Purposes, as in wartime where survival and victory dominated, could be taken for granted. Individual idiosyncrasies, which might influence choice of purpose, or domestic politics, which might destroy the elegance of the game, could be safely ignored, for they were hardly significant in comparison to the external imperative imposed by life in international affairs. All states would respond to the same drummer, irrespective of internal differences, because they had no choice if they wished to survive (as a Great Power).

Is there something beyond its elegance and simplicity that has made this doctrine so popular to the practitioner? The power or fascination of a doctrine ultimately must rest on its apparent ability to provide answers to practical questions. The answers must be attributable to the doctrine, in that some connection may safely be posited between successful practitioners and doctrinal commitment. In the case at hand, the ability to make that connection would imply that a substantive distinction exists between a Realist and a non-Realist.

Is it easy to distinguish a Realist from a non-Realist? The difficulty is that commitment to the Realists' image of world politics—a world scarred by a permanent quest for power by potentially wicked men—hardly guarantees realistic decisions about the practical world. Realists and non-Realists may disagree about the permanence of power as the decisive factor in international politics, but they can still reach similar judgments about specific cases. On the other hand, two confessed Realists may reach totally dissimilar conclusions about the same case—one may even detect difficulties in relating an individual Realist's position on policy to his philosophical convictions. Correlating Morgenthau and Kennan on policy with Morgenthau and Kennan on Realism requires talmudic skill and patience, not to say a willingness to suspend disbelief.

ment, see Michael Oakeshott, *Rationalism in Politics* (New York: Basic Books, 1962), pp. 81-109.

The difficulty is that reality is so complex and ambiguous that the policies we choose to call "realistic" at any moment depend to a significant degree on personal predispositions and perspectives.

What this suggests is that Realism involves more than a temporal perspective on power and the nature of man. Also, lists of characteristics presumably shared by all Realists are irrelevant: statesmen or analysts possessing all the characteristics can act very unrealistically, while others possessing none of the characteristics may act realistically.[88] The more subtle contention that Realists share a realization that full security is beyond attainment, and that compromise and adjustment of interests is necessary, is more helpful. It implies that Realism involves a state of mind with which we approach problems, rather than possession of a few characteristics or attachment to the permanent significance of a single operating principle.[89] Nevertheless, some groups have the same sense of the nature of politics and are not considered Realists (some liberals). Moreover, the difficulty of discovering exactly why one policy position is more realistic than another persists.

These efforts to give Realism an acceptable programmatic content have been inadequate, for the task is impossible. We can define a Realist arbitrarily as someone who possesses certain characteristics or believes in certain doctrinal propositions, but there is no way we can convincingly relate those characteristics or beliefs to specific choices in the world of action. Realism simply constituted belief in the wisdom of certain "eternal verities" about politics, conveniently collected in a few texts and conveniently confirmed by a series of all too recent blunders by non-Realists. The point is not that Realism was unimportant or irrelevant. But its real significance has not been in providing a (nonexistent) direct connection between theory and action. Its power and influence over the choice of specific actions has been—and perhaps remains—pervasive but indirect. Realism has conditioned the political climate so that some actions seemed to stand to reason and others seemed naïve—by definition. And it has furnished an authentic body of scripture to rationalize and legitimize hard choices, to justify the notion that a democratic foreign policy is inconceivable, and to provide psychic support for the acolyte compelled to lie in defense of his interpretation of the national interest.

[88] Kenneth Thompson, *Political Realism and the Crisis of World Politics* (Princeton, N.J.: Princeton University Press, 1960), seems unable to understand this problem. Thompson's glorification of Realism fails to provide any standard by which we can distinguish realistic from unrealistic actions—unless we are to assume that what Thompson favors is, by definition, "realistic."

[89] For this point, see William T. R. Fox, "Who Are the Realists?" *Union Seminary Quarterly Review* 16 (March 1961): 345-348.

The great hero in the Realist canon was always the successful diplomat—as many of the founders and followers of Realism were frustrated Castlereaghs, or better yet, Metternichs—and the great danger in the Realist canon was always the bumbling amateur. Professionals, after all, could always reach an agreement. The very ambiguity and uncertainty of the relationship between the theory and the choice of specific actions guaranteed that the diplomat's role would be supreme. What else but experience and intuition allowed the necessary connections to be made? And who but the diplomat was trained (one should say, "experienced") to make the necessary judgments? The absence of an obvious connection between the theory and a practical action, and the ensuing necessity of relying on a corps of skilled intermediaries, made Realism singularly attractive to the professional diplomat.[90]

There were other themes—and omissions—that made Realism attractive to the diplomatic mind. A sense of limitation, of the need to compromise and balance interests, was one of the pervasive leitmotifs of the Realist doctrine. It meant, above all, that one always had to be satisfied with a piece of the cake, that one's power began to decline as its reach extended. There was probably no tenet in the doctrine so attractive as this to the Realist practitioner. One need only consult the works produced by former members of the Policy Planning Staff in the Kennan and Nitze years: the great message that they wished to impress upon the American people concerned the limits of their power and the imperfections of all solutions to major problems.[91] There is a nostalgia in both doctrine and practitioner for a world in which the supremacy of foreign policy (and the diplomat as its high priest) could be taken for granted, and an underlying contempt for the manner in which democracies make foreign policy, such as that expressed in Tocqueville's famous comments.

The doctrine of Realism presumed a world of similar states: it was based upon, and beholden to, the behavioral styles of the traditional

---

[90] A recent statement by Professor Morgenthau defends traditional approaches to international relations: "The theoretician is here reduced to admitting that what he does is not essentially different from what the practitioner does, and is just as precarious." Hans J. Morgenthau, "International Relations: Quantitative and Qualitative Approaches," in Norman D. Palmer, ed., *A Design for International Relations Research: Scope, Theory, Methods, and Relevance* (Philadelphia: The American Academy of Political and Social Science, 1970), p. 68.

[91] See, for example, Charles Burton Marshall, *The Limits of Foreign Policy* (New York: Henry Holt, 1954), especially p. 17 f., and Louis J. Halle, *Civilization and Foreign Policy* (New York: Harper and Brothers, 1952), especially p. 106. Packenham, "Political Development Doctrines," notes also that the AID officials to whom he talked continually stressed the marginality of American influence in other countries. (p. 228)

Great Power. Totalitarian, revolutionary, underdeveloped, and unstable states—as well as Small Powers, international organizations, and nongovernmental organizations—were all unwelcome anomalies. Such states violated the notion of a shared, if tacit, sense of a range of permissible behavior for states.[92] It is not altogether inexplicable that many events that have surprised us—both theorists and practitioners—in the last twenty-five or so years have been perpetrated by such states: the Nazi-Soviet pact in 1939; Pearl Harbor; the German blitz; Soviet acquisition of a nuclear capability; the Berlin Blockade; North Korean aggression and Chinese intervention; Nasser's reaction to our Aswan Dam diplomacy; the sputniks; the Berlin Wall; the installation of missiles in Cuba; and the more recent internal turmoil in both Indonesia and China. It is not that we could not predict the exact moment or action that criticism of these failures can be made: we were neither politically nor psychologically prepared for them to happen.[93]

Many of these failures resulted from the inability of men trained to deal with concrete contingencies only after they have arisen to understand the actions of men or states committed to an ideological interpretation of world affairs—or to an interpretation not derived from the history of the European state system. In addition, a congenital bias against planning made it difficult to deal with those who did have a plan. A bias toward analyzing and evaluating the world according to habits and precepts drawn from European history was another characteristic shared by both Realists and practitioners. Yet the principles that could be extracted from behavior within the traditional European state system hardly constitute a universally applicable theory of politics.

Another aspect of Realism made it attractive to diplomats and prac-

---

[92] One fortuitous reason for the predominance of Realism through the mid-1950s was the bipolarity of the world it was trying to explain, and predictability is much higher (or simpler) in a bipolar world. Since the single opponent is, by definition, doing the worst everywhere, the only serious questions are specific and tactical: the "immutable" patterns are presumably immutable in a world in which conflict is direct, pervasive, and unmediated—by definition.

[93] Many factors account for each and all of these failures, and there is no way in which a causal relationship can be proved between a doctrine—especially one held with differing degrees of depth and firmness by different people—and actions in the world. That qualification aside, the point is that in each instance one decisive factor may have been the failure of our conceptual framework to adequately prepare us for actions that were not that surprising (retrospectively). More is at issue here than the familiar notion that "noise" interferes with correct perception of relevant phenomena; what constitutes "noise" and what constitutes a significant occurrence are both part of a larger conceptual framework that focuses attention with a high degree of selectivity. For the Realists of this period, selectivity was heavily conditioned by perception of a Eurocentric world.

titioners. Concentrating on interaction between states perceived as billiard balls tended to turn attention away from structural alterations in the international system. The systemic environment was taken as a constant—as a field fluctuating around a metaphorical balance of power. The result was a static theory concerned only with creating or preserving an equilibrium. Thus, only tactical questions—operator's questions about means, not ends—appeared truly interesting. The central preoccupation was never why or where the system was going (it was going no place, by definition), but rather how to preserve the existing order of things.[94]

This order of concerns also meant that long-range planning was irrelevant. The interesting questions, as in times of war, were here and now questions—Keynes's incontrovertible dictum that in the long run we are all dead provides a metaphysical justification for letting the future take care of itself. There was also, however, another argument that presumably justified this attitude. If only tactical questions were interesting, and if the game of politics was concerned only with maintaining or achieving a balance of power, the things that statesmen wanted to know about the future would be just the things that were essentially unknowable. The best the planner or the social scientist could do was pass on knowledge about tendencies or trends. But the operator wanted something more specific and less problematic: who would do what and when. This prediction, insofar as it could be made at all, could best be made by the experienced statesman. (For further comments, see Chapter 4.) Thus, long-range problems were not very interesting; when they were pondered, it was merely to guess whether different players might be joining the game.

No intrinsic necessity compels a Realist to take the structure of the system as a given. Nevertheless, the contention that immutable patterns of politics characterize the behavior of the actors in world politics rests on the presumption that they are all fundamentally alike and that the international system is stable enough at the structural level for those patterns to retain their relevance. The proposition that different normative rules ought to condition state behavior in different international systems (even different balance of power systems) was ignored or treated as irrelevant. It has meant that the Realists have been very poor guides through the thickets of bipolarity, multipolarity, and polycentrism.

We need to summarize the practical effects of Realism: the attitudes

[94] For interesting comments on the static quality of Realism in another area, see Leon Bramson, *The Political Context of Sociology* (Princeton, N.J.: Princeton University Press, 1961), p. 26.

and predispositions it fostered and the choices it seemed to authorize. And then we need to speculate on the effect that continued commitment to Realism might have on our ability to deal with the problems of the future.

The extent to which Realism was elitist and anti-democratic was masked—or ignored—for many years because the policies that dominated American foreign policy rested on a substantial domestic consensus about the proper way to deal with the Soviet and Chinese threats. Not only the mass public but anyone who disagreed with the conventional wisdom could be disregarded, be they reporters, professors, or lost souls in general. What Realism passed on was a romanticism about both policy—for the responsibilities of power meant that we had a stake as policeman or judge in anything happening anywhere—and the policymaker—who had to make hard choices in spite of domestic stupidity or indifference. The professionals would give Americans a good foreign policy even if they had to be tricked into it or misinformed. Realism therefore provided the high tone of necessity for a low range of behavior. Thus, the revelation in the Pentagon Papers of a persistent disregard for the democratic process, and a fascination with fooling the press and obscuring the truth, was entirely predictable.

Realism was also implicitly a conservative doctrine attractive to men concerned with protecting the status quo. It hardly predisposed its followers to look at revolutionary change favorably, for that kind of change threatened all the fences that Realism had erected: it meant one might have to deal with some untraditional states—and "diplomats"—about some untraditional issues. Disagreement about ends and values possibly would begin to creep into the system, certainly an unfortunate development from the point of view of men committed to the notion that only the proper choice of means is ever at issue.

From one point of view, Realism was always an eminently sensible doctrine: its emphasis on the virtues of moderation, flexibility, and compromise was an intelligent response to the difficulties and dangers of living in an anarchic world. But from another point of view, Realism emphasized the necessity for Great Powers to maintain their prestige, status, and credibility. Great Powers, by definition, were compelled to play "prestige politics," that is, a form of politics difficult to compromise or control. Turning the other cheek could be imprudent or disastrous in a world dominated by the quest for power. In fact, it was always necessary to use, or to appear to be willing to use, limited amounts of force quickly to avoid having to use larger amounts belatedly. This sensible proposition, so fundamental to a generation who remembered the follies of Chamberlain and Daladier, was very dangerous for men who could remember—or learn—nothing else. Flexibility, moderation, and compromise had to take a back seat to the necessity of teaching the aggressors a lesson and enhancing the credibility of one's word. Brinkmanship and waiting to see if "the other guy would blink first" could result.

Realism asserted—and it could neither be proved nor disproved—that nothing much could be changed, that the only guide to the future was the past, and that the best interpreter of how to get there safely was the operator skilled at negotiating limited compromises. Thus, the "generalist," the operator armed only with traditional procedural skills, had a central role in the conduct of foreign policy. But it was also a conservative and anti-innovative role; as a result, the doctrine provided a metaphysical justification for the passivity and procedural inertia of the Foreign Service and the State Department, characteristics already built into the policymaking system by incrementalism and bureaucratic politics.

The nature of the role that the practitioner was expected to play also had a crucial effect on the training he was to undergo. The only unanswered questions were tactical questions about applications. And there was no way to train someone to make correct tactical decisions except on the job. Thus, the proper training for the practitioner was never analytical or intellectual: presumably his proper role was simply to apply known principles to individual cases. That task, which rested on a combination of experience, intuition, and familiarity with the latest details, could only be learned by doing—or, more accurately, by imitating. It is one of the few instances of a profession that takes anti-intellectualism as a virtue. The training of the practitioner sharply circumscribed his ability to deal with untraditional events. Again, we can see the extent to which Realism reinforced predispositions that were already part of the Foreign Service ethos. From what other source could the generalist find intellectual support for maintaining his ignorance?

Realism had the ring of truth to men compelled to work in an environment that they could not always understand and could never adequately control. It provided a few simple keys that could facilitate understanding (if only by oversimplification) and an intellectual justification for the failure to control (for all was unpredictable—although hardly unexpectable). None of this meant that Realism was responsible for any policy choice; the doctrine of Realism could be used, for example, to defend not only going into Vietnam, but also staying out. What it did do was foster attitudes that predisposed its followers to think about international politics in a narrow and ethnocentric fashion, and to set clear bounds around the policies that seemed reasonable to contemplate. And once decisions had been made, it provided the necessary psychological and intellectual support to resist criticism, to persevere in the face of doubt, and to use any means to outwit or dupe domestic dissenters.[95]

The appeal of Realism has been deceptive and dangerous, for it rests on assumptions about state behavior that are increasingly irrelevant. It treats one time-bound set of propositions as if they are universally applicable, and thus turns everyone's attention to problems of application—to issues of "how" not "why." Realism has always been a doctrine of the powerful for their survival, and has also been a doctrine that takes for granted the primacy of foreign policy and the dominance of the security issue defined in simple notions of power. It is, in sum, not only the classic version of a state-centered doctrine but also an affirmation of the dominance of the Great Powers and the autonomy of their foreign policies.

This would only be of historical interest except for one fact: despite the increasing irrelevance of Realism as an interpretation of the external world, its hold over the mind of the practitioner is still formidable. Why this should be so can only be understood by considering the predominant—and thus exceedingly attractive—role that Realism assigns to the generalist practitioner (who gets a hunting license on all issues in spite of an absence of substantive expertise) and by considering that all doctrines persist at the practical level much beyond the theoretical point where they begin to be assailed. After all, for the practitioner to abandon or question what he considers to be his expertise is to abandon or question what separates him from outsiders; that is threatening.

The international system is currently in an ambiguous stage of development. Where it is heading is far from clear. Nevertheless, we may be on the verge of the first systemic revolution, which occurs without the intervention of general war or the development of a new kind of military technology. The central point is that the traditional security issue is no longer likely to be the dominant consideration in world politics. I am

[95] Realism also had a profound impact on the relationship between government and the academic world, discussed again in Chapter 5. In brief, since the principles of Realism were already known, *both* theorists and practitioners became preoccupied with narrow issues of policy: in effect, they competed with each other and threatened each other, rather than performing functions that were different but nonetheless supplemental. The failure of the academic world to perform one of its critical roles—questioning the conventional wisdom—merely reinforced the blocking power of the Realist syndrome. This is a serious charge, the significance of which has been ignored by both groups. It is not clear, unfortunately, that the academic doctrines replacing Realism are an improvement: we have moved from the academic-Realists' illegitimate intrusion into policy opinion to the methodologists' indifference to policy issues. Neither position makes much sense.

very far from asserting that security will no longer be an issue or that it will somehow disappear from the calculations of states—some analysts of the emerging system seem to take this position, thus acting as if the realm of security and the realm of interdependence were completely autonomous. It is clear, however, that security will be only one of the issues of world politics, although a crucial one, for it will have to share prominence with a range of issues heretofore left to technicians or domestic politics. (For further comments, see the first part of Chapter 1.)

The growing interdependence of the state system on economic, social, and cultural matters implies a system in which the autonomy and sovereignty of all the members—great and small—is being eroded. Rational decision-making on such issues requires international cooperation well beyond what has occurred in the field of security. (Even in NATO, the United States always determined strategic questions alone even though they affected all the allies.) This is true because there is no guarantee that these issues will reduce the degree of conflict in the international system *unless* they are handled in a manner that is minimally satisfactory to all concerned. Interdependence clearly could just as well lead to trade wars and an insane effort to achieve autarky as to increased prosperity and welfare; only a new style of decision-making and a change in basic thought patterns could turn these developments into an opportunity to enhance the degree of cooperation in the system. Finally, the security issue is becoming (or perhaps one should say, is finally being recognized as) increasingly interdependent, as the recent agreements on the hot line and nuclear accidents attest. It will become more so if nuclear weapons proliferate and arms technology continues to grow in complexity. Even a more mundane, but very critical, security issue such as the control of conventional arms cannot be handled by any traditional formula—if it can be handled at all.

The attitudes and predispositions that Realism fosters constitute a classically inappropriate response to these developments. With its narrow conception of politics, and with its antiquated notions of sovereignty, Great Power dominance, and the autonomy of foreign policy, the Realist response is bound to create conflict and destroy the possibility of working out new forms of cooperation. The potential that these issues have for creating either cooperation or conflict means that they must be deliberately manipulated to encourage cooperation. It may even be necessary to adopt a decision-making style borrowed from domestic politics, or to begin to take functions like planning seriously. We may also shortly be compelled to contemplate other heresies. The Realist is unlikely to be able to even think about these matters in their proper dimension; worse yet, since Realism presupposes conflict, it is likely to turn the politics of interdependence into another exercise in the politics of security.

We cannot argue that the hold Realism has maintained over the realm of practice is unimportant, for we can change nothing substantial until we first change fundamental patterns of professional beliefs. How we should—or can—do this is unclear. Perhaps the most formidable obstacle to change is the absence of a generally acceptable alternative interpretation of world politics—men are unlikely to relinquish faith in one doctrine until a feasible alternative begins to be widely accepted. With a new doctrine, we could begin to educate future practitioners more sensibly. In the short run, until we have rethought what we mean by "international relations," the best we can probably hope for is that continued discussion of these issues will compel the practitioner to think again about the wisdom of what he has taken for granted for so long. An academic social science that took the concerns of the practitioner more seriously, and spent less time celebrating the procedural triumphs of methodology, should be in the forefront of criticism of the old doctrine and the quest for a new one. These are slender reeds on which to base hope for reform, which explains why we seem to oscillate between radical proposals for reform, which have no possibility of implementation, and reassertions of the relevance of traditions that were obsolescent fifty years ago.

Practitioners usually object strenuously to the notion that they believe in any single doctrine. They point to the indisputable fact that there are sharp internal disagreements within the government over major issues like Vietnam and the ABM. This mistakes disagreement about specifics for disagreement about general attitudes and approaches. Anyone who reads the memoirs of former practitioners, or who spends any amount of time talking with them, can attest to the existence of widely shared beliefs and very similar perceptions of what can be taken for granted about the conduct of foreign affairs. These shared beliefs and convictions are not expounded with the formal elegance or coherence that one finds in a Morgenthau or a Kennan text. Nevertheless, they exist and they reinforce—or repeat—the Realist canon. It may be violently unsettling to the political practitioner, but he does indeed "speak" theory. It would be better for all of us if he were aware of it and understood what it implied.

REALISM AS A PARADIGM

It is tempting to treat Realism as the first fully articulated paradigm about international politics. Thomas Kuhn, in a fascinating and by now familiar intellectual history of scientific revolutions, has defined paradigms as "universally recognized scientific achievements that for a time provide model problems and solutions to a community of practitioners."[96] Paradigms, according to Professor Kuhn, have two characteristics: they reflect an achievement significant enough to attract adherents, and they are sufficiently incomplete or open-ended to provide problems for their adherents to solve. They also provide models from which coherent traditions of research emerge, since acceptance of the model commits practitioners to the same set of standards and rules. "Normal science," the activity undertaken by scientists who have accepted the paradigm and its implications, attempts to extend and articulate its substance. It is a "mopping up" operation, concentrating on detailed, small-scale research on the puzzles left standing by the original statement of the paradigm—puzzles that, by definition, have the "assured existence of a solution."[97]

Professor Kuhn's attempt to illustrate how an intellectual achievement affects the regular activity of practitioners in a discipline is not unprecedented. For example, Stephen Toulmin makes a similar point when he argues that scientists begin their labors with the conviction that things are not "just happening," but that fixed laws or patterns account for nature's course. He notes,

> those who build up their sciences around a principle of regularity or ideal of natural order come to accept it as self-explanatory. Just because (on their view) it specifies the way in which things behave of their own nature, if left to themselves, they cease to ask further questions about it. It becomes the starting point for explaining other things.[98]

The "ideal of natural order" seems very similar to Kuhn's conception of a prevailing paradigm—for Toulmin too, it tells the practitioner what to research, what questions to ask, what is mysterious, and what is explicable. The fascination that Kuhn's analysis evokes, however, is not from the originality of the basic idea but from the skill, subtlety, and detail with which he explicates it, and from the fact that his ideas seem to have relevance in other disciplines.

Paradigms, ideals of natural order, principles of regularity, dominant metaphors—call them what you will—serve as frames of reference for an ongoing practical activity. They constitute the most general arrangement

[96] Thomas S. Kuhn, *The Structure of Scientific Revolutions* (Chicago: University of Chicago Press, 1962), p. x.
[97] *Ibid.*, pp. 23-42.
[98] Stephen Toulmin, *Foresight and Understanding: An Enquiry into the Aims of Science* (New York: Harper and Row, 1961), pp. 41-42.

of concepts and categories by which empirical activity can be undertaken and explained. A frame of reference does not explain anything: it merely provides a conceptual standard by which an explanation will be given. Whatever empirical material we have is understandable only in relation to the specific frame of reference we have accepted as valid.[99]

Are there prevailing frames of reference in international politics that serve as a standard according to which practitioners—and even academics—go about their business?[100] On a general level, the answer is yes. Any intellectual activity that is neither random nor incoherent must relate to a frame of reference. Yet if one attempts to use Kuhn's very elaborate and complex description of scientific paradigms, one may carry the idea further than the facts permit. One major difficulty, for example, with treating Realism as a paradigm is that it was never a theoretical achievement even vaguely comparable to the scientific theories that Kuhn had in mind (mainly the emergence of Newtonian and Einsteinian physics). Realism was not even a theory in this sense, and thus, rather than directing and organizing research and practice, it merely provided a justification for any kind of activity—almost any action could thus be described as "realistic" in some scale of time or space. Moreover, even if one maintains that Realism was more of a theory than this argument indicates, it could never attain the power that Kuhn attributes to scientific paradigms. Social science theories are so much less compelling that more ambiguous and ambivalent reactions to their "imperatives" are inevitable.[101] For these reasons, Realism has been discussed as an approach or a doctrine in the preceding pages, and not as a paradigm. It seems prudent to be more inhibited about swallowing analogies with the sciences, simply because the analogy is elegant and aesthetically pleasing.

[99] The influence of frames of reference has appeared in several places. See, for example, Paul Meadows, "Models, Systems and Science," *American Sociological Review* 22 (February 1957): 4; Muzafer Sherif, *The Psychology of Social Norms* (New York: Harper and Brothers, 1936); and Martin Deutsch, "Evidence and Inference in Nuclear Research," *Daedalus* 57 (Fall 1958): 91-94.

There is a degree of conceptual distinction between paradigms and frames of reference. "Paradigm" is a wider and more general term, subsuming various frames of reference within its confines. The paradigm is not only the concepts that prevail but also the state of mind that conditions their choice and their acceptability.

[100] We refer to frames of reference that deal with our most general level of *professional* beliefs: assumptions about international politics, about the way states ought to behave, and about the correct way of studying how they behave. Frames of reference are essentially normative constructs, but, as in all such ventures, descriptive elements are frequently introduced *sub rosa.*

[101] See the comments in Chapter 3. For an interesting use of the paradigm concept in political science, however, see Sheldon S. Wolin, "Paradigms and Political Theories," in Preston King and B. C. Parekh, eds., *Politics and Experience* (Cambridge: Cambridge University Press, 1968), pp. 125-152.

CRITICS OF THE PLANNING PROCESS

The sophisticated response to criticism of policy planning in the Department of State is that planning is an impossible task in the American system of government. That is true so long as the planners perceive their function as an immediate influence on the policymaking process. It is not clear, however, that a redefinition of the policy planning function would be either useful or significant. In what sense is it possible to redefine planning so that it could be more than, or different from, a second-string operating bureau? And how could it possibly make any difference if the rest of the political system continued to treat the planners and planning as irrelevant, irrespective of how their role is defined?

The planners themselves have frequently attempted to define their task. Morgan, for example, has said that planning is "thinking ahead with a view to action."[102] Bowie has noted that its "main function is to relate current actions to future consequences and objectives."[103] Rostow is more overtly operational, arguing that the function of the planner is "to conceive of specific objectives in particular theatres of activity and to determine how to move forward towards those objectives under rapidly changing operational circumstances."[104]

There is nothing intrinsically wrong with these definitions. They have appeared with predictable regularity each time that one planner or another has felt compelled to prove that concern with the future is not visionary—that he did not have his head in the clouds (or in some irrelevant academic treatise). Emphasis has always been on the immediate and concrete significance of the long-range perspective. This is not especially harmful, for one of the most useful roles that any planning staff can play—particularly in a system committed to the virtues of incrementalism—is to illuminate the future consequences of present actions or inactions. But the planners never *consistently* did even this: they simply wrote studies of current problems with no more or no less concern for the future than the operator had. Some problems had significance for the long run as in the decision to deploy MIRVs, and everyone kept it in mind; other problems could be treated more narrowly by both planners and operators. When the planners were truly visionary, and thought about matters not on the Secretary's desk, the morale of the staff appar-

[102] Morgan, "Planning in Foreign Affairs," p. 271.
[103] Robert R. Bowie, *Shaping the Future: Foreign Policy in an Age of Transition* (New York: Columbia University Press, 1964), p. 82.
[104] Rostow, "The Planning of Foreign Policy," p. 43.

ently sank.[105] In the one case, they suffered from a lack of bureaucratic power; in the other, they suffered from a lack of knowledge and skill.

The man of experience has traditionally disliked and distrusted the planner. Planning relies on experience (of others and of the planners), but it also deliberately sets out to transcend experience. It must attempt to shape the future according to conscious preferences. There is nothing revolutionary about this, for we do it irrespective of whether we are driven by a clearly articulated plan. Still, to the Foreign Service mind, which uses assumptions of unpredictability to justify an exclusive preoccupation with the present—rather than as a prod to attempt to limit the worst aspects of uncertainty—planning has appeared potentially subversive.[106] This may have more to do with the fact that planning may be used not so much to direct movement toward desirable futures, but as a pretext for reexamining established policy, altering resource allocations, or becoming involved in actual operations. And none of these functions appears so irrelevant to the operator.

The operators' fear that the planners will meddle in operations is not wholly unjustified. The planners have done little else: since they want immediate influence, and feel they can get it only by jumping on the nearest bandwagon, they have had very little choice. It is also true that planning is not a highly visible occupation, its successes are hard to identify and may be preventive rather than remedial, and its contribution to career advancement obscure, if not negative. The result is peculiar, for the operators, intent on protecting their own territory, attempt to keep the planners out by insisting that only the regional or functional bureaus can effectively plan. They are, of course, perfectly willing to concede the long run to the planners. The planners, conversely, must refuse the gift, for they can define their utility only in terms of meddling in operations. The conflict is merely obscured by the contention that they bring a unique perspective into their meddling.

What would be the effect of transferring responsibility for short-range planning to the bureaus? It might mean that some effort to actually plan would be undertaken. Whatever its effect on the future, there is no reason to doubt that effective planning can improve the nature of imme-

[105] This impression emerged during my interviews—a clear sense that the PPC was not doing important work among the people with whom I talked. Even on "not immediately feasible" projects there was some embarrassment from the realization that they were simply summarizing suggestions made elsewhere.

[106] For another confirmation of the bias against planning and prediction on the part of policymakers, see *The Formulation and Administration of United States' Foreign Policy* (Washington, D.C.: The Brookings Institution, 1960), p. 100.

diate actions. Since the bureaus would concentrate on what is usually called "contingency planning" or on program planning—that is, on short-range planning—it is possible to presume that operations would become more coherent and integrated. The State Department has made some movement in this direction, and now each regional bureau is supposed to include an officer with responsibility for planning. However, March and Simon's dictum—"daily routine drives out planning"—has been amply confirmed: there has been even less planning in the bureaus than there has been in the Policy Planning Council.[107]

Perhaps nothing more effectively illustrates why this should be so than Robert Elder's comment on the way in which one regional bureau functions:

> As is the case in other bureaus of the Department, personnel in the Bureau of Inter-American Affairs find little time for long-range policy planning or for taking a good hard look into the future. The emphasis is upon daily operations. At the Bureau level, one officer has said, "It is not the planning function to pose basic alternatives to policy already decided upon." Rather, the planning function is concerned with "tactics, timing, and priorities."[108]

There is one range of criticism about the failures of planning in foreign affairs that insists that administrative reorganization will be irrelevant unless the men, their training, and the national style are also altered. There is some sleight of hand here, since it merely excludes the need or possibility of organizational reform by positing (ideal) conditions that would make it superfluous. It is reminiscent of the argument that it is unfair to criticize the United Nations for its failures because it has to work in so imperfect a world, but one would hardly need the United Nations in a perfect world. In any case, this criticism can run from the naïve faith of Senator Jackson that the only problem is "getting our best people into key foreign policy and defense posts" to some sophisticated

[107] For the quoted phrase, see March and Simon, *Organizations,* p. 185. For a good summary of the efforts to place some responsibility for planning on the regional bureaus and also to coordinate planning through the so-called "SIG-IRG" system (which I must regretfully leave unexplained), see *The National Security Process* (Washington, D.C.: Institute for Defense Analysis, 1968), Part II. The authors of this report note that "mention of the word [planning] in some 'Foggy Bottom' circles produces a glazing of eyeballs or uncomprehending remarks, such as 'Planing? Why I plan every day of the year.' It is therefore not surprising that State's leadership of interagency planning has been less than fully successful." (p. 82)
[108] Robert Elder, "Department of State Organization for Inter-American Affairs," in *The Formulation and Administration of United States' Foreign Policy,* p. 183.

interpretations of the way in which better men can plan better policies.[109]

How are we to get better planners? That question is usually left unexamined. For example, Stanley Hoffmann, whose criticisms of the planning process have been more interesting and coherent than those of any other commentator, contends that it is wrong to have any division between planners and operators: "In short, the policy-makers must also be the planners."[110] While Professor Hoffmann contends that the problem cannot be solved by administrative reorganization, *this* reorganization will apparently prosper because of a previous change in training procedures and national style. In the abstract, this is very convincing. It is, however, also obvious that the national style changes very slowly, that its influence on planning is hypothetical, that training (or, rather, the lack of it) continues unaltered, and that we are left without direction as to what better training implies.

For any reasonable period of time—say five to fifteen years—our policymakers are not going to become our planners, nor is their training or style going to alter markedly. Moreover, it is not clear that our policymakers *should* be our planners. They have neither the time nor the inclination to do so. Planning and operating are two different ventures, requiring different skills and perceptions, perhaps even a different mind set (in the Gestalt sense), and thus can be amalgamated only by (theoretical) *force majeure.* They occur in different time spheres not only in that planners concentrate on the future and operators on the present (a trivial distinction because concentration on the future is aimed at clarifying present choices), but also in that the planners can influence the policymaker only in the period before the policymaker decides on a course of action.[111] The planner and the policymaker can be one and the same only when the policymaker has all the analytical and theoretical skills of the planner, in addition to his unique skills as a decider.

[109] The quote is by Senator Jackson. See Senator Henry M. Jackson, ed., *The National Security Council* (New York: Frederick A. Praeger, 1965), p. 67.

[110] Hoffmann, *Gulliver's Troubles,* p. 321.

[111] Again, see the discussion in Chapter 3. The desire to amalgamate planners and operators was fashionable during the Kennedy administration. Thus, McGeorge Bundy assured the public that President Kennedy "deliberately rubbed out the distinction between planning and operation." But this is equivalent to saying that Kennedy—after all, a traditional politician—simply rubbed out planning altogether. This perhaps partly explains the excessive fascination of Bundy, Rostow, et al., for the intellectual fashions of the moment, stylishly embellished, but indifferent to where all the "movement" was presumably taking us. For the Bundy quote, see I. M. Destler, "Can One Man Do?" *Foreign Policy,* no. 5 (Winter 1971-72), p. 30.

Another important criticism of the planning function in foreign affairs has come from Zbigniew Brzezinski, who served on the Policy Planning Council for a year and a half. Professor Brzezinski's comments are a curious combination of the very practical and the very idealistic (perhaps grandiose would be a better word). On the one hand, he maintains that the political success of planning depends on how the planning unit is organized and staffed, and on how closely it is plugged into the existing lines of power.[112] This is essentially a restatement of the prevailing wisdom in Washington about the proper relationship between a planning staff and the Secretary of State. On the other hand, Brzezinski's notion of what that planning staff ought to be doing is quite unique. Rather than becoming immersed in details or in applications, or concentrating on solutions to specific problems, Brzezinski wants the staff to develop a broad conceptual framework "to integrate an extraordinary variety of historical patterns into a coherent whole from which meaning and goals can be extracted."[113]

One of the major difficulties with Professor Brzezinski's desire to outfit the planning staff with a broad conceptual framework is that it is in complete contradiction with everything that the Foreign Service and the State Department believe. It strains credibility to imagine the anti-theoretical, anti-intellectual Foreign Service Officer developing "architectural" perspectives that rest on a sensitivity to "the broad sweep of history" and the capacity to define "historically relevant goals."[114] They lack any of the requisite skills, let alone the desire to do so. The result would be a planning staff composed entirely of outside intellectuals, in open and constant warfare with the rest of the Department for whom they were presumably providing guidance.

Aside from the difficulties with the rest of the State Department, it is far from clear that Brzezinski's conceptual scheme would be either useful or desirable. How do we know whose interpretation of history is correct? If there is a consensus, we do not need acolytes to interpret it; if there is no consensus, we have no means of discovering who the acolytes are. In addition, the relationship between a body of doctrine (that Brzezinski indicates should be a nondogmatic ideology, which verges on a contradiction in terms) and specific actions is intrinsically obscure. A resonant statement of historical directions may turn out to be a hitching post for everyone's favorite horse.

---

[112] Zbigniew Brzezinski, "Purpose and Planning in Foreign Affairs," *The Public Interest*, no. 14 (Winter 1969), p. 56.
[113] *Ibid.*, p. 56.
[114] *Ibid.*

The Policy Planning Council was an admitted failure in the 1960s. It neither had any influence nor developed any unusual ideas. Yet a series of interviews with members of the staff during this period yielded very few suggestions for reform. The general consensus appeared to be that nothing significant was wrong beyond the personal and intellectual qualifications of the two directors. Several staffers yearned for the days (in the Truman era) when the Policy Planning Staff prepared most of the position papers for the meetings of the National Security Council—it was a peculiar desire, since the NSC in the 1960s was moribund. The NSC was attractive solely because it appeared to be a shortcut to influence. This notion was especially attractive in Washington, where the assumption prevails that writing speeches and preparing the final (very short) brief for discussion is the next best thing to being a policymaker. No one ever seems to ponder what this implies about the mental level of our policymakers.

Interviews also indicated that all the members of the staff would have preferred to see more outsiders on it. Translated, that seemed to mean one or two professors with sufficient governmental experience not to become irrelevant. They may have merely been polite, on the assumption that the interviewer would be pleased to hear their high regard for academics. When pressed for names, they invariably chose a prominent in-and-outer, whose academic prestige was nil, or a former colleague. Several were quick to praise one academic on the staff because, as one said, "You would have never known he wasn't one of us."

Very few planners believed that the academic world could produce anything that they would find useful.[115] One constant refrain appeared: they were interested not in theories but in the application of theories. An explicit question asking whether they could think of studies that they would like to see done, but that they thought could be done better in a university setting, evoked very little response. In some ways, it was an unfair question, since it asked them to translate the usual rhetoric about helping each other into something explicit and meaningful. A few mentioned studies in which a great mass of data had to be collected, but they could not indicate why this would necessarily be useful to the policymaker (as distinct from being best done in a university). Others mentioned various long-range studies, although it was clear that they felt their utility would be, to borrow an academic term, heuristic. In fact, it

---

[115]Perhaps this should be qualified for the economists, although one staff economist with whom I talked kept insisting that he did not understand theory. He also apparently did not read it.

is quite clear that they did not really believe that academics *could* do much of interest. And as long as they defined the planning function as exerting influence on immediate decisions, they were absolutely right.

THE FAILURES OF POLICY PLANNING: A SUMMARY

When we ponder the record of the Policy Planning Council and examine the backgrounds, the perspectives, and the professional beliefs of the planners themselves, we can begin to understand why so little planning has occurred in the past twenty-five years. The fact that the elimination of the Council as an independent entity provoked so little comment—favorable or unfavorable—is suggestive and symptomatic: no one had the feeling that the Council was doing anything unique or important, or that it would be missed.

The difficulties of creating and instituting an effective planning staff become more apparent when we contemplate the reforms that critics have advocated. The one sure road to improvement has seemed to be the recruitment of better planners. Who could disagree with that? No one, of course, ever bothers to define "better," on the presumption that its meaning is self-evident. In a sense, perhaps it is, for the clear implication is that "better" men are equivalent to men who can manage to manufacture more influence for the staff on immediate policy issues. So long as this remains the criterion by which we judge the effectiveness of the planning function, the quest for better men *may* yield a planning staff that is indeed influential—although it also may not, for the planners in the past have been chosen, in part, according to such a criterion, but have not achieved much influence—only because it has forsaken planning for meddling in operations. Operators disguised as planners may perform some important functions, but we need not assume they have much to do with a properly conceived planning role.

Before we can begin to understand what we mean by better planners, and how to recruit them and train them, we need a clearer understanding of planning itself. The notion of planning encompasses a wide variety of activities, and different planning tasks imply different planning staffs—and planners. Making and understanding these distinctions is a necessary prerequisite to the establishment of a useful planning function; doing so also provides us with an opportunity to move from the rhetorical sloganeering that dominates most discussions of planning—planning can *never* work, or, planning is our *only* hope—to a careful analysis of who can do what for whom.

88

THE NATURE OF PLANNING IN FOREIGN AFFAIRS

Does it make much sense presently to attempt to reorganize the planning function within the Department of State? Does the Department's exclusive preoccupation with immediate issues predetermine the failure of any attempt to institutionalize a concern for long-range factors? The impulse to answer the first question negatively, and the second affirmatively, is quite strong. There are, however, two reasons to resist the impulse. First is that no serious planning has ever taken place in foreign affairs (except for the war-time years, 1941-1945),[116] and any answer to these questions is thus very speculative. We know that the planners have not planned, and have instead sought immediate influence, but we must be less certain about what would transpire if they attempted to do so. Second is that the State Department really has no viable alternative but to attempt *some* kind of planning: the attempt to deal with increasingly complex and revolutionary problems by traditional methods is bound to be futile and irresponsible.

Planning, in the most general sense, is an effort to control or limit uncertainty. As such, it would seem reasonable to presume that it would be a very attractive instrument in international relations—which is, of course, dominated by a high degree of uncertainty. But the State Department has used perceptions of uncertainty to justify passivity, not planning: where nothing can be foreseen, the best hope appears to be to cling to the comforts of the familiar. Since planning is the antithesis of passivity, and clearly implies some active intervention into ongoing affairs, the reluctance of men trained only to pass on traditional formulas to engage in it is not surprising.

Perhaps the antipathy of the operator for planning might be lessened if he had a clearer understanding of what it means. So much discussion of planning is dominated by rhetoric, slogans, and ideology—"planning cannot work" or "we must plan if we are to survive"—that confusion is understandable. The operator, confronted by the charge that he must plan, tends to presume that he is being asked to prepare something akin to a rigorous, comprehensive, and centrally directed "Five-Year Plan." And the planning enthusiast, knowing that there are many useful forms of planning that fall short of the notion of "Five-Year Plans," but confronted by the operator's unqualified contention that planning is impos-

---

[116] The fact that the State Department did a great deal of planning during World War II, some of it quite useful, was directly related to the fact that it had so little else to do.

sible in a complex world, begins to believe that our only hope lies in completely ignoring and bypassing the operator. But the debate is never really joined, for each side is content to rest with a broad indictment of the other's failures: for the detractors, the failure of comprehensive planning in India or Pakistan, for instance, is sufficient to condemn all efforts at planning; for the enthusiasts, any failure of the policymaking system to foresee long-run consequences is interpreted as a mandate for planning.

What do we mean—what activities do we imply—when we argue for or against planning? There is no simple answer to this question, for planning evokes a whole range of images in the eye of the beholder. Moreover, the boundaries of the planning function, like all social functions, tend to waver and shift in response to many different intellectual and technical developments. This means that the term "planning," standing by itself, is an abstraction without any substantive meaning. It needs to be given some substance if we want to get beyond rhetorical exchanges. We probably cannot devise a universally acceptable definition of planning, but we can indicate the attributes and characteristics of the activities that we have in mind when we discuss planning. If nothing else, it will enable us to know what we are disagreeing about.

An attempt to define planning, and to understand what it might accomplish in foreign affairs, must rely somewhat on analogies with disciplines that have implemented the planning process. For the most part, that means economists and social scientists who have attempted to guide the process of change within domestic social systems. That also means that these analogies must be treated with great caution. Planning within a single social system is enormously complex, and its results very uncertain. Yet it is likely to be a more controllable and predictable process than it will be in foreign affairs. The goals that emerge from the domestic political process tend to be somewhat less intangible and amorphous, and success in implementing them tends to be somewhat easier to measure against some standard such as money expended. Provided that we remain aware of the limitations of the analogy, however, the lessons that we can learn from other disciplines are a useful starting point for our analysis.

The most general definitions of planning are so amorphous that it frequently becomes more difficult to discover activities that are not part of the process than those that are. Almost any proposal concerned with the future, for example, bears some relationship to planning. This is also true of any attempt to evaluate alternative proposals or the methods by which they might be implemented.[117] But these are things that all of us do most of the time—at least when we are behaving as good and prudent middle-class burghers. What is it, then, that distinguishes the planner from the run-of-the-mill citizen concerned with assuring himself of a modicum of future security and prosperity?

The usual answer to this question is that the planner is distinguished by a deliberate and conscious effort to make choices on the basis of rationality. Thus one text declares: "Planning is rational, adaptive thought applied to the future and to matters over which the planners, or the administrative organizations with which they are associated, have some degree of control."[118]

The meaning of rationality in this context is obvious: an organized, self-conscious, and judicious attempt to choose the best alternative to reach a given goal. But what if the goal is not sensible or coherent? The result could be a series of rational decisions, which are also subjectively valid, but are nonetheless incompetent because the ends sought (or the intellectual framework employed) are irrelevant or misconceived.[119]

The easy response to this is that any interpretation of the planning function that excludes a constant concern with both ends and means is inadequate. Simply evaluating means and ordering them according to a preference scale is necessary but insufficient: the tactical dominates the strategic only at the risk of stumbling into dead ends. It is also clear, however, that not every planning staff should—or can—raise questions about goals and purposes. Nothing would ever get done, and all decisions would be transitory, as each planning group sought to reargue and redefine the end in sight. One planning staff *must* extend the normal definition of planning to include a concern for both ends and means, but *only* one group ought to have this kind of authority. Moreover, it probably ought not to be a group within an operating agency like the State Department.

There is parallel here with Karl Mannheim's distinction between "substantial" and "functional" rationality. The latter indicated that a series of actions was so organized that it led to a previously defined goal (which did not have to be rational). "Substantial" rationality, conversely, in-

[117] These considerations are part of the definition in Herbert A. Simon, Donald W. Smithburg, and Victor A. Thompson, *Public Administration* (New York: Alfred A. Knopf, 1950), pp. 423-424.

[118] *Ibid.*

[119] See Polanyi, *Personal Knowledge,* p. 374, for an analysis of how to classify reasonable action.

volved an act of thought that revealed intelligent insight into the interrelation of events in a situation.[120] The procedural rules that usually define rational behavior—relying on warranted beliefs, learning from experience, and using all the available evidence—apply to either of Mannheim's categories: they explain how we ought to behave in each case before we act.[121] It is true, nonetheless, that they are much harder to apply when the ends themselves and their interrelations are in question. While all planning staffs must concern themselves with "functional" rationality, only the most highly placed and generally competent staff can afford to become involved in issues of "substantial" rationality.

It is necessary to have a staff with this dual authority in a period of revolutionary change, for the need to continually assess the relevance of ongoing goals rises when the system is in the process of transformation. There is a useful analogy here with the kind of economic planning that is dominant in the developed countries and the planning that is dominant in the developing areas. In the first case, anti-cyclical planning is directed toward maintaining or increasing effective demand within the existing system in order to employ resources optimally. Development planning, conversely, seeks to alter the framework of the economic and social system in order to accelerate the rate of progress: that is, the aim is change plus growth, and not growth alone.[122] The point is that we are in an international system in which the attempt to maintain stability by simply adjusting the traditional mechanisms of control is likely to be insufficient; we must worry about maintaining stability while reorganizing the system to meet a new range of problems and stresses.

What other attributes distinguish a genuine long-range planning staff from a staff solely concerned with short-range policy analysis? The most obvious attribute is the time period that falls within the staff's pattern of concerns. This is usually stated in a specific range of time; for example, short-range staffs deal only with periods up to two years (at the most), and long-range staffs take over from that point. Perhaps this is a useful guideline. It is my feeling, however, that such statements are essentially arbitrary, and obscure more than they reveal. It is not the specific date

[120] Karl Mannheim, *Man and Society in an Age of Reconstruction* (New York: Harcourt, Brace and World, 1940), pp. 53-58.

[121] For a discussion of rationality in the more traditional sense, with the rules to follow before we act if we want our actions to be classified as rational, see Felix E. Oppenheim, "Rational Choice," *The Journal of Philosophy* 50 (June 1953): 341-350. For Oakeshott's position, see the comments in footnote 87.

[122] See Albert Waterston, *Development Planning: Lessons of Experience* (Baltimore: Johns Hopkins Press, 1965).

that distinguishes the two planning staffs, but an entirely different consideration: whether a problem must be perceived in terms of chance deadlines—the policymaker's schedule, the time left in office, and the headlines of the day—or whether the time period in which it is reasonable to perceive the solution to a problem is left to the outcome of the analysis. This distinction usually parallels the distinction of specific time periods. Nevertheless, it need not do so. A long-range planning staff therefore should be characterized by the capacity and the authority—political and intellectual—to deal with problems without arbitrary deadlines.

A long-range planning staff must also be a staff characterized by the realization that its contribution is intellectual and not operational. Its primary commitment must be to ideas and assumptions, not programs. The insights, speculations, and analyses that it develops do not (and cannot, as we shall see in the next chapter) lead directly or determinately to specific policy decisions: these must always remain in the hands of the policymaker. A long-range planning staff is not a replacement for decision-making, nor should it supplant the other methods by which our political system reaches a decision. It is a supplement to the decision-maker's traditional approach to his task, but one that has been seriously neglected in the past. The impact of a long-range planning staff, in the short run, must come from questions about the ideas and assumptions that guide the policymaker; and in the long run, from its ability to discuss probable boundaries of the emerging international system, as well as the possible consequences of short-run actions.

A long-range planning staff must also be capable of using the most advanced techniques that the social sciences have developed. It cannot afford, however, to become exclusively attached to any methodology. One of its most useful functions might be to test and evaluate—and demythologize—whatever the current favorite in the methodological wars happens to be. Technical knowledge in the social sciences has not reached the point where it can guarantee the results of predictions or offer conclusive evidence about the superiority of one course of action rather than another. Perhaps it never will. The necessity of having practitioners who can make wise decisions about available alternatives will never be eliminated, fears (or hopes) notwithstanding.

We stress so commonplace a point only because many methodologists have been inclined to substitute enthusiasm for sense, and the poor practitioner, knowing next to nothing about this, fears that the enthusiasm is justified. But none of the "miracle methodologies" can (or should) ever be more than an aid to human judgment. Program budgeting, systems analysis, simulation, and "alternative futures" will create more illusions than insight if their limitations are ignored.[123]

The warning holds for the planner as well as for the policymaker. In the present state of the social sciences, the contribution that the planner makes to the policy realm will rest on traditional intellectual virtues— "his own mixture of professional training and experience, personal values and beliefs."[124] Significantly, many new methodologies are process-oriented, and thus unable to offer guidance on assumptions and goals. And since the long-range planning staff that we have in mind must deal with goals and purposes, as well as alternative means, the new methodologies can never be more than a useful tool.

Listing the qualities that should characterize a long-range planning staff gives us an idea of what it might be doing.[125] One study that analyzed planning in the State Department argued that the Policy Planning Coun-

[123] Nonetheless, a concern for the potential implicit in new methodologies should be a part, although not a basic part, of a new planning staff's function, not only for the staff to improve policy but also to improve the policymaking system.

For critical comments on the most fashionable new approach, see Thomas C. Schelling, "PPBS and Foreign Affairs," *The Public Interest*, no. 11 (Spring 1968), pp. 26-35; and Aaron Wildavsky, "The Political Economy of Efficiency: Cost-Benefit Analysis, Systems Analysis, and Program Budgeting," in Austin Ranney, ed., *Political Science and Public Policy* (Chicago: Markham, 1968), pp. 55-82.

One study of the relationship between forecasting and available techniques came to a conclusion that is not without relevance for planning: "There is no discernible relationship between good forecasting and the use of techniques. Their most important contributions to practical forecasting can be summarized in the following three points: (1) They elucidate the role of individual input factors . . .; (2) They tend to reduce prejudice and bias; (3) They permit the evaluation of complicated patterns of input information and facilitate the systematic evaluation of alternatives." Erick Jantsch, *Technological Forecasting in Perspective* (Paris: Organisation for Economic Co-operation and Development, 1966), p. 10. One fundamental difficulty is that many new techniques are used as though they were theories or could substitute for theories. This is not the case, and the full use of many such methodologies—particularly those that aim at collecting or ordering data in a useful fashion—awaits the development of a theory that indicates which data are significant and why.

[124] Robert Morris and Robert H. Binstock, *Feasible Planning for Social Change* (New York: Columbia University Press, 1966), p. 87.

[125] In addition to attempts to define planning, numerous descriptions of the planning process attempt to list its components. Most descriptions are only relevant to a planning staff that limits itself to a concern with means. For example, one study contends that the planner first tries to find out what the policy goals are, then forecasts a future designed to indicate the distance that must be traveled to achieve the goals, formulates a program to eliminate the distance, and, finally, modifies the program in the light of experience. Michael D. Reagan, "Toward Improving Presidential Level Policy Planning," in Thomas E. Cronin and Sanford D. Greenberg, eds., *The Presidential Advisory System* (New York: Harper and Row, 1909), pp. 259-270; see also Jan Tinbergen, *Central Planning* (New Haven: Yale University Press, 1964), pp. 9-10, 42-43.

cil should be entrusted with the task of analyzing "strategic alternatives."[126] If that phrase implies a concern beyond the next few months, I would disagree. The Council never had, nor is it likely to have, the talent or inclination to comment critically on either long-run issues or the underlying nature of contemporary issues. That task requires an intellectual curiosity and mental agility—perhaps the playfulness of the intellect rather than the operationalism of the intelligence[127]—that is in short supply everywhere (including the academies), but simply nonexistent in the State Department. Awareness of what is required, and what was missing, in the case of some hide-bound bureaucrats concerned with urban affairs, may provide a useful analogy:

> the planning method can be used to solve problems only when the planner understands the nature of the problem and the relation to it of alternative solutions. It is not sufficient for a planner to predict that certain actions will lead to certain reactions; he must be able to grasp the relationship theoretically. He must be able to explain his predictions . . . using an understanding of the dynamic relationships among sets of relevant variables.[128]

Perhaps we could conceptualize the tasks of a long-range staff by consecutive "why" and "what" questions. The answer to *why* we should want to be doing something must rest on an effort to clarify and explicate the conditions that will affect and determine the kind of environment we shall have to deal with; *what* options we have in attempting to do so, and *what* costs (in a generic sense) each option entails, must clearly be the next task. This does not remove the need for a political decision between the options, but it does set the limits within which the decision will be made. Tactical questions—or "how" questions—should probably be left to a planning unit within the operating bureaus. Questions dealing with the effectiveness of the "how" should, I believe, be a shared concern of both the short- and long-range staffs.

A long-range planning staff might also focus substantially on innovative planning, deliberately seeking new objectives or major changes in old objectives.[129] In this perspective, if a long-range planning staff received enough support from the higher reaches of the bureaucracy to legitimize its endeavors, it might engage in what the French call "indicative

[126] *The National Security Process,* p. 82.
[127] See Richard Hofstadter, *Anti-Intellectualism in American Life* (New York: Random House, 1963), pp. 24-30.
[128] Morris and Binstock, *Feasible Planning for Social Change,* p. 9.
[129] This form of planning is discussed, although with reference to the developing areas, in John Friedmann, "A Conceptual Model for the Analysis of Planning Behavior," *Administrative Science Quarterly* 12 (1967): 225-252.

planning"—an attempt to point to desirable goals, without necessarily having the power to impose them.[130] This could be effective only if the relevant bureaucracies were responsive to change and innovation.

To be more detailed than this in outlining the tasks that a long-range staff might undertake is impossible. It would be futile considering that we have so little experience with serious planning in foreign affairs. Clearly, part of what any planning staff does is so dependent on the needs of the moment, and the state of the art in methodology, that any list of planning activities can only be taken as illustrative.

It would be misleading to leave the impression that this planning staff could be wholly or convincingly apolitical. No institution within the government could ever achieve that level of impartiality, nor is it clear that it would be sensible or wise if it did happen to be possible. A mixture of values, norms, techniques, and objective knowledge is inevitable in the vast majority of cases; this is obviously true when long-range projections are at issue. What we seek is a staff that is sophisticated enough to understand that it is a part of the political system, but that also deliberately seeks—and is given—the opportunity to influence the process of choice with the results of intellectual analysis and the best possible speculations about long-range consequences.

A number of planning tasks of significance should *not* be entrusted to a long-range staff. For example, some planning activities ought to be left to the regional and functional bureaus of the Department of State. The most obvious example is contingency planning "which considers what should be done if some event occurs which radically departs from expectations and which may require the United States to take urgent action."[131] This deals neither with strategic alternatives nor policy guidance, but with possible responses to likely and unlikely specific events. At present, such contingency thinking as there is tends to exist—needless to say, in rough form—in the heads of operating officers.[132] There is some merit in institutionalizing these expectations, not on the assumption that all undesirable events can either be predicted or averted, but because it is more likely that all the relevant factors will be considered if the contingency arises. Preventive measures possibly will be conceived beforehand to avert the worst disasters. Finally, there is an educational

[130] See the discussion of the French experience in Andrew Shonfield, *Modern Capitalism: The Changing Balance of Public and Private Power* (London: Oxford University Press, 1969), p. 84 f.
[131] *The National Security Process,* p. 82.
[132] *Ibid.,* p. 85.

impact on those responsible for thinking through the range of likely contingencies that is potentially useful.[133]

This planning requires intimate familiarity with the problems of an area. It clearly must be undertaken by those who have that familiarity, and who will be called upon to offer advice about dealing with the contingency if it arises—which means the operating officers of the regional bureaus. Some half-hearted movement in this direction has taken place in recent years, but its results have been minimal. Interviews with several regional planning officers indicated that they were very uncertain about the nature of their tasks and that they were usually appointed because they were available, and not because they had shown any interest in or aptitude for planning. It is also revealing that most of them were not asked to do any contingency planning but were left on their own, or asked to do a series of general position papers (related to Rostow's National Policy Papers), or a study of how planning could be made more relevant for daily operations.

Another range of planning probably should be done by a special planning group in the Department of State. One recent study calls it "policy planning" and defines it as a form of planning "which analyzes long-range problems on the assumption that presently discernible trends will probably continue."[134] (In the literature of forecasting, this is occasionally described as the "logical future," which merely extends the present, in contrast to the "willed future," which transcends present trends.) This is a notably confining assumption. It would be fatuous for a *long-range* staff to take any such assumption for granted. It is probably less dangerous, however, for a lower-level unit to do so, provided that the inevitable biases and distortions are recognized. In any case, over any short-range period, it is likely to be an accurate enough assumption to justify its retention. It is also probably true that neither the operators nor a low-level planning staff have the capacity or inclination to work with any other assumption.

What functions should this special staff perform? Essentially, it should concentrate on "spelling out the means of carrying out approved strategies."[135] This would involve not only planning the programs to implement policies but also checking and evaluating the way in which the programs function. This would provide a high degree of authoritative

[133]*Ibid.*, p. 107.
[134]*Ibid.*, p. 82.
[135]*Ibid.*, pp. 106-107.

policy guidance for particular areas and problems. It should not be done by the regional bureaus because they are unlikely to be very objective. In the abstract, the argument that an independent planning staff, somewhat like the Policy Planning Council of old but within the Secretary of State's office, will be more objective seems reasonable; but it is also well worth keeping in mind that its experts usually go back to the bureaus they are supposed to be objective about.

Nevertheless, some unit ought to be given the task of providing authoritative policy guidance to the bureaus. This is probably the only way to prevent or inhibit the kind of free-lancing that has characterized the style of some operating bureaus. This is another way of saying that some unit ought to be monitoring and coordinating the activities of the various bureaus. It should definitely not become involved in operations itself. In fact, in order to avoid the kind of misunderstandings that arose between the regional bureaus and the Policy Planning Council—in which the latter was accused of meddling—this staff probably should be left within the Executive Office of the Secretary of State (and not as an independent entity directed by an Assistant Secretary).

What we have been advocating is a hierarchy of planning staffs and a hierarchy of planning functions. We have been arguing that the short-range planning staffs within the State Department should primarily be concerned with "how" questions—how to deal with unexpected contingencies, how to implement approved policies, how to coordinate them, and how to evaluate them—but that a long-range planning staff, outside the State Department (so long as the Department is run by men trained in the current fashion), should be created to deal with "what" and "why" questions. In the next two sections, we shall briefly discuss some problems of staffing and institutionalizing this long-range unit. But before doing so, we shall add a few comments about our expectations for this kind of operation in our system of government.

Nothing can more easily destroy a planning staff than expecting too much from it. Given the inherent limitations of social theory and social knowledge, and given our lack of experience with planning, we can understand easily enough why it might achieve nothing at all or become another competitor for "a piece of today's action." A negative outcome is guaranteed if we continue to confuse planning with any single activity such as the attempt to create comprehensive Five-Year Plans. This is one kind of planning, although the one least relevant for the staff that we have been discussing; it is also not the only form that planning can assume. Once we recognize this, and begin scaling our demands, our expectations, and our evaluations accordingly, we can begin to move from rhetorical or ideological posturing to an effort to discover who can plan for what ends and by what means.[136]

A new planning staff may also fail because it meets so much resistance from the traditional foreign affairs bureaucracy that it collapses or loses the political support it will need. It may also perform so timidly or ineffectively that it will become nothing more than a set of obscure initials in some bureaucratic corridor. We shall take account of these dangers in our discussion of where this staff ought to be placed and how it should be staffed.

The planning function is such that its successes tend to be preventive and its failures glaring. It will always be impossible to prove that planning was uniquely responsible for favorable outcomes. Even in economics, where there is more data and more experience with planning, "it is virtually impossible . . . to make a theoretically satisfactory comparison between what happens with and what happens without planning."[137] With so many possibilities of failure, and with so many detractors already convinced that what they call planning cannot succeed, it becomes imperative to emphasize that some of the most significant virtues of planning are intangible and subjective. The aim of a long-range planning staff is to reduce uncertainty by accurate forecasting and by enumeration of the alternatives that have some chance of getting us to the future we want—in English scientist Dennis Gabor's phrase, the future we "invent." But we look ahead not for its own sake but in order to give ourselves some standard by which to make present choices and some means by which we can illuminate the biases of the present. However successful we may be in an objective sense in achieving these goals—and one has the hope that our approximations will become increasingly useful—the act of pursuing them has important intangible benefits. It makes all of us more sensitive to the relationship between what we are doing and where we are going, and it also gives us some sense that we are operating in a universe that is not entirely beyond our control. A commitment to long-range planning, from this perspective, is an important indication of the state of mind with which we approach political problems. Getting to where we believe that it is valuable to think about the long run, and to treat the planner seriously, may be far more important than any list of the specific ways in which the planner influenced the choice of goals.

[136] For a similar statement in a different context, see Robert A. Dahl and Charles E. Lindblom, *Politics, Economics, and Welfare* (New York: Harper Torchbooks, 1953), p. 5.
[137] Tinbergen, *Central Planning,* p. 54; see also Waterston, *Development Planning: Lessons of Experience.*

I have not argued that planning will lower the level of conflict in the political system. That would be possible only if we could develop an absolutely reliable scale of personal preferences and if our social theories could replace human judgment. In the present circumstances, planning may lead to as many conflicts as any other approach to policymaking. The difference is that planning should at least make clear what a policy conflict is about—that is, whether values are at stake, or whether the disagreement is about the proper choice of means, or whether the struggle involves both ends and means. Although knowing what we are fighting about may not be an unmitigated blessing, such knowledge seems preferable, on balance, to obscuring why we fight.

I also have not argued that planning should replace all other methods of making political decisions. Planning hardly has a record of accomplishment that would justify any such claims. Nevertheless, we do not have a clear and simple choice between planning and not planning. All policymaking systems must make some effort to look ahead, to choose actions rationally, to evaluate them carefully, and to narrow the area of reliance on "faith, hope, and charity"—which is to say, they must make an effort to plan. Even a system that relies on bargaining to develop incremental decisions can only drift aimlessly and allow its problems to accumulate, unless it spends part of its energies doing these things. The real issue is whether they are done consciously, in full awareness of both the limitations and the possibilities of planning, or whether they are done badly and haphazardly—and then used to rationalize the assertion that since we cannot plan perfectly, we should not plan at all.

THE LOCATION OF A NEW PLANNING STAFF

A proposal for a long-range planning staff runs against the grain of everything the Washingtonian takes for granted. Nothing excites less interest and more genial contempt than another proposal for administrative reorganization. This kind of response is self-confirming, and approaches an explanation of the inertia and passivity of the political system—until it confronts a major crisis, to which it inevitably overreacts. Reorganization is hardly a panacea. Yet it does create new roles and new sets of expectations and may slowly begin to alter behavioral patterns. We may achieve more by moving in this direction than by issuing demands for more revolutionary changes that will be dismissed as utopian or naïve. It is also possible that a properly constituted long-range planning staff could have a major impact on how we think about foreign affairs.

Some advantages that an in-house planning staff has would have to be sacrificed if it was located outside the State Department. The inside staff may have easier access to information and may get better cooperation from the rest of the Department.[138] There are, however, more substantial reasons to justify creating a new and autonomous outside staff. One set of reasons refers to the difficulty of achieving objectivity, resisting pressures and questioning basic assumptions if the planners know that their career in the years ahead must be made in the bureaus and with the men they are criticizing. It is not likely that planners drawn from the bureaus will be able or willing to adjust their thinking to the questions that the staff ought to be raising.[139] Also, both planning and the State Department are held in very low intellectual esteem: the only planning staff that is likely to be influential is one supported by the President, not staffed by the State Department, and run by men of known intellect and integrity.[140] It might be noted that this kind of planning staff would constitute a revolutionary administrative reorganization, not the aimless reshuffling of the same, faceless bureaucrats.

There is yet another reason for placing the planning staff outside the State Department. It is conventional to assert, as Professor Ernst Haas does, that

the possessor of knowledge is impotent to make policy if he is unwilling to be political. But being political calls for compromising, negotiating, giving, and taking. And the sources of the compromises lie in the interests perceived by nations and by groups, not in abstract knowledge.[141]

Haas also contends that the planner must become a political partisan to be effective. This argument, however, rests on a confused notion of just when and how planners and planning can influence the choice of policies. The function of the possessor of knowledge (by which we presume academic or theoretical knowledge) is *not* to make policy. If he tries, he must obey Professor Haas's imperative, but in doing so, he becomes

[138] See Rensis Likert and Ronald Lippitt, "The Utilization of Social Science," in Leon Festinger and Daniel Katz, eds., *Research Methods in the Behavioral Sciences* (New York: The Dryden Press, 1953), pp. 605-606.

[139] See Bruce L. R. Smith, *The RAND Corporation—Case Study of a Nonprofit Advisory Corporation* (Cambridge, Mass.: Harvard University Press, 1966), p. 244. Professor Smith argues that an in-house research group frequently does nothing more than provide ceremonial support for policymakers.

[140] For other criticisms of the in-house group, see Simon, et al., *Public Administration,* pp. 446-447; and Likert and Lippitt, "The Utilization of Social Science," p. 605 f.

[141] Ernst Haas, *Tangle of Hopes, American Commitments and World Order* (Englewood Cliffs, N.J.: Prentice-Hall, 1969), p. 216.

another player in the game of bureaucratic politics.[142] His proper role is to attempt to influence style, assumptions, and training, not to try to intervene in the process of choice. And this means that it is wrong to tell the possessor of knowledge that he must become a partisan in the bureaucratic struggle: his influence, on the contrary, has to come from the intellectual weight he carries, not his political clout. If that role is not recognized by the players, especially the President and the Secretary, the argument should not read that intellectuals must become politicians, but rather that planning is impossible and irrelevant.

A staff of scholars and intellectuals could not survive the working habits of the State Department (and vice versa). If they were placed directly in the Secretary of State's line of command, the result would be a series of specific demands emerging from the Secretary's immediate needs. This would be true at the present moment, when perceptions of what the planners might be able to do remain parochial and myopic. The intellectual who joins a governmental planning staff, either in or out of the existing bureaucracies, is never unattached—at least in the sense that the university or free-lance intellectual is presumed to be unattached. There are, however, relative differences that retain some significance, and in this sense a staff outside the State Department would have more freedom in choosing the problems it wants to work on, the methods that seem appropriate, and the proper time to start thinking about issues.[143]

There are also conflicts of value and perspective between an intellectual and an operating bureaucrat that could perhaps be mitigated by separating them. Merton lists a series of incompatibilities that arise when the intellectual becomes an in-house part of the bureaucrat's world: different universes of discourse, the exploitation of research findings for political purposes, the bureaucrat's demand for immediate answers, and the scholar's unwillingness to commit himself on flimsy evidence.[144] Once again, these considerations merely indicate that bureaucracies are action-oriented agencies, and intellectuals and planning units are (or should be) reflective and critical in temper and outlook. An intellectual may become a good bureaucrat because he is intelligent, well trained, and sensitive to personal nuances; then again, he may not, even though he has all or some of these qualities. But he will not become the kind of planner that we need—someone committed to understanding issues, not just manipulating

---

[142] As a player, he is usually weak and ineffectual.
[143] Robert Merton's essay "The Role of the Intellectual in Public Bureaucracy," in his *Social Theory and Social Structure,* pp. 207-224, is worth reading. On the points we have been discussing, see pp. 217-218.
[144] *Ibid.,* p. 223.

them—if he begins to sacrifice the virtues of his profession for momentary pieces of the action. The planners must be separate from the operators or there will be no planners.[145]

Former government officials are fond of stressing the point that there is a difference between being in and being out of the government.[146] These differences are not at issue here, for we are discussing a planning staff entirely within the government. That explains why Merton's comments on the difficulties an intellectual or a scholar faces working in a bureaucracy are more pertinent than comments on the contrast between the independent scholar and the policymaker restrained or constricted by arbitrary deadlines. The planner within the government, insofar as he is performing an analytical and not a ceremonial function, will confront some of the same problems in dealing with his policymaker as an outside scholar would. The policymaker still lives primarily in a world in which his attention centers on salient issues, not necessarily important ones, and in which he worries about trading off support on one issue for support on another, and not whether particular policies are the best available.[147] The differences, however, are muted and less significant when the planner has the access, the information, and the responsibility of the insider. This may be particularly true if the planner also has the respectability that comes from recognition that he is performing a useful function.

LONG RANGE PLANNING:
THE PROBLEMS OF INSTITUTIONALIZATION

The institutional form that a new planning staff should assume is difficult to establish. If the concept of this staff was sufficiently supported, it probably would not make much difference. In the more likely circum-

[145] Hammond in "NSC-68: Prologue to Rearmament" argues that rationality in the policymaking process can be achieved only at the price of relevance. (p. 373 ff.) This is true if one hopes to bring rationality to bear at the moment of decision. At the moment, however, the clash between the two qualities is only apparent: we have sacrificed rationality for relevance rather significantly. If one hopes to give rationality its due, however modestly, one must create a situation in which its insights can be brought to bear before they clash with the imperatives of immediate relevance.
[146] See Frankel, "The Difference between Being In and Being Out," and Howard Wriggins, "The Scholar and the Policy-Maker—Contrasting Views of What Matters" (papers delivered at the 1968 American Political Science Association Convention). See also Heller, *New Dimensions of Political Economy,* pp. 15-26, as well as the argument in Chapter 3.
[147] See also Raymond A. Bauer, "The Study of Policy Formation: An Introduction," in Raymond A. Bauer and Kenneth J. Gergen, eds., *The Study of Policy Formation* (New York: The Free Press, 1968), pp. 1-26.

stance that the new staff was met by suspicion, distrust, and apathy, organizational form could be significant.

The question of form should not obscure one basic point: the new staff must be entirely within the governmental apparatus, and not half in and half out. This is in response to suggestions that the proper model for the relationship between planners and operators can be found in the workings of the National Science Foundation and its semi-autonomous committees. There is no doubt that the advisory system in science has had a major impact on the government's decisions about science policy (especially in deciding who gets what from whom).[148] These committees, however, have primarily been concerned with questions of resource allocation within and between disciplines. Perhaps the permanent agencies established within the executive branch to oversee and coordinate science policy provide a better illustration.[149] They have not apparently been very successful thus far, which perhaps suggests that other analogies ought to be sought. In addition, it seems true that science and the problems of science are rather unique, and we may be misled rather than informed if we continually turn to the hard sciences whenever we seek models for the social sciences. We are interested in research and planning done for the government and not in research merely supported by government funds.

The Council of Economic Advisers provides another possible model for a new planning staff. A major study of the CEA by Edward Flash notes that it

> has emerged as the government's economic ideologist. It is a source of ideas and information rather than a force in execution and coordination. Characterized by an expertise that is essentially substantive rather than derived, the Council has helped more in policy formulation and analysis than in management . . . Each of the Councils studied went beyond factual analysis and advice (important as these were) to provide the rationale for the economic policies of the respective administrations.[150]

The words that Flash uses to describe the Council's behavior—educator, spokesman, catalyst, sounding board, facilitator—would, in the best of all

[148] See Daniel S. Greenberg, *The Politics of Pure Science* (New York: The New American Library, 1967), pp. 167-168.
[149] See the essays by Harvey Brooks and Don K. Price in Cronin and Greenberg, *The Presidential Advisory System.*
[150] Edward S. Flash, Jr., *Economic Advice and Presidential Leadership: The Council of Economic Advisors* (New York: Columbia University Press, 1965), pp. 276-277.

possible worlds, be the words that should characterize the work of a successful planning body in foreign affairs.

Why and how has the CEA been a success? Flash notes that "its successes have derived from getting things started or changed, and its failures from being unable to prevent things from being undone or delayed or stopped."[151] Its performance has also varied in terms of a number of other factors: its relationship to the President and his bureaucracy, the range of conflict over an issue, the competitiveness of advice from other sources, and the inherent subjectivity of economic analysis.[152] Thus the CEA has not been automatically successful; it has faced the "necessity of creating and maintaining a need for its services, in effect, of nurturing a demand for its supply of analysis and advice."[153] Inevitably, the CEA's chances of having its advice prevail have improved when opinions on an issue are diffused, or when an issue is new and important, or when a crisis arises and the decision-making arena narrows.[154]

There are two major reasons why the example of the CEA may be inappropriate. The CEA was too concerned with immediate policy issues to do any research (although it did encourage research elsewhere).[155] It became a staff to the President, rather than an institution with clearly defined functions that persist in much the same form through different administrations (as in the Budget Bureau). The planning staff that we have been advocating, however, ought to have the capacity not only to advise on policy but also to do research. Also, the planning staff ought to have an independent status sufficiently protected so that it does not necessarily wither and die if a President ignores it. Only this kind of status would allow it to do substantive research and planning; only a guaranteed status and autonomy (within the government) would give the planning staff the time and freedom to find a real role and purpose, and to survive initial failures and hostility. In effect, one hopes to protect the essentially conceptual and abstract functions of the planning staff from the demands for immediate and specific advice and support.

The second reason for distrusting the CEA analogy concerns the nature of the expertise that prevails in economics and in foreign affairs. The economist's expertise may indeed be essentially substantive—he has, at

[151] *Ibid.*, p. 279.
[152] *Ibid.*, p. 296 ff.
[153] *Ibid.*, p. 306.
[154] *Ibid.*, p. 307. An article of faith with several members of the Policy Planning Council was that the best time to get a new idea into the process was during a crisis. An outsider finds this mysterious because the PPC was rarely consulted during crises.
[155] *Ibid.*, p. 291.

any rate, a reasonably good record in that curious combination of macro-analysis and advocacy that constitute the CEA's distinctive contribution to economic policy. The foreign affairs expert is in a more anomalous position. His expertise, especially if he is in the government, may be primarily procedural and not substantive. It tends to be an expertise that is dependent on circumstance and is not self-contained or autonomous. Nor does it have the record of success that (some) economists have. The academic expert in foreign affairs is not much better off: even if he is versed in macropolitical trends and developments, and is not a narrow specialist in palace politics, he confronts the difficulty that his macro-political analyses are not what the policymaker (currently) wants. The economist is more fortunate, because it appears true that macroanalysis is just what the economic policymaker needs (or wants).

An analogy with the Council of Economic Advisers is likely to raise expectations about future performance that cannot be met. This would not be true, I believe, if there were more awareness of the degree to which economic advice combines the advocacy of particular values with technical analysis. There are, of course, areas in which this does not pertain and in which the economist functions as a technician: for example, in macroeconomic efforts to achieve stability. In determining an equitable tax policy, however, or deciding on the degree of competition or monopoly that is acceptable, the economist:

> functions primarily as a propagandist of values, not as a technician supplying data for the preexisting preferences of the policy-makers. Some of his propaganda is directed at those participants in political decision-making to whom the advisers are directly responsive . . . Much of it is directed through his political superiors to other participants in the political process—including the general public—and the adviser becomes, in fact, a supplier of arguments and briefs which seek to gain wider support for economists' political values.[156]

Even if knowledge of the degree to which economic advice rests on values, and not theory, were more widely shared, it would still remain true that differences between economics and politics would persist. The crux of the matter is that the theoretical component of political advice is much weaker: that is, the economist may mix values and science, but the combination is more attractive just because the scientific element itself is more enticing. Until political theories begin to achieve a higher degree of

[156] Carl Kaysen, "Model-makers and Decision-makers: Economists and the Policy Process," *The Public Interest,* no. 12 (Summer 1968), p. 83.

rigor, an analogy between economics and politics may be dangerous and misleading.

Another alternative would be to establish a group modeled on the RAND Corporation or one of its offshoots. This has obvious virtues. A group modeled on RAND suggests a group composed of recognized experts working for the government but outside the normal bureaucratic apparatus. This alternative also implies an effort to retain as many of the advantages of free academic research (and researchers) as is possible for a staff wholly within the government. This implies, in turn, a serious effort to allow the researcher some say in the definition of the problem he is working on and some control over the data on which he is expected to offer conclusions that he is willing to stand behind.

The RAND analogy is appealing because RAND's influence has tended to center on the period before an actual decision has to be made. Thus, Bruce L. R. Smith, who goes so far as to maintain that only outsiders like the RAND analysts can do long-range research,[157] has argued that RAND's major impact has been in "influencing the way in which policy-makers approach their task, define alternatives, and assess criteria for choice."[158] Even more critically, RAND made analytical thinking about strategic issues respectable *within* the government. This is not to say that the thinking was good or accurate. But it does suggest, especially in areas that are new and important, that overcoming the traditional antipathy of the operator to intellectual arguments is not impossible. (The Pentagon was more receptive to these developments than the State Department.)

Two points about a planning staff modeled on the RAND experience ought to be emphasized. First, this group should be staffed neither by Foreign Service Officers (no doubt a blow to the vastly overcrowded Foreign Service)[159] nor by the typical in-and-outer repeating the few

[157] Smith, *The RAND Corporation,* pp. 226-227.

[158] *Ibid.,* p. 28.

[159] A recent piece on the Foreign Service argues that its performance could be improved if its numbers were sharply cut. Although no one can deny that the Foreign Service is overcrowded, it is not clear why reduction would improve its substantive performance–the Foreign Service would remain the same group of untrained, self-designated elites, only smaller. Moreover, there is no strong evidence that the Foreign Service was more effective when it was smaller, although it may have seemed a true elite to its members. The author suggests that the FSOs who would be ousted in such a cutback could be parceled out to other government agencies. However, the thought of inundating neighboring bureaucracies with several thousand officials that the Foreign Service does not want is a bizarre suggestion. See John Franklin Campbell, "What Is to Be Done?"
This article does contain interesting statistical information on the Foreign Service

"lessons" he thinks he has learned. The staff might be a disaster in the best of times, but its only hope of achieving a respectable role is to deliberately seek the best analytical minds—not the most experienced. These men must have training and perceptions different from the usual bureaucrat's, for there is no other way in which they could offer advice and inspiration that is truly different. Second, the new staff probably ought to be attached to the office of the President's National Security Advisor to protect it from the State Department (and the Pentagon).[160]

The analogy with RAND should not be taken too literally. Like all analogies, it should be treated with caution, and used solely as a catalyst to think about an issue, not as a replacement for thinking. The sharp decline in RAND's prestige in recent years, and a concomitant (and justified) tendency to raise questions about the quality of some of RAND's most vaunted studies and methods, must also be kept in mind.[161]

One of the most important functions that this new staff could fulfill is to begin to rebuild confidence in the honesty, integrity, and virtue of government service. The contempt and distrust between the governmental and academic worlds create a critical problem, particularly since academics have so much influence on the quality and quantity of students who are willing to contemplate a government career. A new planning unit staffed with men of recognized intellect might be a useful opening to an outside world that is now thoroughly disaffected. This is, perhaps,

---

and offers serious comments on its problems. I disagree with the unexamined premise that the Foreign Service is an elite institution and that its difficulties have nothing to do with its character, training, and style. In addition, Campbell's belief that power in foreign affairs ought to be centralized in the Secretary of State's hands would make more sense if State had the desire—and the right personnel—to carry out a wide range of tasks—beyond either representation or managing programs. See also my comments on Campbell's views, pp. 49-51 above.

[160] In view of the National Security Council's prominence under Henry Kissinger, I doubt that the planning function, as outlined in this book, could be successfully carried out by the NSC. The NSC seems too political and *personal* a staff of the President and too likely to become totally immersed in operations and current problems to perform the analysis that I have in mind. For evidence supporting the view that the NSC is likely to get too involved with the immediate agenda to do genuine long-range planning, see I. M. Destler, "Can One Man Do?" *Foreign Policy,* no. 5 (Winter 1971-72), pp. 28-40, and John P. Leacacos, "Kissinger's Apparat," *ibid.,* pp. 3-27.

[161] See, for example, the interesting comments by Bernard Brodie, especially in reference to RAND's excessive fascination with systems analysis, in "Why Were We So (Strategically) Wrong?" *Foreign Policy,* no. 5 (Winter 1971-72), pp. 151-161.

another reason why the analogy with RAND should be treated with care. The idea of another RAND Corporation is not likely to evoke much enthusiasm, unless it is made clear that the original idea underlying RAND's creation, and the relationship with its sponsor, was eminently sound.

Many of RAND's successes were in the hard sciences and in economics; the variables and parameters are far more complex in foreign affairs. This is perhaps the major reason why all analogies—the NSF, the CEA, RAND, or any other—designed to indicate the proper form for a new planning staff in foreign affairs are somewhat suspect. The only substantial evidence we have is negative: it is clear that creating another planning staff in the State Department, without a major revolution in that organization (and one not designed to turn out diplomat managers), is entirely useless. All this suggests that the increased complexity of foreign affairs may justify lowering expectations about the immediate impact of an increased commitment to planning, but not giving it up entirely. This is especially true because the problems emerging or likely to emerge in the years ahead will require even more specialized treatment and more concern for their long-run implications than those of the past.

Reflection on the problems that a new planning staff would encounter—the bureaucratic jungle in Washington and the substantive problems that the staff would have to confront—suggests that there may be virtue in attempting to combine the best features of several different alternatives, rather than settling on a single model. From RAND, one might choose to borrow the idea of a research organization doing work of the highest quality on mid- and long-range problems, outside the bureaucratic wars but nevertheless within the government. From the CEA, one might choose to borrow the idea of an organization directed by men of recognized professional standing who are willing to spend a number of years analyzing public policy issues. In addition to their substantive contributions, these men of professional standing might perform significant ceremonial functions: they might lessen the suspicion that the new staff was simply another tool of the bureaucracy, and they might make the possibility of working for the government seem more honorable than it currently does. Finally, from the NSF, one might borrow the idea of consultative committees, composed of highly regarded experts, offering advice and direction in various areas. Whether a hybrid organization such as this would survive more easily or perform more effectively is very uncertain; but mongrels often perform tasks far more effectively than less hardy but purer breeds.

PLANNING AND THE RELATIONSHIP
BETWEEN THEORY AND PRACTICE

It would be possible at this point to bring the substantive part of this book to a close. When my research had just begun, it was my intention to do so. In addition, it is my belief that the arguments in this chapter could stand by themselves: they offer a reasonably self-contained analysis of the failures of planning in foreign affairs and they suggest how the obstacles that have impeded planning might be bypassed. Yet it has become increasingly clear to me that these arguments are necessary but not sufficient.

Perhaps another way of making the point is to note that we have been dealing with symptoms and not causes. This is hardly unusual in cases where causality is unknown—in medicine, for example—or where it has been misunderstood. I believe the latter to be the case here, for the failures of planning have generally been attributed to the peculiar nature of the environment with which it must deal. But, as I have already noted in the Introduction, it is just this kind of environment that should put a high premium on planning, and, provided that we assess planning in comparison with alternatives to it and not against abstract standards of success, there is no a priori reason to assume that planning must fail. It is clear that we have never made a serious effort to see whether planning could be made to work—it is doubtful that our practitioners even understand what that would entail. Moreover, if the security issue is no longer the only issue (or even the dominant one) in international relations, it may well be that the only alternative to planning, no matter how imperfect its results, is the acceptance of chaos.[162] This is especially true so long as foreign policy continues to be made by men schooled in the narrow and increasingly irrelevant traditions of Political Realism.

We can begin to develop a more profound understanding of why planning has failed only if we alter the questions we are accustomed to ask about it. Up to this time, we have been content to describe the nature of

---

[162] The response to this argument is that the alternative is not chaos but incremental adjustments of ongoing policies. As I have argued on pages 24-25, the consensus that facilitated the bargaining of incrementalism is gone. In addition, the problems have become more complex and specialized, and it is no longer satisfactory to handle them procedurally—that is, without attempting to judge the substantive nature of the issue. Failure to do so can lead to the accumulation of small difficulties into a major crisis. Finally, the change in the international environment—to the extent that growing interdependence means that national solutions, no matter how developed, are inadequate—demands a decision-making style that is more coherent, rational, and long-range. In short, I doubt that chaos is too strong a word in light of the record of the last two decades.

the obstacles that combine to create a situation in which serious planning is unlikely. But suppose we ask instead: Why is it that these obstacles persist in spite of the obvious need for new approaches and ideas? Why do both practitioners and theorists believe that it is either impossible or unimportant to challenge these obstacles?

We cannot plan or take concern for the future seriously until the planners and the men from whom they seek counsel have the conviction that these are legitimate and useful functions. Until these men believe that they *should* plan and that they *can* plan, the obstacles to planning will remain overwhelming and unchallengeable. Planning has failed, therefore, not only because of the difficult practical obstacles that impede it, but also—and perhaps preeminently—because we have developed a generation of practitioners and theorists who are convinced *ab initio* that planning must fail and has almost nothing to do with the professional roles they define for themselves. And when such men assert that they want to reform or improve the planning function, what they mean is that they want to discover how the planners can influence current events. They rarely realize that such a role can be played, if at all, only by sacrificing any opportunity to make planning truly useful.

One point about planning is frequently forgotten: planning is the area within a social discipline in which theorists and practitioners are most likely to share interests and to help each other significantly. Thus, an examination of the planning function gives us a good perspective on the relationship between theory and practice and illustrates how the record of planning is heavily conditioned by the theorists' and the practitioners' views of their professional obligations. In the present case, the practitioner's assumption that long-range planning is impossible, and the theorist's view that he can (and should) do nothing for the practical realm until he has first created powerful theories, have created a situation in which they rarely communicate or make any serious attempt to collaborate. In fact, this situation, which should be viewed with deep concern, is accepted by both groups as inevitable, legitimate, and desirable. Even the policy planner, for whom the absence of contact would seem most dangerous and debilitating, has been unfamiliar with and uninterested in academic research; also, the theorist has made no effort to alter the situation—indeed, he has converted indifference into a professional virtue.

In Chapter 3 we shall examine the images of professional behavior that have justified this state of affairs. Upon what assumptions do they rest? Are they valid, or can they be reinterpreted so that cooperation between theorists and practitioners—in planning, in research, and in analysis—can begin to appear useful and necessary? An affirmative answer to the last question will not guarantee the success of planning. The practical obstacles to planning that we have already discussed will remain formidable, and convincing both theorists and practitioners of the advantages of rethinking positions that they now take for granted will be difficult and time-consuming. Nonetheless, unless we make an effort to alter patterns of professional behavior, planning will never be productive. In metaphorical terms, we shall be intent on resetting the boundaries between theorists and practitioners in one social discipline so that they can understand what modes of cooperation are possible and what modes are impossible, and so that they do not assume that a facile analogy with the way the relationship presumably works in other disciplines is all that should be recognized.

To the practical man, accustomed to dealing with political problems in a *terre à terre* fashion, this venture into the abstractions of theory and practice may appear exceedingly irrelevant—the archetype of the professorial passion for the impractical. Nothing could be further from the truth. The attempt to understand, to evaluate, and to alter fundamental professional beliefs has far more significance for the world of practice than any set of practical reforms. One need only recognize that what we perceive as a practical reform is dependent on prior professional beliefs to understand the practical implications of this exercise in abstraction.

Theorists and practitioners within a common discipline can never escape each other. The specific form that their relationship takes may vary widely, according to the nature of the discipline and the sophistication of its theories and methodologies, but *some* relationship is always there. The theorist, after all, would have nothing to theorize about without a flow of problems from the practical world, and the practitioner, conversely, would not even be able to identify problems without a cognitive response to his universe. The only relationship that is *always* wrong is one that asserts the autonomy of either realm. This situation now nearly exists, for the increasingly rare statements that attempt to discuss these issues seem more intent on protecting vested professional interests than on illuminating real problems. Therefore, the effort to analyze the relationship between theory and practice without commitment to the prevailing stereotypes is important; even if my interpretation fails to satisfy everyone, it will at least compel attention to an issue that we can ignore or misunderstand only at our own peril.

The arguments in the next chapter are complex and difficult. Would we lose anything of value if they were excluded? The answer to this question depends on how serious we are about beginning a process of change that will make the policymaking system in foreign affairs more effective in the years ahead.

The creation of a long-range planning staff committed to taking the future seriously could be an important innovation. It would add new and different voices to a political process that has lost direction, self-confidence, and, most critically, its sense of legitimacy. Nevertheless, it would be foolish to assume that a new planning staff, or any other institution, which is merely added to the old political system, could have a profound impact on how we conduct our political affairs. Institutional reform is not by itself sufficient to create fundamental change unless it is accompanied by changes in professional belief systems. New institutions must be staffed by men who understand and believe in their purposes. For that to happen, we must change the minds of practitioners who believe that planning is a waste of time and of theorists who believe that involvement in practical affairs is sinful.

Chapters 2 and 3 thus appear to involve very different things. This chapter argues for a short-range and practical institutional reform; the next chapter argues for more long-range and cognitive changes in individual belief systems. Nevertheless, if we want to institute fundamental changes in our political system, the arguments in the two chapters must converge. There are no shortcuts, no "quick fixes," no magic keys by which we can escape this conclusion. We could attempt to escape it only be asserting that our existing institutions and beliefs will deal with the future better than they have dealt with our immediate past. And who can believe that?

CHAPTER 3

Theory and Practice:
Dilemmas of Coexistence

INTRODUCTION

We normally analyze the relationship between theory and practice by attempting to establish the connection between a body of doctrine and practical actions. Such analysis is important, as I hope the discussion of Political Realism in the preceding chapter indicated, in spite of its difficulties and ambiguities. So many factors can determine the choice of specific actions that it is never possible to assert that the theory, by itself, was directly responsible for the choice of A rather than B or C. We must be satisfied with less than a statement of direct causality: we are limited to indicating how a certain theory affected the intellectual climate in which the practitioner operated. The influence of the theory, therefore, depends on how the orientations it establishes allow us to organize a piece of our intellectual landscape.[1]

We cannot underestimate the importance of illuminating this aspect of the relationship between theory and practice. John Maynard Keynes's well-known contention that practical men seldom realize how indebted

---

[1] We accept such theories because we believe that they illuminate a particular area more accurately or more comprehensively than any alternative. We are usually aware that they do not provide specific answers to all problems, but we accept their authority, although provisionally, because they best offer an element of certainty amid great uncertainty. The judgment of reasonable men can differ sharply about the precise implications of practical events, but preliminary agreement on general principles allows them to perceive what their disagreements are and perhaps even sets limits on them. Commitment to a code of beliefs in an environment dominated by uncertainty is a psychological necessity, for without it we lack confidence in our judgment. In sum, theory is important to practice even when its reins are loose and permissive.

they are to the ideas of "some academic scribbler of a few years back"[2] defines the issue quite clearly: if we want to know why men chose as they did, we must examine the doctrines they believed in. The practitioner who refuses to acknowledge the power of ideas in his own realm is a fool, and potentially a very dangerous one.

As long as the discipline of international relations was dominated by Political Realism, or any other essentially normative theory, an analysis of the relationship between particular theories and particular actions seemed sufficient. The theoretical realm was, in a manner of speaking, all of a piece: the theories were similar in kind, however much they might differ in detail, and attention inevitably centered on how they affected external events. But did the fact that all theories were similar in kind structure the relationship between theory and practice? The answer is obviously yes, but no one bothered about it very much, perhaps because it was an unavoidable effect if all theories were the same (and could thus be "factored out"), or perhaps because the effect was so familiar that it could be ignored.

Of course, normative theories no longer dominate the discipline of international relations. Empirical theory, or the quest for empirical theory and the attendant behavioral styles, is now central to the discipline's concerns. And an academic discipline that concentrates on producing empirical theories will have a very different (not necessarily better or worse) relationship with the practical realm than a discipline that concentrates on producing normative theories. What will these relationships be? Why do they take the form they do? If we want to answer these questions, we cannot be satisfied with an analysis of how a specific theory conditions the choice of specific actions: we must also look at how theorists (and practitioners) define their professional role, what theories they produce, and what use such theories might have for men concerned with practical problems. We move up one level of abstraction, from a concern with particular theories to a concern with how the quest for one *kind* of theory rather than another affects how theorists orient themselves.

To restate this argument more directly in the context of the discussion in Chapter 2, it was obvious that there was very little contact between the realm of the theorist and the realm of the practitioner. Worse yet, what contact there was—in the form of in-and-outers faking the possession of knowledge different from, or superior to, that of the practitioner—took place on illegitimate (and dangerous) grounds. How could

[2] John Maynard Keynes, *The General Theory of Employment Interest and Money* (London: Macmillan, 1957), p. 383.

the relationship between theorists and practitioners within a common discipline, especially one so intimately tied to the practical world, have reached the point where they ignored each other—and, indeed, treated a wholly artificial isolation as if it was a virtue? The only way to find out is by asking how they define proper professional behavior and by illustrating how those definitions affect the style and substance of cooperation. Instead of discussing specific theories, we shall discuss what theorists do and what kinds of theories they produce. This has value whatever the kinds of theory a discipline produces: the ascendancy of normative theories or that of empirical theories—or some combination of the two— conditions the specific form that the relationship takes, but does not affect whether there is a relationship. That is unavoidable.

What attributes define a "theorist"? For the practitioner, the answer is anyone holding an academic title. That helps to obscure the proper relationship between the two worlds, for obviously not all academics do work that can be legitimately labeled theoretical—one reason why it is important to deal with this issue. Improvement in the relationship between theorists and practitioners is impossible unless practitioners have a more sophisticated understanding of who does and who does not possess knowledge different from their own.

Must a theorist theorize empirically, or is normative theory (or some combination of the two) also legitimate? And who has the right to say? The answers we get owe too much to personal taste and current fashion to be universally acceptable. It is difficult to devise satisfactory answers at this moment in time, for the discipline itself is still divided between normative theorists, empirical theorists, methodologists, and policy analysts of various degrees of sophistication. What would be *useful* in this discussion is a definition of the theorist that excludes frustrated practitioners disguised as professors who merchandise their opinions as the "wisdom of theory" and methodologists who mistake practicing the scales for a concert performance. We also want a definition that does not arbitrarily exclude theorists who happen to be working within a tradition momentarily out of fashion.

The limiting condition is that we seek to define a theorist within a particular context: an academic social science discipline. We cannot do so by asking whether he is a behavioralist or a traditionalist or whether he is using one methodology rather than another, for this succeeds only in identifying the theorist with a particular body of doctrine. Nor can we define a theorist by his studies or the problems that interest him, for theory can emerge from *any* kind of research. In addition, to define a theorist by reference to the audience he addresses is, at least in the social sciences, not very helpful: the audience stretches across too wide a spectrum. (For further comments on some of these categories, in a different context, see pages 148-149 below.)

Only two possibilities seem to be left. We might, in the first place, define a theorist by the results of his work, but then our classification would be entirely retrospective. No one would be able to call himself a theorist until sufficient time had passed for his work to be evaluated. Since that might take decades and since the criteria for theoretical work might have altered in the interim, this option is only interesting and useful to the intellectual historian.

That seems to leave us only one possibility. The theorist works with the knowledge that his discipline has produced, and his desire to create or amplify or refine, and perhaps even to replace or restructure, that generalized body of knowledge may be the only *immediate* way we have of distinguishing the theorist from other members of the discipline. These activities are independent of the problem being analyzed or methodology being employed. The critical question is not whether the research is behavioral, traditional, or eclectic, but whether the researcher is asking the questions and seeking the generalized answers that are of legitimate interest to an academic discipline. This does not mean that people who are not doing this kind of research are expelled from the discipline; it means only that their work does not directly contribute to theory.

Great and obvious difficulties attend this definition. The most important is that anyone can say that he intends to contribute to the theoretical knowledge of the discipline; motivation is an extraordinarily elusive criterion to employ in these circumstances. In policy-oriented disciplines, moreover, it is also possible to straddle or move back and forth between categories. Nevertheless, I believe that this is the best approximation currently within our grasp. Inevitably, a definition of theorists and theoretical work will remain ambiguous and unsatisfactory so long as the discipline is split into factions and so long as it remains in a "pre-theoretical" stage. In these circumstances, this definition has two important virtues. First, it is much clearer on its principle of exclusion: researchers who are trying only to influence the choice of policies or who are merely testing methodologies on available data are part of the discipline, but they are not theorists. Second, the definition does *not* exclude from the realm of theory a concern with normative questions. Indisputably, many questions to which we must seek answers lie beyond available empirical approaches. These are relevant questions for the theorist as long as he attempts to answer them in order to contribute to the body of knowledge that the discipline is building.

Most analyses of theory and practice have been written by theorists or from a theoretical point of view, resulting in an analytic bias against the practitioner. What he thinks and does tends to be measured against an idealized picture of what the theorist thinks and does. The practitioner's behavior, measured in its own terms, is frequently so inept that the additional bias imposed by evaluating it by standards that are partially irrelevant is gratuitous.

Nevertheless, the bias persists. It has meant that the conceptual universe of theory has simply been imposed on the world of the practitioner. That theory and practice are different is unquestionable, but the degree of difference and the forms this difference assumes have been heavily conditioned by a mode of analysis that has been abstract and very stylized.

Self-interested interpretations of the proper relationship between theorists and practitioners thus predominate. Each group's interpretation of the relationship protects its own view of its craft and reinforces its own notions of what is prestigious and aesthetically pleasing professional behavior. This is not difficult to do, for any activity can be discussed either in terms of what it aims for and achieves or in terms of what it ignores and misses. Consequently, theorists have emphasized the unreliability and ambiguity of the knowledge upon which practitioners act, and practitioners have emphasized the failure of theoretical insights as guides for action. Neither group has felt it necessary to go much beyond these negative interpretations of what the other can offer. We shall examine the reasons for this below.

One related issue is worth treating separately. Theorists take for granted the assumption—or prejudice—that theoretical research has much more to contribute to practice than practical research has to contribute to theory. Talcott Parsons has made the point explicitly: "groups engaged in relatively pure research and analysis have made greater contributions to practical benefits than the practitioners have to scientifically generalized knowledge by processes of induction from practical as distinguished from empirical research."[3] It is difficult either to substantiate or deny this contention. One assertion is interesting: Does the theorist waste his *professional* time by working on practical problems? If he does, it would hardly be wise to attempt to convince him to alter his behavior.

---

[3] Talcott Parsons, "The Intellectual: A Social Role Category," in Philip Rieff, ed., *On Intellectuals* (Garden City, N.Y.: Doubleday, 1968), pp. 16-17.

THE THEORETICAL VIRTUES OF IMMERSION
IN PRACTICAL PROBLEMS

The most significant period in which academics were forced to concentrate on practical problems was World War II. And significantly, some major theoretical and conceptual advances in social science directly resulted from that concentration: the "culture at a distance" approach (e.g., the work of Ruth Benedict and Geoffrey Gorer); operations research and the beginning of a movement toward its broader offshoots like systems analysis; Guttman scaling; psychological testing; the indirect and qualitative form of content analysis; and the first significant use of computer technology.

Two famous research projects of the time also ultimately resulted in several books that became classics. The studies of the American soldier and the massive analysis of the authoritarian personality were significant in both a substantive and a methodological sense. The methodological disputes that these works engendered were especially important, and they illustrate a point that Karl Popper made: the most fruitful debates on method have tended to be those about the proper way to deal with a practical problem.[4] Many great theories of social science were stimulated by such practical debates—for example, the theories emerging from debates about the struggle between capital and labor, the rise of colonial empires, and the Great Depression.[5]

Concern with practical problems obviously did not inhibit the theoretical creativity of Freud, Durkheim, or Weber. On a less exalted level, it also facilitated the insights of Chester Barnard and George Kennan. Even in a science like bacteriology, many major breakthroughs in the nineteenth century were achieved by men who set out explicitly to solve a pressing practical problem.[6]

[4] Karl Popper, *The Poverty of Historicism* (New York: Harper and Row, 1964), p. 57.

[5] See also Ralf Dahrendorf, *Essays in the Theory of Society* (Stanford, Calif.: Stanford University Press, 1968), p. 273.

[6] The relationship between science and technology has become increasingly close in the twentieth century. In the nineteenth century, however, much technological development occurred independently—that is, before adequate explanatory theories had been developed. See Aaron Warner, Dean Morse, and Alfred Eichner, eds., *The Impact of Science on Technology* (New York: Columbia University Press, 1965).

Walter W. Heller has also pointed out that "many academic economists are themselves at the forefront in providing realistic analysis and policy proposals." *New Dimensions of Political Economy* (Cambridge, Mass.: Harvard University Press, 1966), p. 51. The implications of this truth have not yet penetrated political science with sufficient force.

Academics tend to assume that a university atmosphere is more conducive to creativity and innovation than an atmosphere dominated by concern for practical problems. Yet available evidence questions the accuracy of this happy but self-serving assumption. For instance, one sociological study that compared the originality of research in several social science departments with that in three practical institutions concluded that the work done "in academic social science departments was judged less innovative" and that "marginal research settings stimulate innovation."[7]

Another study by Joseph Ben-David reached the same conclusion. He also attempted to explain why innovation appeared to be more frequent in a practical setting:

> Practice . . . is an invaluable guide in locating relevant problems—rather than finding illusory ones, which happened not infrequently in the history of academic thinking—and in adapting existing methods or devising new ones. The problems of practice are always real, and it usually possesses a tradition which is the result of a long collective process of trial and error and which may suggest the way toward new theory and new methods.[8]

Practice, in effect, directs research to problems that are ignored or not implied by the existing methodology.

Thus, a conservative bias exists in the academic frame of reference. The academic, as Ben-David notes, is confined within the boundaries of his own discipline. If he wants to achieve status and security, he must work on problems and in areas that his peers and predecessors have defined as central. The professionalization of a discipline—and its consequent legitimation by autonomous status within a university—may not only turn it away from practical problems but also impede its ability to be theoretically creative.[9] The university setting reinforces this tendency when

[7] Gerald Gordon and Sue Marquis, "Freedom, Visibility of Consequences, and Scientific Innovation," *American Journal of Sociology* 72 (September 1966): 197.
[8] Joseph Ben-David, "Roles and Innovations in Medicine," *American Journal of Sociology* 65 (May 1960): 558.
[9] For corroborative evidence about conservative implications of professionalization and innovativeness associated with practical problems, see Eliot Dole Hutchinson, "The Period of Elaboration in Creative Endeavor," *Psychiatry* 5, no. 2 (1942): 175; Mary Henle, "The Birth and Death of Ideas," in Howard E. Gruber, et al., *Contemporary Approaches to Creative Thinking* (New York: Atherton Press, 1962), p. 43; M. L. Johnson Abercrombie, *The Anatomy of Judgement* (London: Penguin Books, 1969), p. 61.

rewards and status are granted only to those who exhibit virtuosity in explicating the accepted canon.[10]

Problems arise only when traditional behavior persistently fails to solve significant problems. In this sense we can say that theoretical knowledge, which is old knowledge, is unable to solve practical problems—if it could, there would be no problems. Solving problems requires new (or differently formulated) knowledge. The practitioner does not dwell on his debts to the theorist when all goes well, but when things go badly and he turns to the theorist, he may find that he himself has a better grasp of emerging difficulties.

Theorists may become so lost in admiration of their own handiwork that they ignore or actively resent efforts to clarify or verify what they have done. Theory emerging from a practical orientation is less likely to meet this resistance. There is something bracing about being asked, "So what?" especially if this occurs before ego and theory have congealed into an entity. Of course, it may be impossible to clarify the terms of the theory or to validate (or invalidate) any of its conclusions. Systems theory provides a pertinent illustration; in cases like this, the practitioner can do little for the theorist, at least very little of what the theorist wants done. Nonetheless, in other instances, the practitioner's concern for terms that he can understand and for knowledge that he can trust is entirely salutary.

The evidence presented is hardly conclusive. Still, indications that involvement with practical problems is *theoretically* fruitful and that commitment to the conventional wisdom of a discipline may be inhibiting are surely suggestive. In no sense does this imply that everyone ought to be immersed in practical problems; theory can emerge in many ways and practice is but one of them.[11] Nor does the evidence imply that the

---

[10] The above argument is also consistent with the argument in Thomas Kuhn, *The Structure of Scientific Revolutions* (Chicago: University of Chicago Press, 1962).

Another virtue of research in a practical setting is perhaps that it increases the visibility of the consequences of the research and thus may lower resistance to innovation, even within the university. See Gordon and Marquis, "Freedom, Visibility, and Innovation," pp. 198-199.

[11] It does not appear necessary to stress that theory has a major, although varying, impact on practice, that all practitioners operate on an implicit theory of international relations, nor that practical problems should never become an exclusive preoccupation for an academic discipline. Overemphasis on practice would probably mean that many problems that were either unfashionable or long range would not be studied at all (until they became major problems), and that the discipline might become nothing more than a statistical handmaiden or data collector for the practitioner.

professionalization of a discipline and its emplacement in a university setting are entirely negative characteristics; many advantages are implicit in a secure status, and many useful tasks (both theoretical and practical) can best be done far from the pressures of the practical realm. In particular, the explication and the verification of hypotheses, even those discovered in the course of practical work, almost have to be done in a university setting.

What is involved, then, is a question of emphasis. The discipline of international relations has been inundated with cheerleaders and self-styled "new frontiersmen" of theory, simplistically chanting the virtues of science, defined apparently as the endless creation of research strategies to be pursued by someone else. This is a peculiar version of science. In any case, although work done from this perspective may now or someday be useful and fruitful, it is decidedly not the only road to theory. So long as this is true, and the evidence in this section not irrelevant, there is justification in reassessing the relationship between theory and practice from a somewhat different viewpoint. The arguments that follow are designed neither to praise practitioners nor to denigrate theorists; they are, rather, designed to clarify a problem that both theorists and practitioners apparently prefer to leave in obscurity.

The next two sections attack current views on the proper relationship between theorists and practitioners. These sections cannot tell us what the relationship ought to be, but they should make us more willing to contemplate less conventional interpretations of what theorists and practitioners can say to each other. Over the years social theorists have managed to develop a number of arguments that appear to justify an exclusive preoccupation with their own concerns. We shall examine several of these arguments, especially the contention that we can understand theory and practice in politics by means of an analogy with more mature sciences.

THE THEORIST AND THE WORLD OF PRACTICE: THE RATIONALE FOR WITHDRAWAL

The dangers of a radical disjunction between theory and practice have been obscured by the almost mystical veneration that academics grant to any enterprise labeled "theoretical." Kurt Lewin's assertion that "nothing is so practical as a good theory" has become an article of faith, the first commandment in a new canon. But are all theories equally practical? Is the road from one theory to one practical action always the same? An affirmative answer to these questions, whatever else it does, justifies treating the practitioner's problems as embarrassing intrusions into what would otherwise be an elegant and prestigious—if isolated— academic discipline.

Intellectual contempt for the world of practice has a formidable history. John Dewey, for example, in the course of preparing the ground for his version of pragmatism, contended that thought had always been more revered than action:

> The distinctive characteristic of practical activity, one which is so inherent that it cannot be eliminated, is the uncertainty which attends it. . . . Judgment and belief regarding actions to be performed can never attain more than a precarious probability. Through thought, however, it has seemed that men might escape from the perils of uncertainty.[12]

Sir Frederic Bartlett made the same point from another perspective. He noted that thinking likes to go on in closed systems,

> for this gives it a wide apparent range, and especially rids it, as completely as possible, of all ultimate uncertainty. And there is something in thinking which is sympathetic to the uniform and the universal and antagonistic to uncertainty.[13]

Intellectuals may also denigrate practice because it is so dependent on tradition, and the authority of tradition may appear arbitrary and irrational.[14]

Intellectual fashions within a discipline also influence how the world of practice is treated. The study of international relations before World War II, for example, was dominated by international lawyers concerned with putting an end to power politics and creating a peaceful world community; inevitably, the contemporary world was either ignored or viewed as a particularly pernicious anachronism. Political Realism dominated the discipline after the war, and concern for the practitioner increased. That concern, however, was concentrated on an effort to instill veneration in (presumably ignorant or unaware) practitioners for a particular set of principles. Since the principles were already known, empirical analysis of behavior was unnecessary—it would only confirm the obvious.

In recent years, the discipline has been dominated by a curious combination of methodology and metaphysics. The crucial methodological

[12] John Dewey, *The Quest for Certainty: A Study of the Relation of Knowledge and Action* (New York: G. P. Putnam's Sons, 1960), p. 6.
[13] Sir Frederic Bartlett, *Thinking: An Experimental and Social Study* (London: George Allen and Unwin, 1958), p. 96.
[14] Edward Shils, "The Intellectuals and the Powers: Some Perspectives for Comparative Analysis," in Rieff, ed., *On Intellectuals,* p. 44.

concern has been to produce reliable knowledge (which has led to an emphasis on quantification) or to develop conceptual structures analogous to those in more advanced disciplines (which has encouraged an emphasis on systems theory). Presumably the nature of politics determines the nature of political science, but in fact it has been the nature of other disciplines that has determined or conditioned political science. It has required a great leap of faith to justify this course of events. Whatever the outcome, concern for the problems of the practitioner has declined sharply, for they are hard to quantify or to treat substantively from a systemic point of view.

Of course, more sophisticated arguments can also justify an exclusive preoccupation with theoretical concerns. The most fashionable and the most misunderstood argument relies on the indisputable fact that the theorist's work and the practitioner's work involve different frames of reference, time spans, moral codes, and standards of success. In fact, the theorist and the practitioner simply have contrasting vocational cultures. They want and need different things. It is especially true that politicians "pressed to make decisions highly consequential for society, and for themselves, upon quick diagnoses of and responses to concrete pressures and conditions, want, understandably, hard certainties immediately applicable to complex concrete pressures."[15]

Many interpretations of the relationship between theory and practice stop at this point. Different vocational cultures presumably imply the futility of any attempt to cooperate. Does this mean that the assertion that "nothing is so practical as a good theory" is wrong? Not at all, for the two cultures presumably will be usefully joined when the theorist manages to produce his theories.

If a discipline has succeeded in developing theories of its own, the significance of this argument can be indicated explicitly. It is not difficult, for example, to illustrate the connection between theoretical developments in nuclear physics and the bombs that we dropped on Hiroshima and Nagasaki, or between Keynes's general theory and various governmental ventures into deficit financing. But what if the discipline is immature and has not developed theories of its own? The only alternative is to draw an analogy with the way in which more mature disciplines have managed to prosper and grow.

[15] Harry Eckstein, "Political Science and Public Policy," in Ithiel de Sola Pool, ed., *Contemporary Political Science* (New York: McGraw-Hill, 1967), p. 159. For less sophisticated versions of the same position by two in-and-outers, see Charles Frankel, "The Difference between Being In and Being Out," and Howard Wriggins, "The Scholar and the Policy-Makers—Contrasting Views of What Matters" (papers delivered at the 1968 American Political Science Association Convention).

Science, the argument goes, proceeds by abstracting from and simplifying reality; but the practitioner presumably needs advice that rests on an accurate reproduction of reality. Science, moreover, segments and divides reality as its activities become more and more specialized. Thus, the progress of a scientific discipline and the concern for policy problems are inversely related: as the discipline matures, it inevitably turns away from practical problems. In one sense, the discipline does so because its methodological style makes its work seem irrelevant to the practitioner; in another sense, the discipline deliberately withdraws from the realm of policy to establish control over its priorities, such as relevance and status.[16] The creation of good theories is, therefore, the *only* useful deed that the theorist can do for the practitioner; and the theorist is most productive in isolation from the distractions of the practical world.

Withdrawal from policy has indeed occurred in some disciplines, but usually after these fields of study have achieved some theoretical success. No one could seriously argue that international relations is a mature discipline in this sense.[17] The vocabulary in which political events are analyzed has changed, but improvements in the quality of explanation (and thus theory) remain marginal. Moreover, in the present pretheoretical stage of the discipline, the connection between theory and practice is more intimate and pervasive than theorists are willing to admit. All political research is applied research: it is undertaken with the hope of affecting the conduct of public affairs. The notion that we should attempt to separate the two realms is thus arbitrary and unnatural, for politics is not an aesthetic discipline in which we pursue theory for its own sake.

If the analogy with the way in which mature sciences develop is reasonable, this is an unfortunate conclusion. It means that theoretical involvement in practical affairs delays, perhaps irreparably, the creation of

[16] This position is summarized from David B. Truman, "The Social Sciences: Maturity, Relevance, and the Problem of Training," in Austin Ranney, ed., *Political Science and Public Policy* (Chicago: Markham, 1968), pp. 277-287.

[17] Most disciplines develop as a response to practical problems. In its early period, a field has no alternative but to draw its problems from practice—in fact, the theorist and the practitioner may be one and the same. Isolation from practice and concentration on the problems of and between "theories" await the appearance of bodies of knowledge that the members of a discipline are willing to call theories. In international relations, that "willingness" appears premature. At any rate, in the early period, only concentration on practical problems can keep a discipline from descending into aimless empiricism. For interesting comments on the problems that set inquiry off, see Scott Greer, *The Logic of Social Inquiry* (Chicago: Aldine, 1969), pp. 8-14.

theories and, in turn, the improvement of practical affairs.[18] But is the analogy reasonable? Do all disciplines produce theories that can be converted into practical advice in the same fashion? Is the relationship between the technologist and the scientist in mature disciplines the same as the relationship between the practitioner and the theorist in politics? If there are differences in the way in which theories can be used in practical affairs, and if political practitioners are not technologists applying discrete rules to specific cases, the analogy with mature disciplines may not make sense.

ON MISUSING AN ANALOGY WITH THE HARD SCIENCES

Philosophers, especially philosophers of science, are fond of describing the relationship between theory and practice by elegant and economical dichotomies. The theorist, so the argument goes, follows "intimations of the natural order."[19] The knowledge that he collects is presumably judged according to its truth or falsehood. The practical man, conversely, is concerned primarily with the success or failure of his activity. Rather than truth or certainty, which could be stated in the form of a law-like proposition, he must accept the necessity of acting on the basis of likelihood.[20] Having accepted a different conceptual framework, he has no

[18] This is the standard position within the discipline of political science. For example, David Easton argues that "the understanding and explanation of political behavior logically precede and provide the basis for efforts to utilize political knowledge in the solution of urgent practical problems of society." "The Current Meaning of 'Behavioralism,' " in James C. Charlesworth, ed., *Contemporary Political Analysis* (New York: The Free Press, 1967), p. 16. Professor Easton does not consider the possibility that practical problems may be ameliorated by using knowledge not yet part of a theory nor that problems may be clarified through inquiry. Nor does he discuss the possibility that understanding and explanation may themselves profit from immersion in practical problems. He takes for granted that what was logical in another area is also logical in politics.

This should not be construed as an attack on theory, for there is no reason to doubt, in Arnold Brecht's phrase, that "the better our theory, the better it is for our practice." *Political Theory: The Foundations of Twentieth Century Political Thought* (Princeton, N.J.: Princeton University Press, 1959), p. 14. The difficulty is that this argument may be used to rationalize the assumption that practical problems must await the arrival of developed theories. It also ignores or oversimplifies the complexity of the process by which we get better practices from better theories in different disciplines.

[19] Michael Polanyi, *Personal Knowledge: Towards a Post-Critical Philosophy* (New York: Harper and Row, 1958), p. 187.

[20] See Alfred Schutz, *Collected Papers, II: Studies in Social Theory* (The Hague: Martinus Nijhoff, 1964), p. 72: "As we normally have to act and not to reflect in order to satisfy the demands of the moment ... [w]e are satisfied if we have a fair chance of realizing our purposes, and this chance, so we like to think, we have if we

choice but to evaluate his efforts by an inelegant standard: Were they successful in achieving desired ends? His knowledge is instrumental; the theorist's is an end in itself.

The quest for truth—verifiable truth—does not suffer from the limitations and imperfections of the quest for success. For example, the quest for truth implies that the theorist can concern himself with the universal and the unchangeable, but that the practitioner in his search for success must immerse himself in the particular and the changeable. The theorist also does not confront the deadlines that dominate the practitioner's world; the theorist can begin in the beginning or anywhere he pleases, and he can wait upon events without the fear of being thrust *in medias res*. The theorist can afford to be detached about events, but the practitioner is always involved in them. The products of their labors also differ: theory can achieve a high degree of simplicity, uniformity, and precision, but practice is dominated by mixtures, balances, and compromises. Finally, the theorist is free to innovate without fearing the consequences, for the victory of one thought over another rarely has an immediately pernicious effect, but the practitioner is reluctant to innovate and is happiest with tradition, for the unknowable consequences of untried actions may be irreversible and disastrous.[21]

Treating the relationship between theory and practice as one of opposed polarities has a certain aesthetic appeal; it also has the apparent virtue of bringing the discussion to a satisfactory conclusion, for if theory and practice are completely divergent, no one needs to analyze where and when and how they intersect. Perhaps this is merely the

---

set in motion the same mechanism of habits, rules and principles which formerly stood the test.... The consistency of this system of knowledge is not that of natural *laws,* but that of *typical* sequences and relations."

[21] These dichotomies are borrowed from a number of sources. One of the most complete analyses, however, can be found in Leo Strauss's discussion of Burke's view that theory is insufficient as a guide to practice. See *Natural Right and History* (Chicago: University of Chicago Press, 1953), pp. 304-311.

These distinctions can also be formulated by two models of different social systems. Thus, the goal of the theorist (valid knowledge) implies a particular epistemology and methodology; these are enforced on members of the discipline by a normative culture (in science, norms of disinterestedness, organized skepticism, etc.) and by a principle of integration (in science, peer-group pressure). It is, in principle, possible to derive the same model for the practitioner. For our purposes, these models are too static, for they only organize what is already known into a coherent framework—and it is our hope to go beyond that framework. For such an effort, see Norman Storer, *The Social System of Science* (New York: Holt, Rinehart and Winston, 1966); also interesting is the Introduction in Elisabeth T. Crawford and Albert D. Biderman, eds., *Social Scientists and International Affairs* (New York: John Wiley and Sons, 1969).

inevitable result of a mode of analysis that imposes broad categories of analysis on an activity without submitting either the categories or the activity to empirical examination. Still, this mode of analysis has provided the intellectual rationale behind assertions that we are dealing with two divergent vocational cultures.

Much work on theory and practice has been done by philosophers of science, and many social scientists have assumed that their own efforts could easily be subsumed within the available categories. These categories, however, may not even be accurate on their home ground. Technology, in the past, has occasionally achieved significant results without any understanding of the relevant scientific principles. More to the point, in many cases the conversion of a theory into an artifact is far more complex than a simple statement of the science-technology relationship implies; the process may run from different levels of theoretical articulation to the inventor, then to the technologist (who reduces the invention to a practical form), and finally to the production engineer and the designer.[22]

Whatever the case may be in the sciences, the relationship between theory and practice in politics cannot be adequately represented as a dichotomy. Why has it been so frequently misrepresented? Part of the answer lies in a failure to understand the difference in context between the conversion process from theory to practice in the sciences and in politics. The technologist (engineer) in the sciences does not normally have to understand the scientific principles that explain his activity; he can usually carry out his labors by applying a relatively fixed set of rules.[23] Many social scientists have assumed that the same condition holds in the social and political realm. There may be no handbooks for practitioners with a fixed set of rules—which at least leaves to the social practitioner, as distinct from the engineer, an element of art in applying principles to cases—but they too need not understand the theories that they are applying.[24] The practitioner only needs to be able to direct and

[22] See Warner, et al., *The Impact of Science on Technology*.

[23] Fixed rules can be applied only if the objective is also fixed—as it generally would be for the engineer. The problem is more complex for the social scientist. Perhaps Joan Robinson goes too far to assert that for the social scientist, it is the objective that is at issue. More accurately, the social objective is less firm than it is for the engineer, because it is frequently set by a process of interaction with the available means and because the social scientist himself has so much to do with clarifying (but not deciding between) the available alternatives. This is one reason why the old notion that science is about how, not why, questions is unacceptable in the social sciences. For the comment by Joan Robinson, see *Freedom and Necessity* (New York: Vintage Books, 1971), p. 120.

[24] See Hans L. Zetterberg, *Social Theory and Social Practice* (New York: The Bedminster Press, 1962), for the notion of handbooks for practitioners—and the additional notion that they would not contain laws or theories.

utilize the conclusions of analysis in a way favorable to his interests.[25] As the familiar example goes, knowing that a storm is imminent is sufficient; understanding why it is imminent is a luxury left to academic theorists.

The difficulty with this argument is that it rests on incorrect presumptions about what might or might not be useful to the practitioner. To some practitioners, knowing *why* is a necessary prerequisite for doing *what* about a problem. Only a reasonable, even if approximate, understanding of causality permits sensible plans—and thus policies—to be developed.[26] For example, the statistical generalization that major wars occur every twenty-five years, or that the United States' mood in foreign policy shifts from introverted to extroverted and back again in a regular pattern, is undoubtedly useful to the planner—even if he knows nothing else, there are certain prudential measures that become imperative. Nevertheless, it is ludicrous to argue that neither the planner nor the policymaker needs to understand why these fluctuations occur. It is beyond useful debate that the measures that they can take in anticipation of a new fluctuation, or to ward off an unwanted one, will be far more powerful if they know why certain variables are significant. And this understanding is far more important to the social practitioner, who is enabled to intervene to achieve desired ends, than it is to the technologist or engineer, for whom understanding would permit only minor variations in a given product.[27]

If we insist that knowing why the storm occurs is a luxury for the practitioner, then it is clear that practical investigation and theoretical

[25] See Polanyi, *Personal Knowledge,* p. 187, where he notes that a statement has value to the technologists only if it reveals an ingenious operating principle or promises to achieve a material advantage.

[26] For a contrary view, see Robert Jervis, *The Logic of Images in International Relations* (Princeton, N.J.: Princeton University Press, 1970): "But since decision-makers, unlike scientists, need only to be able to predict how others will act, not understand why they act as they do, knowledge of correlation could be an adequate substitute for knowledge of causation." (p. 29) It is dangerous to accept the notion that knowledge of correlation is sufficient, although I am aware that in many instances it is the best available. It seems to underestimate what the practitioner's function entails, and implies that he need know little beyond the latest facts and the prevailing, habitual categories of analysis.

[27] Another way to phrase this argument is by a principle of standardization. For example, the principles by which we construct a house or a car engine are highly standardized. In effect, the loss of flexibility that is implicit in the builder's or the engineer's inability to understand the theories on which his activity is based is not too costly. On the other hand, in many activities standardization is much less rigorous. Thus, both chess masters and the average chess player may know the same set of principles—development, control of the center, open files, etc.—but application is only very loosely standardized. The loss of flexibility implicit in not knowing why the principles hold and in not having a "sense of the board" is serious. And most social science cases come closer to the chess case than to the house-building case.

investigation will concentrate on different variables. Practical investigation will seek variables that can be controlled by the observer or can serve as catalysts to alter the direction of an outcome.[28] Theoretical investigation, on the contrary, will seek variables that cause events or predict outcomes accurately. The notion of catalysts and controls is presumably alien to those who seek truth, not results.

This is an elegant argument. But it is elegant, just as the previous argument was elegant, because it rests on an oversimplified analogy about how the engineer or the technologist behaves. This should be clear to anyone who looks at the way in which problems actually confront the practitioner. The variables that produce practical problems frequently have more than one cause.[29] Also, even if the practitioner knows which variable is relevant, and has access to it, he may not be able to control the outcome because he cannot control enough of the environment. The practitioner is not tinkering with a machine to find the part that is malfunctioning in order to replace it. Catalysts and controls are thus frequently impossible to discover or use. What the practitioner actually seeks—or can get—is less elaborate than catalysts and controls: perhaps indicated by points of leverage, insight, or degrees of influence. And for this venture, the process of inquiry that we associate with theory-building is useful. In addition, treating the quest for control as the distinguishing characteristic of practical activity is partially inaccurate; it mistakes one aspect of the practitioner's activities for the whole. In order to know where to begin to look for catalysts and controls, however rigorously, the practitioner must have an understanding of the nature of the problem that he confronts. Without such understanding, whatever success he has can only be attributed to chance or habit.

We can extract two principal and related points from this discussion. First, the analogy between the technologist or engineer in the sciences and the political practitioner obscures more than it reveals. We are concerned with what happens when they attempt to make use of a theory or a hypothesis that they have had no part in developing. The alternatives confronting the engineer are limited, for he works within a sharply defined frame of reference. He also knows more and is far clearer than the political practitioner about what will and what will not work. The number of intervening variables between the theory and the product is limited, they are usually known beforehand, and they can frequently be

[28] See Robert M. MacIver, *Social Causation* (New York: Harper and Row, 1964), p. 162.
[29] Arthur L. Stinchcombe, *Constructing Social Theories* (New York: Harcourt, Brace and World, 1968), p. 41.

controlled by manipulation. The political practitioner's position is different. He knows nothing for certain, and very little that can even be stated in high probability. Moreover, the subjects to which he must apply his theory are not inert. Their relatively uncontrolled and indeterminate behavior guarantees that the application of social theories will always be an ambiguous and uncertain art. He has no rule book that promises success ceteris paribus.

The second point is more fundamental, for it involves the theories with which the engineer and the political practitioner must work. The theories that the political scientist is likely to produce will probably be nothing more elegant than a collection of tendency statements bound together by creative insight and intuition. It is unlikely that he will produce a deductively compelling hierarchy of propositions, or even, except for unique areas such as voting behavior, a very strong statement of probabilities.[30] Thus his theories will be loose, informal, and—the central point—will require a strong element of judgment in application.

We can see this difference even in sciences that presumably come closest to approximating the conditions in the social and political realm. For example, in meteorology, which is frequently offered as the correct model for political scientists, the essential indeterminacy resides in the complexity of the subject matter, not the theory. That is, if enough adequate data can be collected, the resulting theory, while not deductive, will still hold with a high degree of probability. There are only limited areas in political science in which this kind of probability statement is possible.[31]

[30] For the idea of theories composed of tendency statements rather than more rigorous probability statements, see Abraham Kaplan, *The Conduct of Inquiry* (San Francisco: Chandler, 1964), pp. 298-300.

Note that my discussion of the differences between the social and physical sciences has concentrated on one issue—the different theories they produce—and has ignored many other differences not central to my concerns in this chapter. For example, we have not discussed the significance of the social scientist's dual role of observer-participant, or the discovery of new knowledge in the social sciences which can change both our knowledge of a subject as well as the subject itself. Thus a scientific study of the causes of poverty *may* lead to significant changes in the problem itself, but a study of the structure of DNA has no such effect. I feel that these points are sometimes overemphasized, especially when they are taken to imply a dichotomy between the social and physical areas; nevertheless, they reflect real differences.

[31] It might be argued that the logical structure of a prediction based on probability is the same whether the prediction is in physics, meteorology, or politics—the only difference being in the degree of probability that is possible. This overlooks the fact that social predictions differ from scientific predictions: in the latter, a falsified prediction always involves some mistake by the predictor (bad data, bad calculations, or bad theory), but in the social sciences, the prediction can be wrong *without* the predictor having made an error. A trend may fail to hold, even after we

Perhaps this implies that the proper scientific analogy for politics is not with a hard science, or even with meteorology, but with a weak, ambiguous science like clinical psychology. The parallel is not exact and need not be taken literally. But it is not an irrelevant model, especially if we keep in mind the conditions under which clinical psychology functions: an evolving body of doctrine, constantly adapted and altered by the practitioner-theorist, pointing in significant directions, but always at the mercy of the clinician's judgment and the patient's condition. Above all, clinical psychology is a science in which the practitioner contributes to theory and in which he must understand theory in order to use it wisely.

Social theories can never be automatically converted into social decisions on particular issues: they are neither reliable or rigorous enough, nor are they likely to contain all that the practitioner needs to know in order to choose wisely.[32] The act of choice remains an act of judgment, that is, an act that demands skilled, knowledgeable practitioners. The practitioner must be able to do more than the technician not only because he must deal with a more complex realm, but also because the theories he works with are much less useful. The analogy with the way in which mature disciplines have developed thus fails on two levels, for we cannot understand either social theories or the relationship between social theorists and social practitioners by a simple extrapolation from the way in which mature disciplines have developed.

If we believe that social theories are useful *only* if they can be directly converted into explicit advice—choose A, not B or C—this is a devastating conclusion. Different vocational cultures *apparently* imply that the theorist and the practitioner cannot cooperate in the short run, and the inability of social theories to tell the practitioner what to do *apparently* means that the theorist will not be very useful even if he succeeds in producing theories during his period of isolation. Perhaps, as Lucian Pye has argued, we need a class of social engineers to convert the ideas of theorists into practical form.[33] But a theory passed on by a group of

---

have specified the initial conditions that set it off (which, incidentally, sets it apart from a true law), because human decisions affecting the trend are not determined (alone) by the specific set of initial conditions. Thus, even probability statements will be looser in the social sciences. For a good short discussion, see Peter Winch, *The Idea of a Social Science* (London: Routledge and Kegan Paul, 1958), pp. 91-94.

[32] This issue will be analyzed in more depth in the next chapter when we discuss how predictions based on probability can be used.

[33] Lucian Pye, "Description, Analysis, and Sensitivity to Change," in Ranney, *Political Science and Public Policy*, pp. 239-261. It is also difficult to imagine how such a group of social engineers could emerge. In general, engineers have a low intellectual status—note the usual form "science *and* engineering." The status of

professional middlemen does not thereby become a better theory; it is still a social theory that can be successfully applied only by those who understand it well. Professor Pye's argument also assumes that a theory is useful *only* if it can be converted into the hard currency of specific decisions.

The situation is not so hopeless as it appears. There are indeed two vocational cultures but they are not *completely* different: they share not only a common subject matter and common concerns but also cognitive patterns that frequently parallel each other. Moreover, theories—as we shall see—are useful to the practitioner even if they cannot tell him what to do. We cannot understand the force of these arguments unless we shift the focus of our discussion. We have, up until this time, looked downward from the nature of theory to its impact on the world of practice. This exaggerates the differences between the two realms, for we see only the final products: abstract, elegant theories and concrete, compromising practices. If we alter our perspective, and work upward from what theorists and practitioners actually do to an understanding of how and when they can cooperate, we may find the differences narrowing. We shall begin by looking at the professional activities of the theorist.

ON THE BEHAVIOR OF THEORISTS AND THE UTILITY OF THEORIES

We shall be concerned with two questions in this section. The first concerns the working style of the theorist: What is it in this style that makes it difficult for him to work on practical problems or to communicate easily with the practitioner? Our answer is in the dominance that the principle of verification has established in the theoretical realm.

The emphasis on verification creates a bias among theorists toward a particular theoretical statement. But the result frequently is a theory or a hypothesis that seems irrelevant or useless to the practitioner. Theorists tend to ignore this problem, for they feel that a theory is useful by definition. Yet it is not clear that this is always or even generally true. Thus our second question will involve an effort to understand whether there are characteristics that a theory must possess if it is to be useful to the practitioner.

This is a complex question in which rigid conclusions are out of place.

---

this group would not likely be higher in the social sciences. In addition, for a middleman to be useful, he ought to know *both* theory and practice—but then his status would (or should) be higher than that of either the theorist or the practitioner.

We must attempt, however, to deal with this question, and to be aware of the issues at stake, for the theorist's belief that all theories are useful, and the practitioner's belief that none are, undermine any attempt to establish a meaningful relationship between theory and practice.

The theorist and the practitioner begin their activities in the same place—in confrontation with a problem that has arisen in their domain. The origins of the problem may be very different. For the practitioner, a problem normally emerges in the form of a persisting practical difficulty. For the theorist, problems can emerge, as Greer has argued, either from questions raised by major social philosophies or, in a mature discipline, from conflicts between theories.[34] This categorization is incomplete until we note that theoretical problems may also arise during an analysis of a practical problem.

What is to be done with the problem? The answer of the theorist is clear. The problem has no intrinsic (theoretical) interest unless its implications can be generalized. At first, that merely involves an attempt to place the problem within a classification scheme or within a group of categories. The emphasis is on homogeneity, on what makes the problem similar to other problems. Differences are submerged within those useful, elusive phrases: ceteris paribus and mutatis mutandis. Thus, the drive in theory is to go beyond events. In a psychological sense, the theoretical mind is always—and can afford to be—"optimizing," for today's categories are always contingent, always part of the quest for better and better categories.

Ultimately, the theorist seeks laws, and then a relationship between laws that can be described as a theory, all of which must be open to verification. This emphasis on verification fundamentally distinguishes the theorist's approach to problem-solving from that of the practitioner. It significantly influences the kind of theory that can be legitimately sought, for some statements are more easily verified—particularly quantified statements. Successful prediction of a future sequence of events, one of the more prized forms of verification, has a special allure, and may force concentration on areas dominated by habitual, involuntary behavior: concern may decline sharply in areas where the outcome can be significantly affected by unpredictable human intervention. In any case, the emphasis on verification may become consuming, with the result that propositions and hypotheses of great merit may be ignored if their verification is beyond the current state of the art. The primary concerns of a discipline may indeed shift to forms of macroanalysis because they prom-

[34] Greer, *The Logic of Social Inquiry,* pp. 8-14.

ise easier verification.[35] A discipline, of course, must be in a mature state—it must have some laws or theories—in order for verification to establish dominance over other aspects of the theoretical process.[36]

Are theories useful to the practitioner merely because they exist? Can they tell the practitioner what decision he ought to make? If we answer affirmatively, the emphasis on verification in the construction of theories is beneficial, for it means that the practitioner would be applying better (that is, more rigorous and reliable) theories to the problems he confronts. If we answer negatively, however, and insist that the intrinsic weakness of social theories clearly implies that they are neither always useful to the practitioner nor *ever* capable of telling him which choice he ought to make, we shall be closer to the truth.

The practitioner who believes that theories are useful only if they can be readily converted into policy decisions is unlikely to be surprised at this answer. But the theorist who believes that this is the proper role for social theories is in a more difficult position. The only alternative he has, insofar as he cares about questions of utility, is to attempt to establish the characteristics that a social theory must possess that would make it *relatively* more attractive to the practitioner.

What are these characteristics? First, useful social theories have to be readily understandable: they cannot employ a vocabulary or concepts that the generalist practitioner finds totally incomprehensible.[37] Second,

[35] For an attack on this tendency in sociology, see Barney G. Glaser and Anselm L. Strauss, *The Discovery of Grounded Theory* (Chicago: Aldine, 1967). Bernard Crick has also made the same point with political science, although I am not convinced that it holds with as much force as in sociology or psychology. He argues that "it is clear that what the modern proponents of a 'science of politics' have sought for, above all, from philosophy has been an exclusion of empirically nontestable statements." *The American Science of Politics,* p. 220.

[36] This is not simply an attack on the principle of verification. Verification is a necessary part of making social science (and thus international relations) rigorous and useful. What is at issue is not its value but its costs, especially when verification becomes the sole criterion by which one distinguishes science from wholly normative enterprises. An exclusive preoccupation with verification not only limits the research that a discipline does and the hypotheses that it develops, but also overlooks the fact that verification is a shifting standard, changing over time and from discipline to discipline. Less emphasis on verification and more emphasis on creating hypotheses and generalizations—even if they are beyond verification for the moment—is entirely salutary and not necessarily less scientific. If we define science according to neither verified knowledge nor a particular method, but rather as a quest for generalized explanations of political behavior, we can avoid the dangers implicit in the analogy with the physical sciences. Such an approach, though hardly free of ambiguity, does not limit the explanations which are sought to those appropriate only for an entirely different subject matter.

[37] For example, the tendency of many proponents of systems theory to state obvious or trivial points in terms borrowed from other disciplines is not helpful—

the theory ought to be comprehensive enough to encompass all the essential elements of the problems within its domain.[38] Many theories are relevant—in their pertinence to important issues—but impractical. Thus, the third characteristic of a useful theory is that its variables not only have substantial explanatory power but also be open to control and revision.[39] If these conditions hold, and it is not often that they do outside the laboratory, the possibility of directly converting a theory into practical advice should rise appreciably.

Very few theories will ever possess all these characteristics. This is a melancholy conclusion if one assumes that theories are useful only if they can be applied directly to a problem. It means that the attempt to compensate for the intrinsic weakness of social theories by creating theories with particular characteristics is unlikely to succeed. This does not mean that theories that can be readily understood, that have wide-ranging explanatory power, and that emphasize accessible and controllable variables are not *relatively* more useful to the practitioner than theories that are esoteric and excessively abstract. It does mean that we are unlikely to get such theories and that, even if we manage to do so, the need for practitioners who understand how and when they can be applied will not disappear. In addition, the emphasis on verification in theory construction inhibits the possibility of creating theories that possess the foregoing characteristics: the elements that might make a theory more useful *in terms of actual decisions* are least likely to be found in theories primarily structured to facilitate verification.

It would be wrong to put more weight on these points than is necessary. We cannot develop theories that remove the need for fallible human judgments: the practitioner who applies such theories must know and use knowledge that is not contained in the theories. Moreover, the attempt to compensate for this weakness by creating theories with special characteristics is not only unlikely to be successful but also may force the quest

---

perhaps not even to the proponents themselves. The same observation, of course, has been made many times about the tendency to put anything that can be so stated into numerical form without worrying about whether it is necessary. This does not imply that systems theory and quantification are useless, but that on occasion they are used (or misused) unnecessarily.

[38] This point can be carried too far if it creates a belief that less comprehensive theories are completely useless. The area of uncertainty in the practical realm is so vast that even partial theories are helpful, or as much aid as intuition or serendipity —although the practitioner may be the last to believe this.

[39] Glaser and Strauss, *Discovery of Grounded Theory,* pp. 237-250. This is the best discussion of the factors that make a theory useful to a practitioner. I have not, however, followed it completely and am more dubious about the importance of these attributes.

for theories into unnatural channels. The attempt by *both* theorists and practitioners to understand the utility of theories in this narrow fashion is responsible for much of the confusion surrounding the issue of social theory and social practice. We must begin to understand that the ease with which a theory can be transformed into practical advice is not the only criterion by which to judge its utility. To understand why this is so we need to examine the behavior of practitioners.

ON THE BEHAVIOR OF PRACTITIONERS
AND THE LIMITS OF EXPERIENCE AND INTUITION

Dean Rusk, whose contempt for academics was notorious, was fond of quoting an aphorism to his colleagues: the academic argues to conclusions, but the policymaker to decisions. Presumably one task is harder than the other. Yet one wonders about the wisdom of policymakers who believe that they can make decisions without first coming to conclusions about the problem in question. The point, of course, is that both the theorist and the practitioner must argue to conclusions; the problem of choosing a specific course of action is an addition to that argument, not a substitute for it. Perhaps Rusk will be able to ponder the matter in depth now that he has become a professor.

Rusk's fondness for this aphorism is the center of our concerns. It reflects an interpretation of the practitioner's behavior that is inaccurate and unduly constrained. We shall attempt to illustrate why this is so and to indicate why the practitioner has tenaciously held to a view of his activities that is vastly oversimplified. Finally, we shall cite evidence from other disciplines to indicate the dangers and weaknesses of the style of judgment that Rusk and his cohorts fancy. If nothing else, this section should indicate why the blame for the gap between theory and practice has to be shared.

The theorist generalizes from a particular problem to a set of categories. The practitioner does essentially the same, although the intellectual process may be less self-conscious. Still, they both abstract and develop a body of knowledge that is more than a description of cases.

Is it possible, then, to describe the practitioner's activities as theorizing?[40] If we define theory elaborately as requiring a formal explanation

---

[40] There is an interesting attempt to do so in Ernest Greenwood, "The Practice of Science and the Science of Practice," in Warren G. Bemis, K. D. Benne, and Robert Chin, eds., *The Planning of Change* (New York: Holt, Rinehart and Winston, 1966). Greenwood's definition of theory, however, is very vague and may obscure more than it reveals.

and perhaps even prediction, the answer is no. And if we loosely define theory as any body of generalized knowledge, the word begins to lose all meaning. This has occurred consistently in international relations: theory has become a residual category, encompassing all activities remaining after policy-oriented work has been subtracted.

It is premature to debate the point. In the current stage of development, theory in international relations primarily has involved elaborate attempts to construct classification schemes or to order research according to a shared strategy. It is thus "pre-theoretical." Similarly, practical activity is limited, from a theoretical point of view, to the construction of implicit typologies and the discovery of principles by which specific cases can be fitted to proper categories.[41] However, the fact that both theorists and practitioners are currently limited to the same kind of activity should not obscure the point that they will begin to diverge more rapidly as laws and theories emerge.

This is true because the practitioner has neither the intention nor the desire to improve the range of his theorizing. His aim is to prescribe a solution for a bothersome problem. Once he has managed to incorporate the problem within a particular category, he turns from diagnosis to treatment.[42] And treatment is indeed dominated by the quest for variables that can be controlled and to which access is possible. Thus, the theoretical activity of the practitioner is cut short at the point where sufficient information is available to know the kind of problem that must be dealt with; how the problem should be dealt with is a question that demands a different focus. It is, moreover, in the treatment stage and not in the classification stage that the practitioner begins to emphasize the unique and contextual elements of the problem, for these elements may

[41] This issue implies more than the fact that the practitioner's classifications and categories are implicit and less formalized. Logical studies of method always emphasize that classification must come after observation and description and before comparison. This is true whether we first observe isolated facts or, more sensibly, problems that we cannot solve. See F. S. C. Northrop, *The Logic of the Sciences and the Humanities* (Cleveland: World Publishing Company, 1967), Chap. 1. Clearly this progression is violated frequently in the physical sciences and the social sciences. The violation, however, is more blatant in the social sciences, where there are innumerable instances of classification schemes deliberately imposed on material to facilitate observation and description, and not having emerged from sustained prior research. The worst examples are essays cataloging all variables that might affect a particular problem—the shopping list as a substitute for insight. That this is what science is about requires a willing suspension of disbelief.

[42] Greenwood is interesting on this point because he includes the principles of diagnosis and treatment as constituent parts of the principles of practice. See *ibid.*, p. 79. In this book we are more interested in diagnosis than in treatment, for diagnosis has parallels in the world of theory, whereas treatment is something uniquely part of the practitioner's art.

provide the leverage for control that he seeks. Thus, theories that *merely* enhance understanding, and do not possess characteristics that facilitate conversion to practical advice (noted in the preceding section), are useless for treatment.

Psychologists make a similar distinction when they separate perceptual, cognitive, and decisional behavior. There is an overlap between these categories, but they are a useful analytical convenience. The distinction between cognitive and decisional phases is critical and has important parallels with the distinction between diagnosis and treatment. The central point in both cases is that the knowledge necessary to make a decision about an issue is different from the knowledge necessary to diagnose the case. Decisional knowledge is specific, up-to-date, and applicable only at a moment in time; cognitive knowledge is abstract, generalized, and applicable whenever or wherever the necessary conditions hold.

One might speculate that one reason why practitioners have had difficulty in understanding these distinctions relates to a confusion between practical judgments and practical decisions. The latter is in the realm of the practitioner, as we have already indicated. Practical judgment, however, which sounds much the same, is another matter. *All* judgments are intellectual—that is, they flow from the same source—and practical judgment differs only in that it refers to a particular subject: actions to be taken.[43]

Failure to recognize this distinction and to understand practical activity in depth is primarily responsible for continuing misinterpretations of the relationship between theory and practice. Rusk's aphorism is symptomatic: so long as the practitioner believes that he makes decisions in a cognitive vacuum, neither the theorist nor anyone can help him. It is undoubtedly true that some practitioners behave in this fashion, and make their decisions according to the ad hoc, parochial factors that are present in each case. There is, however, no compelling need to base an interpretation of practical behavior on the stupidity of some practitioners.

The central point is that the *direct* help that the theorist can offer the practitioner can only come during the period when they are engaged in parallel activities: that is, when the practitioner, like the theorist, is intent on sorting the facts of the problem that troubles him, organizing them coherently, and coming to a conclusion about the problem with

[43] Useful comments on this issue appear in John Dewey, "The Logic of Judgments of Practice," in Amelie Rorty, ed., *Pragmatic Philosophy* (Garden City, N.Y.: Doubleday Anchor Books, 1966), p. 216 f.

which he is dealing. The theorist is (or, rather, could be) useful in this period because the self-conscious and organized fashion in which he performs these functions provides an effective standard against which to judge the more rudimentary efforts of the practitioner.

This argument allows us to determine the proper questions that a practitioner should address to a theorist. They are questions about questions: What is it I want to ask, and thus know about this problem, or what is useful to think about before I decide what to do? Acceptance of this point of view would also have a peripheral virtue of aesthetic value. We might no longer have to contend with another round of lectures by practitioners and in-and-outers gleefully informing their academic friends that their theories were completely useless because they had nothing to say about whether we ought to bomb Hanoi or install an ABM system. And we might no longer have to contend with academics, from either the behavioralist or the traditionalist wing, who presume that the practitioner's argument is justified.[44]

We should be careful not to carry this argument beyond reasonable bounds. We are not arguing that the theorist can aid the practitioner *only* before the time for decision arrives. There are indirect ways, as we have already indicated, in which theory persistently influences the practitioner, although he may be unaware of it. Keynes's well-known reference to the unconscious debt that politicians owe to an unknown "academic scribbler" makes the point graphically. Nevertheless, the role of the theorist *should* be limited to the period when the practitioner is still trying to organize his conceptual universe into a meaningful pattern. The theorist can do much at this stage—anything that he would normally do in attempting to study a problem—but, once the practitioner has come to

[44] For example, Ernest Lefever, whose misunderstanding of these issues is pristine, asks whether the new "techniques are of any real value to the President in issuing instructions to our negotiators at the Vietnam peace talks in Paris?" Of course, these techniques are not a substitute for political judgment, but used well and wisely, an aid to it; thus the answer to Lefever's question is hardly as obvious as he believes. On the other hand, J. David Singer, in discussing the question of the utility of social science findings, believes that it would be useful if the practitioner "confronted with an emerging situation that seems to call for one or more major decisions, could turn to a file which would help identify and classify that situation and tell him the probable consequences of each of several alternative responses." The difficulty is that knowledge of probabilities is only marginally useful to a practitioner faced with a single case; in addition, a statement of probabilities based on historical comparisons (which may not be generally comparable) may leave out factors decisive to the case at hand. The file Singer desires could only be helpful before a decision was on the "front burner." The quotes are from Lefever's and Singer's contributions to Norman D. Palmer, ed., *A Design for International Relations Research: Scope, Theory, Methods, and Relevance* (Philadelphia: The American Academy of Political and Social Science, 1970), pp. 201 and 145, respectively.

conclusions, the theorist has no right to pretend that he knows which practical action should be chosen. This judgment *might* be challenged at a future time, but only if social science begins to produce theories that can be directly converted into practical advice. As I have already indicated, I doubt that this is a real possibility.

We should also be careful to note the differences of degree between the theorist and the practitioner even in the cognitive or diagnostic phase. These differences may become important, especially if the practitioner does not understand this argument and accepts it only rhetorically. As a result, either through ignorance, willfulness, or a lack of detachment he may attempt to use the theorist's analyses indiscriminately. This is most likely to happen during the present period when everything the practitioner has learned conspires to convince him that theory can only be used in this fashion. This is one major reason why initial efforts to help the practitioner will be exceptionally difficult and probably possible only with the determined and persistent support of the higher reaches of the establishment. One might suggest that a special effort be made to concentrate on analyzing practical problems in the least abstruse language: one or two successes at this task perhaps might begin to alter habitual assumptions.

The notion of similarities at the stage of diagnosis necessarily implies dissimilarities at the treatment stage (that is, when specific policies must be chosen and implemented). The theorist must presume a world with sufficient stability and order for his generalizations to hold. Practical activity, conversely, when it is at the point of attempting to realize a specific goal, presupposes a world of *unstable* facts: a world of facts that can be altered to achieve a desired end. Practice thus presupposes not only a world of change but also a world of value.[45] Science, political or otherwise, has no right to pass judgments on the choice of ends or, with qualifications, about assured behavior in a world of uncertainty. Science can analyze alternatives and can ponder their consequences, but it cannot choose between them.

This also has significance for the problem of verification. Verification is necessary for valid knowledge. The practitioner's conception of what constitutes acceptable verification has little in common with the rigorous methodological norms of the theorist. If treatment is successful, the validity of method and knowledge is taken for granted: it is, therefore, a verification criterion that provides no test of the process, but only of its outcome. There is no way of knowing whether success or failure resulted

[45] See Michael Oakeshott, *Experience and Its Modes* (Cambridge: Cambridge University Press, 1933), pp. 262-263, p. 289 f.

from extraneous factors or from the intrinsic qualities of the accepted mode of behavior.

The distinction is less precise if we focus on the diagnostic stage. Presumably a practitioner who intended to stay in business would prefer to have his analyses and judgments verified in the best possible fashion. In the abstract, there is no reason to suppose that the theorist would disagree. In fact, the theorist would stand to benefit both from testing his own hypotheses and the hypotheses that emerge, however crudely, from the practical realm.

This benevolent picture of hands joined in a common effort to provide reliable knowledge is a pleasant fiction. The reason has little to do with the nature of the verification problem, but much to do with professional images of desirable behavior. The traditionalist has assumed that the practitioner is indifferent to theory and desirous of policy advice—a decidedly unsurprising assumption. The theorist has used his interpretation of the wide gap between his efforts and the practitioner's as a justification for ignoring the practitioner. When he has turned to the problem of verification, he has tended to emphasize the necessity or desirability of quantitative verification, which has meant that the crude hypotheses emerging from the practical realm have not been tested.

The practitioner's record is less inspiring. He appears to have few doubts about the essential rightness of his approach. No one who is familiar with the recent history of American foreign policy could assume that a record of worldly success lies behind this complacency. Perhaps it is a lack of imagination, or a fear of questioning a familiar mode of behavior. Whatever the rationale, the practitioner remains committed to the notion that he does nothing that scholarly advice could improve. Insofar as he ever feels compelled to call for outside assistance, leaving aside the propaganda function that assistance may serve, it is usually only to be briefed on the facts—the scholar as the substitute for an out-of-date *Statesmen's Yearbook*.

Does the practitioner really need help? Is intellectual understanding a prerequisite for accurate diagnosis, or can the practitioner function effectively aided only by experience, common sense, and intuition? Certainly these characteristics are necessary in the treatment or decisional stage of his activities. Are they, however, sufficient, or does his vocation demand other characteristics also? The practitioner clearly believes that the characteristics that facilitate decision-making are all he needs. We have no studies that either confirm or refute this belief. But perhaps we can get useful insights by examining similar arguments in other areas, and by studying tests that have actually attempted to evaluate the record of practitioners with similar decisional styles.

The practitioner places enormous faith in maxims that he and his predecessors have generalized from their personal experience in the field. He incorporates these maxims in a system of beliefs that is almost impervious to change. Why should this be so? Why should new experiences or new ideas not have the power to alter a conceptual structure that, after all, is an organization of (older) experiences?

One answer is that "the new idea presented to thought must also be *soluble in old experiences,* be recognized as like them, otherwise it will be unperceived, uncomprehended."[46] It is, however, easy for the new to be unperceived or dismissed because most systems of belief are circular:

> the convincing power possessed by the interpretation of any particular new topic in terms of such a conceptual framework is based on past applications of the same framework to a great number of other topics not now under consideration, while if any of these other topics were questioned now, their interpretation in its turn would similarly rely for support on the interpretation of all the others.[47]

Moreover, new evidence normally comes in piecemeal, which lessens its cumulative impact. The absence of accepted concepts to deal with anything but variations on the old theme also weakens the effect.

It is indisputable that the practitioner possesses experience that he does not share with the theorist. Oakeshott has made a similar point in a different way. He has argued that two kinds of knowledge are present in any concrete activity, inseparable but not identical. The first is technical knowledge, which can be formulated precisely in a set of rules. The rules can be learned and applied by anyone willing and able to expend the effort. The second is practical knowledge, and it cannot be precisely formulated: it exists only in use, and is shared only by those who are familiar with the tradition of the activity. Practical knowledge cannot be taught or learned, but must be imparted or acquired on the job.[48]

[46] See Abercrombie, *Anatomy of Judgement,* p. 60.

[47] Polanyi, *Personal Knowledge,* p. 289.

[48] Michael Oakeshott, *Rationalism in Politics* (New York: Basic Books, 1962), pp. 7-12. Oakeshott's views are not universally accepted. He perceives the practical sphere too narrowly: some aspects of it must be learned on the job, but there are aspects that are clearly intellectual.

One might rephrase the distinction as a contrast between intellect and intelligence, the latter presumably referring to the mental qualities of the practitioner, the former to the mental qualities of the theorist. One such attempt notes that intellect is "the critical, creative, and contemplative side of mind," whereas intel-

Proponents of the view that the practitioner has a superior insight into his activity because he has experienced it or shares its tradition draw an important inference about who is worth listening to: the answer is other practitioners. According to Whitehead, other practitioners are members of a craft, which is "based upon customary activities and modified by the trial and error of individual practice," and not a profession, "whose activities are subject to theoretical analysis, and are modified by theoretical conclusions derived from that analysis."[49] And craft members can learn useful things only from other craft members.

A critical practical question remains to be answered: Does his special knowledge and experience help the practitioner to think and act more effectively? Is he thus a better problem-solver?

The answer is that we do not know. The difficulty, once again, is the absence of an independent standard by which we could make the judgment. The success of statesman A and the failure of statesman B may both rest on extraneous or accidental factors having nothing to do with the quality of their experiences or their choice of policies.

Insights and intuitions that rest on experience may have notable limitations as a guide to practice. They can do no more than confirm what we already know, since they utilize only what is already known.[50] And a man's experiences are more limited than the range of experiences in his field. In addition, the verification problem is implicit in any analysis that is not only subjective but also confident in its lack of submissiveness to tests of reliability.[51]

---

ligence is described as "narrow," "predictable," "manipulative," and "unfailingly practical." It is not surprising that intellectuals like this breakdown (need one add, they possess intellect, by definition). See Richard Hofstadter, *Anti-Intellectualism in American Life* (New York: Vintage Books, 1962), pp. 24-30. For our purposes, this is not a useful distinction, because many scholars who develop theories in social science would be excluded from, or ambiguously included in, the category contrasting them with practitioners. In any case, one doubts the significance of these ideal types, apart from their propaganda value.

[49] Alfred North Whitehead, *Adventures of Ideas* (New York: Macmillan, 1933), pp. 73-74.

[50] See Theodore Abel, "The Operation Called *Verstehen*," *The American Journal of Sociology* 54 (November 1948): 216.

Popper's comment in *The Poverty of Historicism* on intuition is worth noting: "By their intuition, some people are prevented from even imagining that anybody can possibly dislike chocolate." (p. 138)

[51] This argument is not against subjective knowledge or its significance, but it is against those who claim to possess it but who treat it as beyond discussion.

No academic discipline could accept the obscurantism implicit in most arguments of the intuitionists. The practitioners (and their defenders) have insisted that the judgments they make cannot be understood or evaluated by outsiders—except by ex post facto success or failure, and perhaps not even then. The weakness in this

Psychologists who have analyzed the process of problem-solving have also raised questions about the utility of experience. For example, Max Wertheimer noted that "the role of past experience is of high importance, but what matters is how and what one recalls, how one applies what is recalled, whether blindly, in a piecemeal way, or in accordance with the structural requirements of the situation."[52] Wertheimer also emphasized the extent to which attitudes that the individual had developed in previous problem situations were significant: for example, whether his experiences had been successes or failures, or whether he was confident or insecure.[53] The contention that experience alone is not a sufficient guide to problem-solving is a persistent theme in this research. N. R. F. Maier has argued that the effort to use experience may actually obstruct a solution.[54] One recalls Disraeli's definition of a practical politician as "one who practices the errors of his predecessors."

We can question the reliability of the practitioners' judgment in another way. In relying on experience and intuition to reach a judgment about a case, the practitioner's mode of inquiry corresponds somewhat with clinical analysis. Many criticisms that clinicians make against those who base their diagnoses on statistical correlations sound like the criticisms practitioners direct against theorists (especially behavioral and quantitative ones) in international relations: they cannot deal with latent factors or with changes resulting from contingent events, they overemphasize the tangible and measurable, and they cannot grasp the intangible complexities that only the clinician can sense.[55]

---

position involves a failure to understand that some empirical generalization is at the root of *both* subjective and objective judgments and that both judgments are plausible hypotheses until they are tested. The test in one case may be more difficult than in the other—at least it may be more difficult to find out why a subjective generalization was right or wrong—but clearly both hypotheses can be stated in an intelligible fashion and tested for reliability. It may also be possible to make useful conclusions about how the judgment was made, even though *both* processes may have subjective elements. The practitioners' reluctance to have their claims of special genius tested is understandable.

[52] Max Wertheimer, *Productive Thinking* (New York: Harper and Brothers, 1959), p. 62.

[53] *Ibid.,* p. 64.

[54] See N. R. F. Maier, "Reasoning in Humans: The Solution of a Problem and Its Appearance in Consciousness," p. 27, in P. C. Wason and P. N. Johnson-Laird, eds., *Thinking and Reasoning* (London: Penguin Books, 1968). Several other essays in this collection emphasize the limitations of experience as a guide to problem-solving.

[55] For a classic discussion, see Paul E. Meehl, *Clinical versus Statistical Prediction* (Minneapolis: University of Minnesota Press, 1954). For a more recent treatment of the history of the debate, see Harrison G. Gough, "Clinical versus Statistical Prediction in Psychology," in Leo Postman, ed., *Psychology in the Making* (New York: Alfred A. Knopf, 1962), pp. 526-584.

Some psychologists became bored with the interminable repetition of verbal dispute and attempted to do something about it: a series of empirical investigations of the diagnostic process to see who was detecting what and with how much success. One general conclusion that emerged was that neither mode of analysis was good.[56] Another was that they needed each other: without the clinician, there was no problem to solve; without the statistician, no reliable solution. Without tests of reliability, the clinicians' diagnoses may become a prey to the winds of fashion.[57]

Detailed analysis of what practicing clinicians were doing produced startling results. For example, an elaborate cross-national analysis of British and American psychiatric diagnoses of the same patient (done by a movie recording a patient's consultation with a doctor) indicated substantial differences between the two national groups. They disagreed about the meaning of the relevant concepts—which would be bad enough, but is primarily a problem of clarity—and about the nature of the symptoms manifested by the patient.[58] The extent to which diagnosis was affected by cultural factors, even within a common discipline and between analysts using the same language, is a useful warning to practitioners in any discipline.

Another study, which was limited to clinicians in this country, may be more relevant. It showed more agreement on the nature of the symptoms, but sharp disagreement on what diagnosis they implied. These disagreements varied according to age, theoretical attitudes (e.g., whether the analyst was a Freudian or not), and ethnic background.[59] In addition, it has become increasingly apparent that diagnosis derived solely from observation of the patient in a hospital or medical setting is not sufficient: this diagnosis must be supplemented by an understanding of the patient's socio-cultural milieu before he came under medical care.[60]

This evidence is hardly conclusive, but it does suggest that exaggerated confidence in the superior judgment of practitioners is unjustified. The practitioner ought to be more skeptical about the significance of his

[56] See Gough, *ibid.,* p. 573.
[57] See Joseph Zubin, "Biometric Assessment of Mental Patients," in *The Role and Methodology of Classification in Psychiatry and Psychopathology* (Washington, D.C.: Public Health Service, 1965), p. 374. The paragraph in the text is not without relevance for international relations.
[58] Morton Kramer, "Cross-National Study of Diagnosis of the Mental Disorders: Origin of the Problem," *The American Journal of Psychiatry* 125 (April 1969 supplement): 1-11.
[59] Martin M. Katz, et al., "Studies of the Diagnostic Process: The Influence of Symptom, Perception, Past Experience, and Ethnic Background on Diagnostic Decisions," *The American Journal of Psychiatry* 125 (January 1969): 937-947.
[60] Zubin, *Classification in Psychiatry,* p. 374 f.

experience. Unfortunately, as La Rochefoucauld said, "Everyone complains of his memory but no one complains of his judgment."

It is impossible to grasp the nature of decision-making in foreign affairs without understanding the degree of fear besetting men who know that their actions are to become part of the historical record. An extra dimension separates them from normal decision-makers. This is particularly true when their actions involve survival, and when they stand the chance of exposure by the press—or even by former colleagues grinding out their unanswerable version of events.

Excessive prudence becomes a way of life, a psychological necessity. Continuity with the past, deliberately not breaking new ground, provides effective protection against accusations of irresponsibility or stupidity. The emphasis falls on avoiding failure rather than on seeking success. Old rules of thumb must fail saliently and persistently before questioning what stands to reason becomes legitimate. By then it is probably too late to do much about it.

The theorist has more freedom. He can choose his problems and his pace. In contrast with the practitioner, for whom mistakes and errors can be disastrous, the theorist loses little except time by choosing the wrong road—he knows where he need not go again. Moreover, skepticism and a sense of the contingent and hypothetical are presumably intrinsic to the theoretical enterprise. They provide an important degree of protection against the tendency to treat tradition as sacrosanct.[61]

The practitioner is thus in a very difficult situation. His judgment suffers not only from the weaknesses and biases of all judgments based on intuition and experience but also from the additional uncertainties attendant upon decision-making in international events. Yet he has been reluctant or unwilling to seek aid, because of an unfounded faith in his judgment and a misunderstanding about the aid that a theorist (or a theory) can give him. But if the practitioner does want to evaluate and improve his judgment, he must turn to the theorist—the alternative is an endless and pointless search for more and more experience. On one level, it is only the theorist who can effectively test the quality of the practitioner's judgment against the judgments of others. On another level, qualitative improvements in the art of choosing policies, i.e., in the treatment phase, must rest upon improved understanding and performance in the pre-decisional (diagnostic) phase. It is here that the theorist and the

[61] Thomas Kuhn in *The Structure of Scientific Revolutions* might contend that the tradition was capable of taking care of itself, and that skepticism was permissible only within the bounds of tradition. Skepticism and a sense of the contingent may reflect aspiration more than reality, even in the sciences.

practitioner operate on parallel tracks, and it is here that the theorist can indirectly help the practitioner to choose well by directly helping him to think well.

We should now say something about the research that a group of theorists might do for a practitioner. Such research is usually described pejoratively as "applied" research in contrast to something called "pure" research. We must see what meaning these distinctions have before we can understand whether it is legitimate for theorists to perform applied research.

RESEARCH: "PURE" AND "APPLIED"

What makes one piece of research pure (or basic) and another applied? One answer, which is both self-serving and fashionable, is that the pure researcher is motivated by curiosity or his sense of taste. Conversely, the applied researcher's motives are less exalted, if not suspect. But basing a distinction between different kinds of work on something as nebulous and uncertain as motivation is bound to be dubious. After all, the pure researcher could have been motivated by nothing more elaborate than the norms of his vocational culture, that is, the desire to achieve professional rewards. And the applied researcher might have been motivated by pure curiosity, even if his work had immediate practical significance. If motivation alone is to provide the criteria to distinguish pure and applied research, a great deal of purely trivial research may have to be described as basic or fundamental.[62]

It might be possible to avoid these ambiguities if the distinction between the two kinds of research came to rest on eventual consequences. This has the virtue of referring to the qualities of the research, rather than of the researcher. It means, however, that one would have to wait for a long period before accurate labels could be attached to a piece of work. Moreover, by the time the distinction could be made, what was once pure may well have become applied.[63]

Another alternative, which is currently in vogue, stresses not so much the originality of the research but the audience to which it is addressed. In this formulation, pure research is research that is of interest only to theorists, while applied research is of general concern.[64] This approach

---

[62] See Storer, *The Social System of Science,* pp. 106-107.

[63] A good short analysis of this issue is in M. D. Reagan, "Basic and Applied Research: A Meaningful Distinction?" *Science* 155 (March 17, 1967): 1383-1386.

[64] Storer, *The Social System of Science,* p. 92, especially stresses this point.

may make sense in areas where the prevailing theories are so complex that only other experts can comprehend their significance. It is misleading in a discipline like international relations, which has no real theories and in which even the most advanced work can be readily understood by outsiders. In addition, if it is true that the practitioner in political and social affairs needs to understand the theories in his area if he is to apply them successfully, then the audience for theory may be more extensive than the proponents of this approach believe.

Many efforts to distinguish pure from applied research restate criteria that purport to distinguish theory from practice. If the normative and vocational cultures of the theorist and the practitioner are radically different, it stands to reason that their research interests and styles also differ. The pure theorist, for example, can choose both his problems and his approach freely; the applied researcher's problems are generated by someone else, and he is compelled to work to that outsider's tune. In addition, the pure theorist tests hypotheses to develop new knowledge. The best that the applied researcher can do is to test theories, that is, to determine whether existing knowledge is true or false.

Perhaps the attempt to define the two kinds of research is irrelevant. What we have come to define as pure research is research done in a university setting; applied research is a residual (and inferior) category, referring to work done elsewhere or by academics who have "sold out." This has nothing but convention to justify it.

In what sense is applied research inferior? It is inaccurate to maintain that application involves nothing more than a simple extrapolation from laws or theories. The uncertainty and instability of the practical world guarantee that the application of any theory to reality will require a measure of art. Nor can it be denied that application goes on without the aid of academic theories, or that in some cases the relationship runs from innovations or discoveries in the practical realm to codification in the theoretical realm. Disbelief in these propositions rests on naïve faith in the necessary similarities between all sciences. The differences between kinds of research are sharpest in a field like particle physics in which it is difficult at present to predict any practical applications. On the other hand, molecular biology, involved with pure research, nevertheless has had a continuing and persistent impact on practical affairs.[65] The ambiguities are more salient in the social sciences. No single pattern can be imposed upon all disciplines that sensibly delineates inferior practical

[65] Reagan, "Basic and Applied Research," pp. 1383-1384.

work from superior theoretical work. In fact, the discussion suffers from a tendency to impose categories *on* descriptions, rather than extrapolating them *from* descriptions.

Perhaps the most useful distinction is the simplest: applied research is research commissioned by an outside source.[66] That does not necessarily mean that the problem to be studied is defined entirely by that outside source, although it may, but it does mean that the results may be used, not used, or misused in whatever manner seems fit to the buyer. Pure research, from this perspective, would differ only in the origins of the problems it chose to study.

The implication is that the two kinds of research do not differ in subject matter, methodology, or goal: the intention is to produce the most reliable knowledge by the most appropriate or convenient means.[67] If true, the contention that applied research is inferior is not a logical proposition. It makes sense only in that some practical problems are more complex and less amenable to empirical analysis than the problems that interest the theorist. The difference between applied and pure research, from the point of view of the discipline, is, then, a matter of degree. Applied research may involve more compromises, it may be less rigorous and more inelegant, and its conclusions may be difficult to verify, but nonetheless it produces knowledge according to the same epistemological standards.[68]

What practical conclusions can we draw from this argument about the kind of work that a new planning staff, committed to producing the best applied research, could do? From a theoretical point of view, one conclusion emerges: a practical orientation would not inevitably inhibit the development of theory. Practical conclusions, however, are more difficult to draw, for the analytical force of the argument that applied research is not necessarily inferior may be overwhelmed by several other considerations.

Both kinds of research involve observation, description, and classification. And they both want to proceed beyond classification to the crea-

[66] See also the editors' introduction in Paul F. Lazarsfeld, William H. Sewell, and Harold L. Wilensky, eds., *The Uses of Sociology* (New York: Basic Books, 1967).

[67] See Edward Shils, "Social Science and Social Policy," pp. 38-39, and Philip M. Hauser, "Social Science and Social Engineering," pp. 247-248, in Crawford and Biderman, eds., *Social Scientists and International Affairs.*

[68] There is a danger that the compromises can go too far, and a difference in degree may become a difference in kind. The only safeguard is the professional conscience of the researcher; if he is asked to make more compromises than the problem requires and to debase even further the quality of his work, he should tell his employer that he is no longer getting the best possible results. Maybe he ought to quit.

tion of explicit hypotheses. To the extent that he is permitted to do so, the applied researcher's efforts may yield a real contribution to theory. But if the practitioner asks for explicit policy advice, or even a hard prediction about the future (of more interest to the practitioner than an analysis of why something happened in the past), the applied researcher may never produce any testable hypotheses. The possibility of making a useful contribution to theory will be lost in the course of making a contribution to practice that has nothing to do with either pure or applied research.

Should we conclude that the opprobrium usually directed toward applied research is misplaced, and ought instead to be directed toward the unrealistic demands that the practitioner thrusts upon the researcher? There is a large measure of truth in this, but we must be careful not to carry this conclusion too far. The practitioner may indeed ask the researcher the wrong kind of questions, but his desire to ask the right questions rests not only on his ability to understand what contributions a theorist can actually make but also on his experience with the theories that he is being asked to apply. The point is that applied research, like pure research, is heavily affected by the styles and values of the researcher. If the epistemological standards that the applied researcher attempts to approximate emphasize quantitative verification, at the expense of the creation and investigation of hypotheses, applied research may appear as irrelevant to the practitioner as pure research. In effect, he may ask the wrong questions because he believes he cannot get any useful answers by asking the right ones.

Theorists and practitioners can get along only if they both make reasonable compromises. The theorist must turn his attention away from processes that are *merely* easily observed and consistently recurring, and toward the substance and content of issues. In addition, an emphasis on recurring processes has introduced a static bias into many analyses, since the description and classification of "what is" in abstract categories have left little room for an analysis of how those categories change (except by definition). Since the practitioner is primarily concerned with the direction in which the present is moving—rather than with the reasons why it became the present or the forms in which it can be most efficaciously described—it has seemed obvious to some observers that what he needs is a theory of change.[69] And presumably the theorist ought to make an effort to provide it.

This change in emphasis is surely justified, but it is prudent to point

[69] For interesting comments on this point, see Alvin W. Gouldner, "Explorations in Applied Social Science," *Social Problems* 3 (January 1956): 169-180.

out that it is *only* a change in emphasis. In the best of all possible worlds, the theorist would provide the practitioner with a theory of change that not only forecast future trends but also employed variables that were accessible. In this world, the political practitioner is never going to be handed a theory that yields specific solutions or explicit predictions. The critical point, however, is that undue emphasis on the desirability of this kind of theory is unhealthy: it detracts attention from the fact that the practitioner may find less elaborate theoretical constructions useful. In sum, the theorist ought to make concessions—in what he theorizes and how he does it—but, as the last point indicates, some concessions he need not make if the practitioner understands the proper way to use theories and theorists.

The practitioner's compromises are more fundamental than the theorist's. Rather than changing emphasis within a normal pattern of concerns, he must alter his view not only of theory but also of the nature of his function. The distinction between diagnosis and treatment is decisive in this context. So long as the practitioner recognizes that diagnosis is an intellectual activity separate from the choice of specific actions, and that one must ask different questions during its tenure than one asks about treatment—"why" questions, not "how" questions—the virtues of theory, and the quest for theory, become clearer. The questions to be asked during diagnosis, the categories to be used, and the conceptual universe to be employed emerge during the quest for theory: that is, theorizing helps the practitioner to think about a problem, not to choose a solution. This means that the practitioner should have no qualms about commissioning the best possible applied research.

The issues that the practitioner *should* want clarified at the stage of diagnosis can only become clear by a theorist attempting to analyze a problem according to his best standards. The theorist may do it badly, or he may use arcane language, or he may concentrate on irrelevant (but quantifiable) variables, but if anyone is going to analyze the problem well, the theorist is the logical candidate. (And if he makes a few compromises, he may also be a very practical candidate.)

This position casts a different light on one of the practitioner's favorite aphorisms. The contention that he is interested in the results of theories, and not theories themselves, is misleading. The results are interesting, but they cannot relieve the practitioner of the difficult task of choosing specific policies. Contrary to this conventional wisdom, it is the cognitive impact of theorizing, not its immediate practical impact, which is useful and important. Understanding what the theorist is trying to do, by whatever means, is more likely to improve the conduct of practical affairs than trying to impose his results on an obdurate world.

If the practitioner wants advice on treatment, on the choice of policies, he cannot get it from any legitimate form of academic research. What he is asking for is "applied opinion," which may be wise or foolish, better or worse, but has nothing significant to do with either theory or research.

The practitioner's current aversion to theory and to research (even *applied* research) is not difficult to understand. It rests on something stronger than a simple dislike for theories that are hard to understand or simplify. The practitioner calls for research only when the traditional modes of behavior persistently fail to solve important problems. It is thus a reluctant call, for it implies that the practitioner's knowledge is inadequate or out-of-date. The practitioner clearly has no interest in undermining the validity of the only knowledge that he (alone) has, and the researcher may appear to be threatening to do just that. This is, once again, an illustration of the failure to understand what the relationship between the theorist and the practitioner can be. Whatever else he may do, the theorist will never be able to challenge the practitioner's dominance as a maker of decisions.

The tension between the theorist, who seeks new knowledge, and the practitioner, who values stability and has a vested interest in protecting traditional modes of behavior, is thus the result of a failure to understand what interests they share and what provinces they hold autonomously. Still, for the moment, the practitioner envisages the theorist as an alien intruder. The ritual avowal of the virtues of research and the promises of theory should not obscure the fact that the practitioner thinks he has much to lose from research into his problems and his methods. One study of research policies in a large organization provides an interesting analogy. Joseph Eaton noted that much research done had only symbolic value, for the practitioner feared "disturbing positions of power or raising questions about existing operations. . . . Findings may raise questions, not only about technique, but also about their own competency as users of the technique."[70] He also found that they were reluctant to interpret research data or to communicate its results, especially when they were discouraging. "Symbolic research" (without substantive significance and cheerfully ignored by all) was the unsurprising compromise between a rhetorical commitment to research and a practical commitment to the traditional interests of the practitioner and the organization.[71]

The belief that new knowledge or new approaches are either irrelevant or threatening limits the practitioner's interest in supporting any research. When he does do so, out of desperation or a desire to placate

[70] Joseph W. Eaton, "Symbolic and Substantive Evaluative Research," *The Administrative Science Quarterly* 6 (March 1962): 422, 427.
[71] *Ibid.*, p. 442.

critics, he will normally turn to an expert whose views are already known and whose style of inquiry is predictably traditional. The narrower the range of the expert's knowledge, the better—the paradigm is the veteran area specialist, preferably one with substantial previous experience in the government.

The deck is stacked so that the worst that the expert can do is to suggest variations on the prevailing wisdom: discovering something new, or even radically attacking an old idea, is perceived as very inconvenient. In some instances, the practitioner may commission research for political, not intellectual purposes. The results, provided they are suitable, can be used in a variety of ways: to persuade doubters, to delay action, or to develop information to rebut critics.[72] The outcome is that the values and perspectives of the practitioner, the material and psychological costs of funding research, and the narrow and contrived description of the problem to be analyzed combine to insure that the gap between theory and practice will remain wide and unbridgeable. And the theorist will have no reason to question his firm belief that applied research is inferior—a form of propaganda for a practitioner concerned only with protecting his flanks.

THEORISTS AND PRACTITIONERS—
CONFLICT AND COOPERATION

The problems that will dominate the international system in the decades ahead seem likely to be increasingly complex and specialized. Neither our doctrines nor our institutions seem capable of dealing with these issues effectively. The creation of a long-range planning staff could be an important response to these developments. But a planning staff in the American system of government can succeed—that is, can attempt to respond rationally to problems that can be foreseen—only if its members and its clientele sharply alter the views they currently hold. This clearly means that the relationship between theorists and practitioners must be reordered: we need to develop theorists who are willing to become involved in the planning process, and practitioners who understand what the planning function is meant to accomplish.

Two sets of beliefs have frustrated any serious attempt to create a better relationship between theorists and practitioners. First, the theorist has maintained a persistent contempt for the world of practice and has

[72] See the comments by Robert K. Merton and Daniel Lerner, "Social Scientists and Research Policy," in Daniel Lerner and Harold D. Lasswell, eds., *The Policy Sciences* (Stanford, Calif.: Stanford University Press, 1951), pp. 282-307.

insisted, on the basis of an analogy with more mature sciences, that the theoretical realm can prosper only by isolating itself from practical concerns. I have argued against both views in the beginning of this chapter. Second, the practitioner has contended that the only useful theories are those that provide specific solutions to problems and, until such theories are produced, that the practitioner does well as a decision-maker aided only by experience and intuition. I have argued in the latter part of this chapter that these views are mistaken; quite to the contrary, theories are useful to the practitioner, once he understands the nature of his profession, even if they do not provide precise answers, and the practitioner's record hardly justifies ignoring any help that he can get.

The theorist who works for a planning staff need not sacrifice his integrity by doing so—although some obviously have. By involving himself in practical affairs, the theorist not only fulfills his obligation (which is implicit in our discipline) to improve the conduct of public affairs, but also enhances the possibility that useful theories will be created. Any attempt to list in detail what tasks these planners should undertake is bound to be futile.[73] Too much depends on the circumstances of the moment, such as the problems that compel attention, the political climate, and the point of view of the men in power. This argument, however, should make us more optimistic that a meaningful relationship can be created, and more willing to risk experiments and innovations that could demonstrate it.

For the practitioner, the argument in this chapter should remove the anxiety that the planner and the theorist somehow intend to do away with the need for men skilled in the art of practical judgment. Once the practitioner recognizes that he cannot seek answers from the planners, but rather the right questions to ask about his universe, it should be clear that the planner and the theorist can only supplement his skills, not replace them. Moreover, since theories are more properly used in the diagnostic stage, it should also be clear that *all* kinds of theory can be useful: what helps us to think about our problem is not necessarily dependent on methodological norms. It may even be true that in the

[73] Such attempts usually list the virtues that presumably characterize academic (and not other) work. For example, the academic has the time and detachment to do in-depth studies, and the in-house researcher does not; the academic may also be more alert to new ideas or problems and a less biased critic of existing programs; he might also force the practitioner to be self-conscious about the criteria he uses to choose between different pieces of advice.

The generality of these propositions illustrates the difficulty of compiling activities for a unit that is meant to be new and different, thus having few parallels in our government's history.

diagnostic stage the qualities associated with the quest for theory are almost as important as the theories themselves.

The practitioner believes that he is both a pragmatist and a generalist. In fact, however, his behavior violates the fundamental norms of pragmatism,[74] and his lack of expert knowledge means that he is always at the mercy of another's knowledge. Rather than seeking research that might remedy these deficiencies, he usually asks only for descriptions of (or anecdotes about) the latest configuration of power. Not much else is of any use to someone whose expertise is essentially procedural. This research falls well within the province of an in-house staff, for it requires little imagination and no questioning of premises.[75] Such research, which merely buttresses familiar, comfortable positions, is very attractive to men compelled to labor in a field without accepted boundaries or criteria of success; few practitioners are willing to have their actions tested and evaluated by outsiders.[76] All these views must be challenged—and revised—if we hope to improve the conduct of public affairs.

I have *not* argued that the practitioner should become a theorist or the theorist, a practitioner. I *have* argued that the theorist who works on practical problems can maintain his integrity and still help the practitioner—provided the practitioner understands what the theorist can do.

---

[74] Labeling American policymakers as pragmatists is so conventional that one does it without thinking. Yet there is an almost unbridgeable gap between any reasonable definition of pragmatism and the behavior of our policymakers. Pragmatism emerged as a doctrine that advocated testing the truth of social theories by the experimental method and that sharply criticized all intuitionist theories of knowledge. Our policymakers, however, are bogus pragmatists, for their willingness to test the consequences of their actions is minimal. Their theory of knowledge is almost wholly intuitionist, and they like to adopt the guise of hardheaded problem-solvers, contemptuous of both metaphysics and theories. What that means is that they have to use their theories and their metaphysics on the sly. In fact, there is probably no group less hardheaded about examining its actions than our policymakers—because they lack the substantive expertise that would give them a chance of getting a decent grade. For comments on the meaning of pragmatism, see W. B. Gallie, *Pierce and Pragmatism* (Harmondsworth: Penguin Books, 1952), and Philip P. Wiener, *Evolution and the Founders of Pragmatism* (New York: Harper Torchbooks, 1965). [75] There are useful comments on the policymaker's attitude toward research in Max Millikan, "Inquiry and Policy: The Relation of Knowledge to Action," in Crawford and Biderman, *Social Scientists and International Affairs*; and Henry Kissinger, "The Policymaker and the Intellectual," *The Reporter* 20 (March 5, 1959): 30-35. [76] Lyons comments that because the results of research are usually inconclusive, "the policy-maker must still perform a difficult act of judgment based on his own views and experience; so he may well question the relevance of a social science that, for his purposes, is inconclusive, and yet raises questions about the limited basis of his own evaluation." Gene M. Lyons, *The Uneasy Partnership: Social Science and the Federal Government in the Twentieth Century* (New York: Russell Sage Foundation, 1969), p. 10.

This means that the practitioner should receive sufficient training early in his career so that he recognizes what the theoretical enterprise is about, and what services it can and cannot perform for the practical world. Perhaps such training would enable the practitioner to understand the meaning of a theory, even if he cannot understand how it was created. That may be too optimistic; we may be forced to settle for a practitioner who does not attempt to apply a theory he does not understand. At any rate, some process of continuing education for practitioners is likely to become increasingly necessary.

A sound relationship between theorists and practitioners and a planning staff functioning as an effective bridge between the two realms do not guarantee that new and better doctrines will be devised or that all our decisions will be easier. They do mean, however, that we would have an institution and a group of men who understood the need to develop new doctrines, who were not afraid to ask "why" rather than "how," and who kept open the possibility that the learning process within the government need not always be thirty years out-of-date.

The likelihood that we will make any or all of these changes is very small. Even the contention that prevailing views would be reconsidered if a disaster of sufficient proportions occurs is dubious. The Vietnam debacle is a case in point. The willingness of those responsible for it to place blame everywhere but on themselves, and the striking ability of many of the least appetizing figures of the past decade to survive and prosper in new positions of power, do nothing to refute the charge that this system can be changed only by wholesale replacement of the political establishment. But there are no available replacements, except a younger generation of practitioners schooled in the past and without the ability to devise new doctrines of their own. There are no easy solutions to this problem. It does, however, make an effort to create the new doctrines we need, and to devise new means of educating practitioners, imperative.

Demonstrating that meaningful cooperation between theorists and practitioners is possible provides the intellectual rationale for changing a moribund relationship. The arguments that I have attacked are, however, deeply embedded in our political culture. We can refute arguments more easily than we can change behavior. In the short run, I believe, this means that we can hope only for occasional cooperation between a few far-sighted theorists and practitioners. At least it is a beginning. In the long run, our best hope lies in changing what both theorists and practitioners learn in the universities.

We shall return to these issues in Chapter 5. Prediction is an intrinsic part of any effort to plan or to make policy in a rational manner. It is also a complex and confusing process, with claims and counterclaims, enthusiasts, and skeptics in constant warfare. What the practitioner needs, before he can use or subsidize studies of the future, is a guide that will explain what can and cannot be predicted, what dangers to keep in mind, and what questions are useful to ask. The way in which the theorist might provide that guide is illustrated in the next chapter.

CHAPTER 4

Predictions, Prophecies, and Policymakers

PREDICTION: AN INTRODUCTION

We scarcely realize how much of our behavior rests on a prediction about the likely course of future events. In politics, even the naïve practitioner who insists that he makes every decision solely on the facts at hand operates with an implicit conception of what the future will be like. As Arthur Schlesinger has noted:

> Public decision in rational politics necessarily implies a guess about the future derived from the experience of the past. It implies an expectation, or at the very least a hope, that certain actions will produce tomorrow the same sort of results they produced yesterday. This guess about the future may be based on a comprehensive theory of historical change, as with the Marxists; or it may be based on specific analogies drawn from the past; or it may be based on an unstated and intuitive sense of the way things happen.[1]

However much we need to predict, the difficulties of doing so—or of explaining our successes and our failures—are so manifest that an effort to evade the whole problem is understandable. One could, for example, argue that we are concerned *only* with success or failure of a prediction, not with the ground on which it rests. That hardly improves our understanding of the art of prediction, but it does provide compensations: acquisition of a reputation as a seer becomes a statistically interesting possibility, provided one predicts frequently enough (and the memory of failure fades fast enough).

---

[1] Arthur Schlesinger, Jr., "On the Inscrutability of History," *Encounter* 32 (November 1966): 10.

The proof of the pudding may be in the predicting—we want to know who predicts well even if we cannot explain why—but we cannot be satisfied with knowing so little. To predict better and to lessen our dependence on the fortuitous appearance of skilled or lucky forecasters, we must try to understand a wider range of issues: What can we predict about the social world? Why and how can such predictions be useful to the man of action? How can we begin to break down the prejudices that impede cooperation between men with the skill to predict and those who might use predictions wisely?

To make this effort is especially important in international relations. The more we can control events, the more we produce and determine changes, the less important prediction becomes. How well we predict makes little difference if we possess the ability to adapt events to confirm our foresight. We merely enlarge the principle of the oracle: rather than predicting nonfalsifiable events, we manipulate events so that the prediction is nonfalsifiable.

Politics in the international arena, however, occurs within a classically "open" system. The future in open systems is uncertain, changing, and contingent. No one controls or determines events with sufficient force to make the problem of prediction irrelevant. With less control of events the importance of prediction increases.

How the international system is structured also affects the degree to which prediction is important. In stable international systems, experience and habit suffice in dealing with the future, for patterns of behavior repeat themselves with regularity. We need not worry about prediction when we already know that the future will only be another form of the present. But we no longer have the luxury of ignoring prediction when we confront a revolutionary international system in which patterns of behavior change rapidly, vary more widely than before, and no longer remain within traditional limits.

The need to treat the problem of prediction seriously seems self-evident. The need, however, has been ignored due to the power and persuasiveness of one fundamental idea: the predictions that the social scientist can legitimately produce and the predictions that the practitioner needs are diametrically opposed. So long as this idea is true, any effort to understand and improve the predictions of the social scientist are irrelevant to the practitioner. This complex argument shall be dealt with shortly. Before doing so, we must examine what a "scientific" prediction in social science is, what its limits are, and how it differs from other scientific predictions. We shall then understand what the practitioner finds useless—and perhaps what he should *not* find useless.

SOCIAL PREDICTIONS AND SCIENTIFIC PREDICTIONS

What is a "scientific" prediction? This question has no simple answer. The best we can do is establish a hierarchy of predictions in which the use of the term "scientific" becomes increasingly debatable—and more a matter of taste—as we get farther and farther away from the controlled conditions of the laboratory. For example, in the experimental sciences, once we have established a relationship between variables and so long as we control the underlying conditions, we can assert absolutely that if A occurs, B will follow. There is no guarantee that A *will* occur, but there is a guarantee that B will follow *if* it does. This kind of prediction, whatever its attraction as an ideal, is of almost no practical interest to the social scientist, for he cannot control the "if" sufficiently to absolutely guarantee the appearance of the "then."

Are all "if-then" statements that rest on a known relationship between variables (but in which the "if" is beyond anyone's control) "unscientific"? Take the warning of a storm as an example. We know that when certain conditions occur, a storm is likely, but we can warn only that it is probable, not that it is certain, because factors beyond our control can alter the probability sharply. Outside the controlled conditions of the laboratory, then, we must be satisfied with a statement of relative frequencies.[2] Most of us would probably agree, however, that it is reasonable to call these predictions scientific.

Economists frequently predict business behavior on the basis of interviews with businessmen during which they are asked to set forth their intentions over a period of time. This is soft "hard" data, for intentions can be disguised or can change with time. Are predictions based on such data scientific?[3] The answer is somewhat a matter of taste. Nevertheless, since such predictions have been reasonably accurate (and useful), it does not seem illegitimate to describe them as scientific.

As we descend the hierarchy of predictions, it becomes increasingly difficult to guarantee the results of the predictions we make. Outside the laboratory, the best we can do is offer statements of probabilities. To achieve certainty, we would have to know all relevant conditions and be able to evaluate them in quantitative terms. Since this is impossible in the social sciences, in which only some relevant variables are known and quantifiable—both ignorance and inherent unpredictability are at issue

[2] For further discussion, see Karl R. Popper, *The Poverty of Historicism* (New York: Harper and Row, 1964), p. 43 f.
[3] For a discussion of these predictions, see Henri Theil, *Applied Economic Forecasting* (Chicago: Rand McNally, 1966), especially Chaps. 10 and 12.

here—the *best* one can hope for is good odds. As Reichenbach has noted, "Any statement concerning the future is uttered in the sense of a wager."[4] What constitutes a good bet? That depends on the event to be predicted (we can get good odds in the social world only in areas where voluntary acts are not significant) and on our knowledge (which, needless to say, is less than perfect, but better for macroanalysis than for microanalysis).

Since predictions can legitimately be made on the basis of probabilities in the social sciences as well as in the natural sciences, clearly distinction between them, in the abstract, is a matter of degree.[5] The correlations that the probability statements of the social scientist can suggest are likely to be considerably weaker—less elegant, less rigorous, less useful—than they are in the hard sciences. The absence of theory (limiting the possibility of knowing which variables to relate), the impossibility of controlling all relevant variables (even if known), and the unavailability of reliable data make firm social predictions unlikely.

Does it make sense to describe predictions that rest on weak theories and unreliable data and offer very low correlations as scientific? My belief is that it is useful as long as the prediction combines two elements: a general proposition (a hypothesis, a law, ideally a theory) and observations or data that attempt to establish the relevance of the proposition. Without this combination of elements, we are in the province of the seer and the prophet.[6]

---

[4] Hans Reichenbach, *Experience and Prediction* (Chicago: University of Chicago Press, 1938), p. 315.

[5] Are predictions that rest on statements of probability identical, irrespective of whether they occur in the physical sciences or the social sciences? The answer, in my opinion, is clearly no. Take the case of a falsified prediction—one in which the stated probabilities did not hold. In the hard sciences, in which the probabilities rest on a verified law, falsification implies a mistake by the predictor (not the law). His data may have been faulty, or he may have calculated mistakenly, or the law may have been incorrectly integrated within a theory. In the social sciences, however, the prediction may turn out badly even though the predictor made *no* error. The probabilities may not hold, even after specifying the initial conditions on which they rest, because the human decisions that affect the outcome are not determined *alone* by these initial conditions. Here the possibility of wayward action is increased when the probabilities refer to the actions of men and not molecules. See also footnote 31 in Chapter 3.

[6] I do not imply that this is always a bad province. We need as much intelligent, normative, and utopian thinking as we can get—especially since our political system has drifted away from these considerations. In this context, I imply only that the social scientist, though he may produce such work, has no reason to presume that he can produce it better than anyone else—it does not engage that much of his professional skills.

It is worth reemphasizing that predictions based on probabilities are the best the social scientist can produce.[7] In practice, he usually (conventionally one adds "as yet" here) must settle for forms of prediction that are even less rigorous and less elegant. Before discussing these efforts, we shall examine the practitioner's argument that the social scientist produces the wrong *kind* of prediction—from the practitioner's point of view. If the complaint against the best that the social scientist can do is valid, it is, of course, also valid against his lesser efforts. But if the complaint is invalid, and if the practitioner misunderstands what he can rightfully seek from the social scientist, and the way in which he can use his efforts, we should be able to demonstrate that the practitioner can learn useful things from predictions that are not detailed and specific—that is to say, from scientific predictions.

PREDICTION AND POLICYMAKING

What predictions are useful to a policymaker? The traditional answer has been clear: the policymaker wants a specific, unconditional forecast "about possible consequences of given lines of action under probable circumstances of the historical world of politics rather than in the hypothetical universe of science."[8] He specifically does *not* want a scientific prediction—a hypothetical "if-then" statement—which seeks only to discover regularities and limits, and is therefore only "an isolated and fragmented particle of the whole."[9] What he does want is something that will tell him which practical action to choose or what will make that choice simpler and more apparent. By definition, nothing that the social scientist can produce is useful, for statements of varying degrees of probability are insufficient.

[7]Other factors distinguish scientific from social predictions, but will only be touched on here. One such factor is that future knowledge itself is an independent factor—not knowing what we will know, we cannot predict what we will do. Another factor, frequently discussed, is that a social prediction can affect the predicted event—to the extent that the prediction can be falsified by public dissemination. A prediction can even *cause* the event it predicts (as well as preventing it from happening). See the discussion in Popper, *The Poverty of Historicism,* p. 15. The literature on self-fulfilling prophecies is also relevant, but too lengthy (and well-known) to cite. These factors can be partially controlled—summarized in the virtues of self-consciousness—but they can never be completely eliminated or safely ignored.
[8]Mulford Q. Sibley, "The Limitations of Behavioralism," in James C. Charlesworth, ed., *The Limits of Behavioralism in Political Science* (Philadelphia: The American Academy of Political and Social Science, 1962), p. 71.
[9] *Ibid.,* p. 65.

We can readily sympathize with this position, for the poor practitioner is aware that he will be maligned someday for not perceiving the future more accurately. Moreover, it is easy to make specific predictions—as any gambler can attest—but it is something else again to guarantee their accuracy (or adequately state the grounds on which they rest) in an open system beset by human vices from ignorance to illness. We would all like sure bets, but the social scientist can *only* offer the best available odds— and sometimes not even that. And the practitioner, as de Jouvenel has stressed, "does not want to know all the possible states and their respective probabilities; instead he wants the predictor to commit himself to one of the states and to suggest that it is so probable as to allow a decision to be based on it."[10]

The social scientist cannot legitimately respond to this request: probabilities cannot be converted into certainties. To the extent that he attempts to do so, he must rely on the same combination of intuition, experience, and luck that the practitioner employs. Also, even if the social scientist has managed to establish a set of probabilities, there is no reason to presume that he is any better at using them as a basis for a decision than the practitioner. There is no road from theory to action that bypasses the need for skilled practitioners in the social world.

We must be clear about the boundaries of this argument. Indisputably, the practitioner's ultimate function *is* to choose a course of action. And when he reaches the point where he must make a choice, a mere statement of probabilities is not likely to satisfy him. Too many factors may have been omitted in calculating the probabilities, and these may be critical in a particular case. That is, the decisive factors in a single case may not be those that were weighed in establishing the odds for a *general* category of events. In addition, the odds may not be good, and in important decisions even a high probability like 81 per cent may not be sufficient. The central point, from this perspective, is that the practitioner is correct in asserting that a probability statement does not eliminate the need for subtle acts of human judgment. The most that a probability statement can do is supplement a choice that must be made on wider and more inclusive grounds.

What confuses the situation is the notion that this is the extent of the argument. It should be obvious why this is not true. Social predictions are not designed to eliminate the need for an act of choice by the social practitioner: to assert that predictions cannot do what they are not capable of doing is a useless tautology. Worse yet, this assertion sustains

[10] Bertrand de Jouvenel, *The Art of Conjecture* (New York: Basic Books, 1967), p. 145.

the belief that the practitioner is a mere "chooser"—that he makes decisions without first intellectually diagnosing his problems—and it diverts attention away from understanding how such predictions can and should be used.

Once we begin giving the conceptual and diagnostic elements in decision-making their due, we can begin to understand why predictions can be helpful even if they do not tell us precisely what will happen on a certain date. They can help a practitioner (*who wants to be helped*) organize his conceptual universe so that he can think more clearly not only about the context of future decisions and the kinds of problems we will be facing in the decades ahead, but also about the questions he should be raising *now* and the consequences he is ignoring *now*. They sensitize him, in short, to what he should be thinking about, and they warn him about the things he is not. This does not guarantee a better future, but it does offer us the best chance of improving the odds for creating the kind of future we want.

THE PRACTITIONER AS PREDICTOR

The last person to accept this argument is likely to be the practitioner. Superficially, this seems odd. Why should the practitioner accept an interpretation of his role that deliberately and artificially limits it to making decisions in an intellectual vacuum? There are several answers to this question, and we must understand them if we intend to make an effort to change the way in which practitioners are recruited, trained, and ultimately practice their calling.

The most obvious reason is that everything in the universe that the practitioner inhabits—the political system he participates in, the bureaucracy he works in, the beliefs he learns to take seriously—is preoccupied with the problems on today's agenda. The long run is left to shift for itself, and thus prediction is ignored or transformed into another effort to get a piece of the action. Only operator's skills are valued, and, consequently, only predictions that directly affect the conduct of operations are valued. This does not mean that no thinking gets done about the long-run consequences of short-run actions but that the thinking is implicit, rudimentary, and inadequate.

A significant psychological factor is also at work. The practitioner's distaste for theory, for research, and for statements of probability (or any generalized prediction) reflects subjective biases and fears that are profoundly felt—as anyone can affirm who has discussed these matters with practitioners. This gap between the operator's mentality, emphasizing intuition, experience, and habit, and the theorist's mentality, stressing generalization, innovation, and precision, is perhaps inevitable. It will continue to be unbridgeable so long as we continue to recruit and train practitioners in the accustomed style. Yet the two modes of analysis are not in complete contradiction, and one can supplement and clarify the other. Failure to do so implies decision-making without intellectual analysis, a form of gambling with bad odds.

Perhaps the most important reason for the practitioner's insistence on the utility of only one kind of prediction is a territorial imperative. Unconditional and specific predictions of events must be based on intuition, experience, familiarity with the latest information, and perhaps even a little luck—and combining these elements is, to most practitioners, the substance of their profession. Thus, the notion of only one kind of prediction being useful is closely tied to the belief that *only* the practitioner has the skills necessary to produce a useful prediction.

But is the practitioner a good predictor of specific events? We have no studies that have directly attempted to analyze the predictive record of political practitioners.[11] Nevertheless, I think that our chances of enlarging the practitioner's conception of what might or might not be useful is dependent on a prior challenge to the presumption that he predicts as well as he thinks he does. We are willing to contemplate change from established and rewarding patterns of behavior only when they become manifestly dissatisfying. The practitioner's dissatisfaction is currently far from epic; it needs a push.

The argument that the practitioner makes certain predictions better than anyone is not new. A classic debate in psychology between advocates of "clinical" and "statistical" prediction provides a useful analogy—provided we consider it with caution. We may presume, without doing harm to the argument, that "clinicians" correspond to practitioners, and that "statisticians" correspond to theorists.

To avoid misunderstandings, I should like to emphasize one point about the following discussion. The debate concerns the proper way to make predictions about a unique event. This does not directly parallel our analysis of prediction in the previous section, for we were not concerned with predictions of a single event. What is at issue here is: If we

[11] In my interviews with members of the Policy Planning Council I asked each member what kinds of prediction were useful (and received the expected answer) and how well he thought he had done as a predictor. The Council members all noted the difficulties of predicting, but they also felt that they performed as well as, or better than, anyone else—failures were attributed to bad luck, or lack of accurate information, or to the fact that "no one could predict that event." Nevertheless, they certainly had no feelings of inadequacy about their performances.

want or need to predict such events, what is the best way to do it? How can the social theorist make a contribution to the practitioner in this context?

All prediction presumably deals with events (defined broadly enough to include, for example, the development of particular capabilities or the alteration of various attitudes). We seek knowledge of the conditions under which an event occurs: we can predict, therefore, only after observation of repeated instances of the events in question. According to this formulation, there is no such thing as "clinical" (or "single case" or "unique") prediction, because we predict the outcome of one case according to our knowledge of other cases of similar behavior.[12] Without previous instances of the case at hand, there is no way to predict probable outcomes. The operational principle is clear. Order each case into a class on the basis of observation; examine a statistical table to find the relative frequencies of behavior for events in that class; and then predict. (Or read the number off the table; taken literally, this kind of prediction is done best by a machine.)[13]

The "clinicians" would agree that we can predict nothing with certainty and some events with a degree of probability. But they would not agree that we can predict unique cases according to frequencies of behavior within a class. The clinician depends on data, impressions, and intuitions to form a subjective (in the psychological, not the biased sense) hypothesis about the structure and dynamics of the case at hand, and then he predicts. The clinical method is superior to the statistical only if the clinician can apply knowledge to a specific case that cannot be found in a table of relative frequencies: that is, if he knows something more than membership in a class would suggest. If factors relevant to the case do not appear in the statistical table, because they are rare or unknown, the clinician has an advantage: his hypothesis *may* be superior to one based *solely* on probability.

An illustration may be helpful. Suppose we know that Congressman X votes against foreign aid appropriations with a frequence of 0.90; also suppose that our clinician-practitioner knows that Congressman X has been bribed to vote favorably for the next aid bill. There is thus a probability of zero, not 0.90, that he will vote negatively. The statis-

[12] See Reichenbach, *Experience and Prediction,* and Karl R. Popper, *The Logic of Scientific Discovery* (New York: Harper and Row, 1965), Chap. 8.

[13] See Paul E. Meehl, *Clinical versus Statistical Prediction* (Minneapolis: University of Minnesota Press, 1954), for a reasoned statement of the issues in dispute; for a more recent summary and analysis, see Harrison G. Gough, "Clinical versus Statistical Prediction in Psychology," in Leo Postman, ed., *Psychology in the Making* (New York: Alfred A. Knopf, 1962), pp. 526-584.

tician-theorist has a ready response: the likelihood of bribery can also be put into a statistical table. But the crucial question is, would it be? Insofar as outright bribery is a rare occurrence in Congress, it would not be statistically significant in any attempt to forecast congressional voting behavior. Thus it *could* be in a statistical table, but it is not *likely* to be, for the statistician-theorist can afford to ignore rare factors—in fact, he probably must if he wants to achieve correlations that are statistically interesting. And yet, for the clinician-practitioner, knowledge that X has been bribed is more critical than other information about him. Therefore, from an analytical point of view, the superiority of the clinician-practitioner in single case prediction rests on knowledge that is unlikely to be in a statistical table because of its rarity.

Whether "clinicians" are better (or, simply, good) predictors is a complex empirical question. Whereas it is possible to test the validity of a prediction by various techniques, it is never possible to know whether the predictor's premises were accurate (and thus responsible for his success) or whether his biases happened to coincide with the course of events. In effect, we may be able to confirm a prediction; but we are not able to confirm whether the prediction rested on valid ground, at least by any statistical method. Still, this is not wholly disabling. The initial formulation of a predictive hypothesis may be as obscure as any creative act, but we cannot dismiss the possibility of discovering who actually predicts well or badly.

The evidence that we do have hardly justifies the clinician's faith in his predictive judgment. There are instances of different individuals using the same data and predicting differently and of the same individual predicting differently from the same data over successive runs.[14] The clinician's judgment, as we have already noted, is fundamentally affected by national style, theoretical approach, and ethnic background.[15] In addition, the range of the clinician's previous experience is significant in limiting what he is likely or able to predict.[16]

Bad prediction by clinicians does not imply that statisticians are likely to be better predictors of single cases. Some things are unlikely to appear either in statements of trends or statements of probability: latent factors (e.g., the relative quiescence of nationalism from 1871 to 1914 when compared to its significance before and after those years); new develop-

[14] See Paul Wallin, "The Prediction of Individual Behavior from Case Studies," in Paul Horst, et al., *The Prediction of Personal Adjustment* (New York: The Social Science Research Council, 1941), pp. 183-239.

[15] See the references in footnotes 58 and 59 in Chapter 3.

[16] See James Bieri, et al., *Clinical and Social Judgment: The Discrimination of Behavioral Information* (New York: John Wiley and Sons, 1966), p. 40.

ments (e.g., the recent emergence of potentially significant transnational interactions); or subjective trends that cannot be (reasonably) stated statistically. And in a particular case there is no guarantee that the decisive considerations will appear in any table. The statistical approach also presumes that the same numbers, or the reality they represent, have the same meaning for all individuals—that we will react similarly.[17] Finally, all prediction rests on an implicit notion of stability, but this is a compelling imperative for the statistician. He has no way of handling unprogrammed or fortuitous change by numerical sleight of hand.

What we have, then, is a situation in which neither the clinician nor the statistician predicts unique cases very well. The statistician could respond that he never claimed that he could, but that if anyone wants to try, he must begin by using his knowledge of cases of similar behavior. The clinician is in a more difficult position, for it is his contention that he not only can predict unique cases but also can predict them better than anyone.

Whether the weaknesses of clinical judgment are more or less blatant than the weaknesses of political judgment is impossible to say. It would be worthwhile to investigate the matter, but both practitioners and academics seem uninterested. That is probably a prudent attitude for the practitioner to assume—he has nothing to lose but his reputation. This is one area, however, in which the academic could help not only himself— by attempting to establish criteria of success and failure and to relate them to other qualities of the predictor, thus reversing the usual relationship between dependent and independent variables—but also the practitioner. He would be doing this not by making predictions but by studying the predictions of others. That is not necessarily an easier task, but it is useful and could not be done by the practitioners.

Evidence that the practitioner's predictive judgment is frequently faulty, and that it is superior only when it incorporates rare or secret knowledge, is probably not sufficient to alter his view that the only useful predictions are predictions of specific, unique events. But it is a step along the way, for shaking the practitioner's faith in one part of his beliefs may ultimately shake his faith in another. A more direct challenge to his beliefs, with any chance of success, would require persistent failures in the realm of practice, a new style of education, and many beneficent accidents. For the moment, we have only the failures, and they do not *yet* appear sufficient to alter self-interested and satisfying patterns of behavior. As a result, the practitioner still asks the theorist

[17] See Gough, "Clinical versus Statistical Prediction in Psychology," p. 555.

for the wrong things—if he asks for anything at all—and still believes in his unique skills to unravel and understand the world of "hard choices" and "great operators."

THE "LESSER" FORMS OF PREDICTION

It is foolish for the practitioner to insist that only specific predictions are useful, for it means that he ignores the potential that other sorts of prediction have to improve the quality of his thinking about the environment he confronts. Once we begin to realize the effect that generalized social predictions can have upon the practitioner's ideas, values, and norms—and thus *indirectly* upon his actual decisions—the rationale for taking such predictions seriously begins to be more convincing. In this section, we shall discuss social predictions that fall short of the rigor of a probability statement—the latter remaining, as we have said, more an ideal than an actuality. We shall be operating on the spectrum between scientific predictions and the intuitive or subjective prophecies of the seer and the oracle. But these are useful operations if they stimulate insights about where we want to go and where we can go—and perhaps even if they compel attention to the future.

The most important of these methods, and the one closest to scientific predictions (it uses numbers, although its proponents claim other virtues), involves extrapolation from current trends. It is less than a scientific prediction primarily because it involves *only* an extrapolation of data—and not a correlation between different trends. Also, trends and probablity statements tend to use different kinds of data: the trend analysis requires data over time, while a statement of probabilities can be based on a single set of observed regularities. Discerning a relationship between trends is one way of establishing probabilities, but it is hardly the only way. A trend does not by itself involve any estimate of probabilities beyond its own continuation. But it is useful for discovering and verifying various hypotheses.

Trend analysis has become so fashionable that it may be helpful to take a closer look at its virtues and vices. This will, moreover, give us a clearer sense of the problems involved in using social science data about the past and present as a guide to the future.

If the trend line is accurate, and if the predicted event is not too far off, trend analysis can be a useful exercise. The dangers are obvious.[18]

---

[18] On the dangers of using trend lines, see William F. Ogburn, *On Culture and Social Change* (Chicago: University of Chicago Press, 1964), p. 107.

Successful extrapolation requires not only clear knowledge of the trend (which means that it must have lasted over a period of time) but also the persistence of the original conditions for the duration of the prediction. In effect, prediction by trend is more valid to the degree that it occurs within a closed system in which change is minimal or controllable—there is no other way in which we could safely assume that events will recur or processes continue.

Where measurement is not available, or where it is suspect, differences in degree cannot be computed. The data on which we base many trend lines are extremely unreliable: it is very difficult to know what has been happening, let alone what will happen. Moreover, beyond the unavailability or inaccuracy of much of our data, no one seems sure of what to measure in order to predict well—a problem engendered by the lack of real theories.[19] Knowing a trend line is also not identical to knowing the fluctuations around it, which is the major reason that trend lines are suspect as a source for decisions. If we try to help the policymaker by deriving specific forecasts from trends, we can do so only by subjectively guessing which factors will be significant at what moment—hardly a scientific venture.

Trend extrapolations are also suspect because they involve human judgments. De Jouvenel notes one of the psychological problems this creates: "If the movement is a fairly pronounced one, we tend to predict that it will proceed in a rather less pronounced manner, as though we unconsciously calculated a weighted average of our two most natural assumptions—'No Change' and 'Same Line of Change.' "[20] There is empirical evidence that even in economics, with quantitative data, forecasters tend to be consistently conservative: they underestimate increases more than they do decreases.[21] Additional evidence shows that trend extrapolators may have their views distorted by prevailing social forces, the techniques they use, and the inertia of habit and tradition.[22]

[19] On the unreliability of available data and the absence of theories, see Donald N. Michael, *The Unprepared Society: Planning for a Precarious Future* (New York: Basic Books, 1968), pp. 10-11.

[20] De Jouvenel, *The Art of Conjecture,* p. 195.

[21] See Victor Zarnowitz, "Prediction and Forecasting, Economic," *International Encyclopedia of the Social Sciences* (New York: Macmillan, 1968), p. 436. Another investigator notes that "individuals overestimate the probability of unlikely events [and] underestimate the probability of likely events." Joseph L. Bower, "Descriptive Decision Theory from the 'Administrative Viewpoint,' " in Raymond A. Bauer and Kenneth J. Gergen, eds., *The Study of Policy Formation* (New York: The Free Press, 1968), pp. 112-113.

[22] A number of available techniques attempt to compensate for, or dilute the effects of, all these weaknesses. They are discussed in William F. Ogburn, *The Social Effects of Aviation* (Boston: Houghton Mifflin, 1946), pp. 47-57, and in Irving J.

Assuming that the trend will continue in a straight line perhaps represents the greatest practical danger in this form of analysis. There is no mathematical reason for this judgment, for a cyclical pattern or a pattern of exponential growth may be equally likely. Without better theory and better data there is no way of knowing. But unless we know when the trend will alter, the most we can offer is a statement of what will happen if the rates remain unchanged (whether they *will* do so remaining beyond the predictor's abilities).[23]

This explains why trend analysis is most successful in forecasting economic conditions, in studying elections and demography, and in predicting technological developments. In each of these cases, the available theory is good, or the data are reliable, or the forecast can be safely made on the basis of current knowledge. The key is that an accurate forecast can be made without worrying much about the impact of intentions or random behavior—or about the forecaster's lack of imagination.[24] The projection of capabilities, of tangible relationships, thus tends to be reliable, especially in the near future.

The most pernicious examples of the misuse of trend analysis probably emanate from the Pentagon. The "missile gap" argument between 1957 and 1962 is a classic illustration of the dangers of projecting trends without worrying about why or whether they would continue. As a result, an ugly spiral of reaction and counter-reaction began, the end of which is not yet in sight. In fact, the Pentagon's obsession with "worst case" projections is an illustration of how to use trends as a substitute for thinking.

If trend analysis is so uncertain and dangerous, why use it at all? Some of the answer reflects current fashions in social science: trends are numerical, they are a form of macroanalysis, and the techniques and data employed are sufficiently esoteric to repel outside assertions of expertise. But this answer is too simple, for some trend analyses are quite accurate, and they can provide a basis for making sensible judgments about the direction in which policy ought to be going.

Bross, *Design for Decision* (New York: Macmillan, 1953), p. 34 ff. A good short study of how demographers had their judgment of trends distorted by social fads and forces is in Otis Dudley Duncan, "Social Forecasting: The State of the Art," *The Public Interest,* no. 17 (Fall 1969), pp. 89-93.

[23] Interesting, useful comments on these matters are in Bruce M. Russett, "The Ecology of Future International Politics," *The International Studies Quarterly* 11 (March 1967): 12-31, and in his *Trends in World Politics* (New York: Macmillan, 1965).

[24] For illustrations of the failures of nerve and imagination in forecasting, see Arthur C. Clarke, *Profiles of the Future* (New York: Harper and Row, 1962), Chap. 1.

One illustration of this argument refers to the data collected during the last decade indicating that cohesiveness within the European Economic Community was growing much faster than cohesiveness with either the United States or Great Britain. Closer ties between France and Germany, and growing neutralist sentiment in France, constituted an early warning about the state of the "Atlantic ideal": close attention to this data might have allowed those who were promoting the "ideal" to have discovered earlier that it was (or might become) a fantasy.[25] The limitations of this kind of data as a guide for specific decisions must be recognized and emphasized. The utility of this data for helping us to raise important questions, and to rethink the conventional wisdom, however, can be immense. From the social scientist's point of view, it has another virtue: testing of trend analyses against actual outcomes is very useful in developing and searching for new hypotheses and relationships. In addition, since trend analysis is inevitably concerned with change, it is a counterpart to the normal emphasis on stability and continuity.

Other forms of prediction in the social sciences are less scientific than trend analysis. Or perhaps one should say that they use less quantitative data and more qualitative judgment. Model-building, systems analysis, less formal uses of analogies, and even the organized use of expert judgment (the "Delphi" technique) are illustrative.[26] So, too, are normative predictions that appear to defy any scientifically acceptable methodology. These methods share one common characteristic: they are "unscientific" (though not unreasoned) inferences in which the "ifs" and the "thens" have to be connected by a combination of intuition, experience, and analytical judgment. For the most part, they also involve an effort to use or discover relevant similarities with the past.

POLITICAL SCIENTISTS AND THE LESSER FORMS OF PREDICTION

It is not difficult to understand why the practitioner has ignored these lesser forms of prediction. They provide none of the certainties he seeks, they are difficult to turn to political advantage, and they are written in a language that is frequently esoteric and difficult. Professional political scientists also have never paid much attention to these ventures, however.

[25] For the data, see Chapter 3 of Russett, *Trends in World Politics.*
[26] Attempts to list predictive efforts can be found in de Jouvenel, *The Art of Conjecture,* p. 65 f; Karl F. Schuessler, "Prediction," *International Encyclopedia of the Social Sciences,* p. 420; and Eric Jantsch, *Technological Forecasting in Perspective* (Paris: Organization for Economic Cooperation and Development, 1966).

And when they have done so, it has rarely been from a perspective that seemed likely to provide results of interest to the practitioner. We need to understand why these efforts have been ignored, for there is not much point in attempting to convince the practitioner that they are useful if the theorist has neither the intention nor the desire to produce them.

One major reason why political scientists have disregarded "unscientific" forecasting resides in a fascination with the argument that explanation and prediction are equivalent terms.[27] An explanation (i.e., a theory) in the standard argument differs from a prediction only according to the time dimension: explanations refer to the past, predictions to the future, but their formal structure is identical. There are undoubtedly instances where this is true in the sciences. However, there are also many cases (some in the hard sciences, and all instances in the social sciences) in which the two terms are not equivalent. We have cases in which we can predict outcomes, but cannot explain why (e.g., we could predict the movements of the tides before Newton, but could not explain why they moved; or we could relate changes in the weather to variations in the level of mercury in a vacuum, but no one could explain the relationship for a long time; or we could predict much about future voting patterns on the basis of previous votes, without being able to explain why certain patterns prevailed). Toulmin maintains, moreover, that the proposition is reversible: there are theories or explanations in science that do not yield predictions.[28]

In general, however, the more formal the explanation, the more certain its conclusions must be; predictions, conversely, can be made not only on the basis of less evidence, but their disconfirmation does not necessarily mean—in the social sciences—that the explanation from which they were derived (or created) was wrong. In the sciences, as we have already indicated, a wrong prediction means that a mistake occurred: either the theory, the data, or the calculator was mistaken.[29] Thus, an explanation and a prediction are not equivalent terms in the social sciences. Recogni-

[27] The argument is stated in C. G. Hempel and P. Oppenheim, "Studies in the Logic of Explanation," *Philosophy of Science* 18 (1948): 135-175; it is disputed in Nicholas Rescher, "On Prediction and Explanation," *The British Journal for the Philosophy of Science* 8 (1957-1958): 281-290.
[28] Toulmin, *Foresight and Understanding*, pp. 36-38. Other differences between scientific and social predictions, noted above, make a social prediction inadequate as a formal explanation; see pages 161-163.
[29] On these issues see Rescher, "On Prediction and Explanation"; Winch, *The Idea of a Social Science,* pp. 91-92; and Olaf Helmer and Nicholas Rescher, "On the Epistemology of the Inexact Sciences" (Santa Monica, Calif.: The RAND Corporation, R-353, 1960).

tion of this might make less fashionable the notion that all predictions must have a rigorous, elegant form. This analogy with the hard sciences is misleading, for it obscures the degree to which weaker theories, weaker predictions, and more ambiguous applications make the parallel between explanations and predictions academic.

The insistence that predictions must be as rigorous as explanations has also reinforced the tendency to stress quantitative data. Only results that can be presented in this manner appear able to be confirmed or refuted in the required style. Other forms of prediction have been dismissed as the province of charlatans or the concern of witch doctors, and a self-fulfilling prophecy rationalizes this attitude. The quest for rigor, carried beyond what either the nature of the subject matter or the current state of theory justifies, has become a principle of exclusion. An area of political and social activity, with enormous normative, theoretical, and practical significance, has hardly been studied because it cannot be done without appearing to sacrifice the visionary and perhaps unrealizable gains of one scientific canon.

In the last few years this situation has been altered by an outburst of interest in "futurology." This interest reflects neither a commitment to reorder priorities in the academic world nor the discovery of new techniques to remove the uncertainties of social prediction. It only shows that our social problems have become so overwhelming that concern for and about the future is imperative. Futurology is also fashionable, which means that book publishers and foundations are willing to pay to express that concern. Whatever the underlying motivation, there is more receptivity to the notion that studying the future is both necessary and legitimate.

A SUMMARY: THE PRACTICAL UTILITY
OF SOCIAL PREDICTIONS

What is the practical significance of our attempt to delineate the limitations and possibilities of social predictions? Perhaps one result is a clearer understanding of why theorists and practitioners have rarely cooperated in the area of social predictions. The practitioner, on the one hand, has mistakenly insisted that only one kind of prediction is useful to him, and that he is better equipped to produce it than anyone. We have stressed repeatedly that this is true only if the practitioner does not understand the extent to which sensible decision-making rests on an intellectual base, which the theorist can improve, criticize, and evaluate, and that it is

175

doubtful that the practitioner is effective at the single-case prediction he believes he does so well. The latter issue is one that could be clarified by research studies well within the capabilities of the theorist—if the practitioner cooperated. The theorist, on the other hand, has accepted the practitioner's argument because of a mistaken notion that he will some-day be able to provide the precise predictions the practitioner demands; and because, in the interim, he can do as he pleases, convinced that ignoring the problems of the practical world is justified and wise.

We can extract another lesson from this discussion. In the current situation, little that the social scientist can (legitimately) do appears useful to the practitioner. But if we begin to educate practitioners differently, so that they develop a wider appreciation of their function and a more subtle understanding of what the social scientist is capable of, then the possibilities of cooperation may be significantly enhanced. In the new circumstances, the social scientist will not be asked to provide what he cannot provide, but, more critically, the undertakings that he can perform may suddenly appear interesting and useful to practitioners who are trying to understand their field, and are not seeking substitutes for their own judgment.

There is another way in which the theorist can aid the practitioner. Some obstacles to prediction are not intrinsic to the function, but emerge from the biases of individuals and the political system that they operate. These factors affect not only how individuals perceive the future but also their willingness to think about the future and its opportunities. We shall, in this context, discuss the nature of the political system and the bureaucratic entities that populate it. Other obstacles relate to the intrinsic psychological difficulties that any individual faces in making objective predictions. We shall discuss these in the next section for they affect anyone, practitioner or theorist, who believes he has kept values out of his forecasts.

The function that the social scientist performs in discussing these issues is a warning one. He is not predicting, but rather warning those who do predict to beware of factors that may distort their judgment. As in all therapeutic exercises, such as psychoanalysis, we may profit from the experience, but no law says we will. Whatever virtues the following discussion has rest on the belief that self-consciousness about possible biases and distortions opens the way to improved performance. This does not allow us to see the future much better, but we may be less surprised when it actually arrives and more capable of coping with it.

176

PSYCHOLOGICAL FACTORS IN PREDICTION

Prediction can be defined as a psychological inference about the future, based primarily on past experience.[30] These experiences and the forecasts we base upon them inevitably have been limited. As Bergson noted, "Of the future, only that is foreseen which is like the past or can be made up again with elements like those of the past."[31] To foresee a truly revolutionary future would imply that what we have learned in the past and what we currently know are irrelevant.

Since there is a "strain toward consistency" in us all, it is unlikely that we would forecast events that break sharply with our current perceptions. The problem is not only that "the individual strives toward consistency within himself" but also that "there is the same kind of consistency between what a person knows or believes and what he does."[32] We are epistemological conservatives, which means that we are poor forecasters in contexts where the relevance of experience cannot be taken for granted.

That would not be devastating, at least in nonrevolutionary periods, if our experiences provided reliable analogies with current situations. Experience, however, does not make our perceptions more sophisticated. It comes to us in relatively uniform contexts. We may be omitting relevant factors from that context or introducing irrelevant ones. Moreover, as Ogden and Richards have noted, "When a context has affected us in the past, the recurrence of merely a part of the context will cause us to react in the way in which we reacted before."[33] We do not reliably test the validity of the analogies that appear relevant to us; worse yet, the analogies are normally based on the partial reappearance of apparently similar pieces of a puzzle. The strain toward consistency—the effort to eliminate dissonance—leads us to assume that we have to put the same puzzle together again. It is psychologically comforting to act as if the parallels are real, for it justifies the relevance of our experiences and the accuracy of our perceptions.

[30] See Douglas McGregor, "The Major Determinants of the Prediction of Social Events," *Journal of Abnormal and Social Psychology* 33 (1938): 179; and also Leonard S. Cottrell, Jr., "The Case-Study Method in Prediction," *Sociometry* 4, no. 4 (1941): 376.
[31] Henri Bergson, *Creative Evolution* (New York: Modern Library, 1946), p. 28.
[32] Leon Festinger, *A Theory of Cognitive Dissonance* (Evanston Ill.: Row, Peterson, 1957), p. 1.
[33] C. K. Ogden and I. A. Richards, *The Meaning of Meaning* (New York: Harcourt, Brace and World, 1946), p. 53.

The psychological difficulties of anticipating novelty are thus enormous. We perceive only an "unchanging kind of change"—in which the future will differ from the present just as the present differs from the past—because it is the only perception of change with which we can live on amicable grounds.[34] Like Goethe, who preferred injustice to disorder, we prefer myopia to instability.

The contention that forecasting is heavily influenced by psychological factors is commonplace. Subjectivity is built into any situation in which individuals must make a choice. And one scarcely needs to be reminded that we usually see only what we want to see and forecast only what we desire to see happen. It is still useful, however, to run through a check list of situations in which judgmental error is likely to be highest, as a warning against complacency.

Several studies have indicated that subjective factors increasingly influence our forecasts as the predicted event grows in importance—the less involved we are, the more objectively we make our judgments.[35] The significance of subjective factors is also dependent upon the ambiguity of the external situation confronting the decision-maker and upon the intensity of his attitudes toward the event in question. For example, Douglas McGregor, reporting the results of a series of experiments on prediction, notes:

> If either importance or ambiguity were zero, the influence of subjective factors upon prediction would be zero. In the first case there would be no wishes to influence prediction, and the predictor would simply record, by the chances he gave, the ambiguity of the existent stimulus situation. If ambiguity were zero, on the other hand, the stimulus situation would be completely coercive. Even an intense wish would be imperative. . . . If both ambiguity and importance were maximal, subjective factors would be completely determinative of prediction.[36]

If we cannot resolve into a coherent pattern the factors affecting an event, that event is also less uniformly forecast. If an event is too complex to be structured externally, a relevant internal frame of reference will determine what we predict.[37] Different men will predict with uniformity only if they share common attitudes, values, and experiences.

[34] Bertrand de Jouvenel, *Futuribles* (Santa Monica, Calif.: The RAND Corporation, P-3045, 1965).

[35] See, for example, Hans H. Toch, "The Perception of Future Events: Case Studies in Social Prediction," *The Public Opinion Quarterly* 22 (Spring 1958): 64; and McGregor, "The Major Determinants," p. 189.

[36] McGregor, "The Major Determinants," p. 192.

[37] Hadley Cantril, "The Prediction of Social Events," *Journal of Abnormal and Social Psychology* 33 (1938): 387.

However, in situations where external ambiguity is high and the forecast rests wholly or substantially upon an internal frame of reference, objectivity is rare—ego involvement is too high.

Evidence indicates that experts do *not* differ significantly from nonexperts in this situation. Their objectivity also declines as internal involvement increases.[38] The reason is that the *nature,* not the *amount,* of information we have is decisive: what information we have on an issue depends on its ambiguity and how important we consider it.

Sidney Verba has summarized other hypotheses about individual behavior that are relevant to any analysis of prediction. In brief, they suggest that the influence of nonlogical factors will be inhibited if the decision-maker has a great deal of information about the event in question, if he has a high level of skill in international affairs, if he believes he has influence on the event, and if he is in some way responsible for the consequences of whatever decision he makes. In addition, if the decision is specific, detailed, and made within a group context in which the decision-maker's biases are canceled out by countervailing biases, the chances for objectivity increase.[39]

Of these considerations, perhaps the one with the most direct relevance for planning in foreign affairs concerns the effect of believing or not believing in the predictability of events. One study has indicated that when we confront a problem and *also* believe that events are predictable, we think more about it, make a more serious effort to devise a solution (not merely a temporary palliative) for it, and have a higher level of aspiration for our efforts.[40] The planners in foreign affairs, like their operating colleagues, take unpredictability as an article of faith. As a result, they respond to events with hackneyed formulas, think about them only in the limited sense of wanting to know all the facts, and have no aspirations beyond getting the event off the front pages of *The New York Times.*

External ambiguity, a high level of personal involvement by the decision-maker (whose historical reputation is at stake), a low level of substantive skill, and a set of attitudes antipathetical to prediction

[38] *Ibid.,* pp. 388-389; see also A. Kaplan, A. L. Skogstad, and M. A. Girshick, "The Prediction of Social and Technological Events," *Public Opinion Quarterly* 14 (Spring 1950): 98.

[39] Sidney Verba, "Assumptions of Rationality and Non-Rationality in Models of the International System," *World Politics* 14 (October 1961): 99-105.

[40] See Orville G. Brim, Jr., et al., *Personality and Decision Processes: Studies in the Social Psychology of Thinking* (Stanford, Calif.: Stanford University Press, 1962), p. 55; on levels of aspiration, see Sidney Siegel and Lawrence E. Fouraker, *Bargaining and Group Decision Making* (New York: McGraw-Hill, 1960).

characterize many international situations. It is less than surprising that nonlogical factors exert a substantial influence. Of course, if the decision or prediction concerns a specific event, and if the decision-maker is skilled, informed, and ensconced in a bureaucracy that values intellectual conflict, the effect of these factors can be controlled. But the statement of limiting conditions indicates why the problem is so profound.

The best that one can hope for is improved controls on the tendency of policymakers to predict on the basis of nonlogical factors. On a minimal level, persistent articulation of the influence of bias and selective perception might be helpful. Self-consciousness about the dangers involved no more guarantees a cure than it does in Freudian analysis, but it does open the possibility of improved performance.

Institutional devices that might limit the effects of individual biases and prejudices hardly promise to be more effective. Discussion or confirmation of a forecast by a group is reasonable *only* if its members do not share the same predispositions.[41] The group may confirm an error and reinforce unwillingness to accept conflicting evidence and opinions. In particular, since forecasts are usually exposed only to experts with similar inclinations and training, dissenters can be ignored as irrelevant or uninformed. The difficulties are especially acute *within* an organization that makes a concerted effort to enforce a single view and that equates loyalty with conformity—like the State Department.

The ideal solution to some would be the creation of an institutionalized devil's advocate who eternally asks, "why?" and "What do you mean by that?" Aside from the fact that he would probably be shot within the month, obvious difficulties arise. Who should he be, what should he know, and what should he advocate in order not to be ignored (or shot)? And who is to devil the devil's advocate? There is no way in which a devil's advocate can eliminate the distortions produced by individual biases, which are in turn reinforced by like-minded colleagues, unless the deviling is done by men of intellectual stature within an organization that values intellectual evaluation of its activities—which is to say, not the Department of State.

POLICIES, POLICYMAKING, AND PREDICTIONS

How policy is made and which policies are implemented impede accurate forecasting. We have already commented on the antipathy

[41] See Verba, "Assumptions of Rationality," pp. 104-105, and Festinger, *A Theory of Cognitive Dissonance,* Chap. 8.

between a policymaking system that is incremental in style and the planning function.[42] Certainly not all policies are made in this fashion. Enough are, however, to make this the central point of departure for any analysis of policymaking because the major exceptions to incrementalism either cannot be substantively planned for—like crisis decision—or resulted from adequate efforts to plan. The latter point refers to the contention during the Kennedy and Johnson presidencies that "cost-benefit" or "cost-effectiveness" analysis had superseded the old style of making military decisions. How true that contention is remains uncertain; it is doubtful in reference to the Pentagon of Melvin Laird. It is not directly relevant here, for we are primarily interested in foreign policy decisions.

The most significant effect of an incremental policy process is that predictions will inevitably be foreshortened, parochial, and conservative. The policymaker looks far enough ahead only to choose between the limited and familiar options he perceives. The differences between the choices are limited, and this cancels out any marked concern for the future—that is to say, whatever effect a choice might have is not likely to differ much from the effect that any other choice might have had. Today is the best and only guide to tomorrow, and concern for either the lessons of the past or the dangers of the future is a waste of time. The search for relevant novelty never begins; quite the contrary, novelties are dangerous and only similarities are relevant. This makes for a short search, since there are very few familiar futures that one has to worry about. In fact, an assumption of unchanging change is a necessity: paradise for lovers of trend lines.

The inherent myopia of this process is reinforced by the bureaucratic setting within which most incremental haggling takes place. As Kenneth Boulding has noted:

> In a hierarchy there is an inescapable tendency toward pleasing the superior, and hence confirming his ideas. Hierarchy in organizations, therefore, produces a condition akin to paranoia in individuals. The information-gathering apparatus always tends to confirm the existing image of the top decision-makers, no matter what it is.[43]

This is incorrect only to the degree that it implies a real conflict in values between higher and lower echelons of the hierarchy—in reality, shared values make the lower ranks more perfervid "true believers" (more be-

[42] See above, pp. 29-33.
[43] Kenneth E. Boulding, "The Learning and Reality-Testing Process in the International System," *The Journal of International Affairs* 21, no. 1 (1967): 10.

cause they may be less cynical). A strong probability exists that the received wisdom of the top will pass unchallenged, and myopia will persist uncorrected.[44]

Realism, insofar as it encapsulates the reigning beliefs of the foreign affairs establishment, also sharply circumscribes the significance of any attempt to plan for or predict the future. The truly interesting projections are bound to be specific and absolute: so and so will do such and such on date X. These projections are similar in style and emphasis to the wartime conception of the intelligence function.[45] Any other kind of prediction can be safely ignored because the principles of politics are both known and unchanging—excessive concern with emerging trends is unnecessary. Continuity always prevails over change.

Whatever the style and circumstances, policies ultimately emerge. Governments become committed to a kind of behavior toward other states, and to a range of expectations on which that behavior rests. Both the policies and expectations inhibit accurate forecasting. Roberta Wohlstetter illustrates the point in discussing the Cuban missile crisis:

> The Administration did not want open conflict with the Soviet Union. It was working on a program of trying to relax tensions, of which a test-ban agreement was one important though distant goal. It most definitely did not want an offensive Soviet base in Cuba. And just as FDR wanted no war in the Far East, no war on two fronts, and didn't want to believe that it could happen, so we didn't want to believe that the Soviets were doing what they were doing.[46]

She concludes that

> this policy background [of relaxing tension] was much more subtle in its influence. For when an official policy or hypothesis is laid down it tends to obscure alternative hypotheses, and to lead to overemphasis of the data that support it, particularly at a time of increasing tension, when it is important not to "rock the boat."[47]

Another investigation of the Cuban missile crisis also illustrates the

[44] For an excellent analysis of why organizations do not obtain or use information about the environment and why "information pathologies" result, see Harold L. Wilensky, *Organizational Intelligence: Knowledge and Policy in Government and Industry* (New York: Basic Books, 1967). Wilensky relates characteristics of the organization to intelligence-gathering styles in an interesting fashion.
[45] See Willmoore Kendall, "The Function of Intelligence," *World Politics* 1 (July 1949): 548-549.
[46] Roberta Wohlstetter, "Cuba and Pearl Harbor: Hindsight and Foresight" (Santa Monica, Calif.: The RAND Corporation, RM-4328-ISA, 1965), p. 21.
[47] *Ibid.,* p. 27.

extent to which a set of expectations about an opponent's most rational behavior affected the situation:

> The predisposition of the intelligence community to the philosophical conviction that it would be incompatible with Soviet policy to introduce strategic missiles into Cuba resulted in intelligence judgments and evaluations which later proved to be erroneous.
>
> Moreover, there seems to have been a disinclination on the part of the intelligence community to accept and believe the ominous portent of the information which had been gathered. . . . In addition, the intelligence people apparently invariably adopted the most optimistic estimate possible with respect to the information available.[48]

Dean Acheson made a similar point about how expectations about Communist behavior influenced our analysis of events in Korea:

> The view was generally held that since the Communists had far from exhausted the potentialities for obtaining their objectives through guerrilla and psychological warfare, political pressure and intimidation, such means would probably continue to be used rather than overt military aggression.[49]

The Commander-in-Chief, Far East, had also noted in March 1950, that it

> seems likely that Communist overt military measures in Korea will be held in abeyance, at least until further observations made by Soviets of results of their program in such places as Indochina, Burma, and Thailand. . . . If checked or defeated in their operations in these countries in Asia they may divert large share of their effort to South Korea.[50]

Harvey De Weerd draws a suitably harsh conclusion about why we were surprised twice in 1950:

> The response of the United States to intelligence indicators seemed to

[48] "The Cuban Military Buildup," Interim Report by the Preparedness Investigating Subcommittee of the Committee on Armed Services, U.S. Senate, 88th Congress, 1st Session (1963), pp. 2, 10. See also the interesting analysis by Klaus Knorr, "Failures in National Intelligence Estimates: The Case of the Cuban Missiles," *World Politics* 16 (April 1969): 455-467.

[49] "Military Situation in the Far East," Hearings before the Committee on Armed Services and the Committee on Foreign Relations, U.S. Senate, 82nd Congress, 1st Session (1951), p. 1990.

[50] *Ibid.,* p. 1991. The influence of the prevailing academic dogma about totalitarian states and the personality types who rise (or rose) to power in them might also have been great. Works like Hannah Arendt's *The Origins of Totalitarianism* and Nathan Leites's *The Operational Code of the Politburo* created or reinforced an impression of the Soviet Union as a monolithic totalitarian state run by a suspicious, power-hungry but calculating autocrat; the image did not leave room for perceptions of the Soviets muddling through, drifting, or mellowing—or changing.

be preconditioned by the official belief that any war in the 1950 time period would be an all-out affair involving the Soviet Union. We did not believe that war was likely in Asia; what we feared there was subversion. . . . It was not the absence of intelligence which led us into trouble but our unwillingness to draw unpleasant conclusions from it. We refused to believe what our intelligence told us was in fact happening because it was at variance with the prevailing climate of opinion in Washington and Tokyo. We also refused to believe it because it would have been very inconvenient if we had. We would have had to have done something about it.[51]

Our failure to anticipate the Japanese attack on Pearl Harbor is another familiar example of how expectations color perceptions.

The assumption was still, as Marshall had put it much earlier, "If we lose in the Atlantic, we lose everywhere." This meant that the Far East simply had to stay quiet. The power of this wish was certainly as effective in limiting the range of our Far Eastern policy as it was in delaying our response to the last-minute military signals.[52]

Mrs. Wohlstetter concludes that

it is rather unlikely that new matter upsetting previous hypotheses will find its way into a periodic intelligence estimate without a significant time lag.[53]

We form expectations about state behavior by selectively extrapolating from whatever experiences or historical material we consider relevant. We then base policies on these expectations, and henceforth view the world—to an important degree—through a policy prism that obscures events that would suggest that the policy is erroneous. The futures we forecast are implicitly designed to confirm the wisdom of our actions.[54] Whether there is an objective reality or an objective fact about which we would all agree is uncertain. In the realm of policymaking and prediction, however, it is clear that there are only interpreted facts and interpreted reality. We may easily disagree because our experiences, expectations,

[51] H. A. De Weerd, "Strategic Surprise in the Korean War" (Santa Monica, Calif.: The RAND Corporation, P-1800-1, 1962), pp. 13, 34.
[52] Roberta Wohlstetter, *Pearl Harbor: Warning and Decision* (Stanford, Calif.: Stanford University Press, 1962), p. 273.
[53] *Ibid.*, p. 300. For a historical study of distorted images in American-Asian relations, see Akira Iriye, *Across the Pacific: An Inner History of American-East Asian Relations* (New York: Harcourt, Brace and World, 1967).
[54] See Festinger, *Cognitive Dissonance,* for many examples of efforts to avoid situations or information that would increase the gap (dissonance) between what we believe and what we do.

and perceptions differ. But once we have made a commitment, we stick to it as if our faith depended on it.

That we have been surprised in these circumstances is less astonishing than the fact that we have also sometimes not been taken unawares. Perhaps this suggests that the forces that favor objectivity—the institutional setting of most policymaking, the necessity to touch base with other centers of influence, the perception of the international arena as dominated by threat and conflict, the notion that politics should stop at the water's edge (especially when the policies are uncontroversial)—are stronger than we have implied. More likely, however, we have simply been very lucky, for we have lived in a homogeneous world in which biases and expectations were shared and the costs of failure or muddling through did not seem disproportionately high.

Is the best that we can hope for the expectation that awareness of bias and prejudice will lead to improved performance? So it would seem, for skilled and knowledgeable commentators continue to insist that more is impossible. Or, conversely, they insist that anything is possible if only we let our most qualified people make policy. But our best people in this scheme of affairs always appear to be those who exemplify the conventional wisdom best—the Dean Rusks.

Why is it so difficult to go beyond these commonplaces? Perhaps the reiteration of the same limited point of view implies a lack of imagination of expert analysts bound by the dogma of their calling. Yet this may be too harsh, for the problem is too complex to yield a single explanation. No one, no matter what the field, has much advice to offer when confronting bias, error, and organizational rigidity—except the same pious hope that awareness will be a virtue. Improvement will not come from the in-house expert, or the insider temporarily masquerading as a professor, for they are committed to the same perception of the futility of forecasting and the necessity of incrementalism. Unfortunately, however, although the limitations of the insider cannot be denied, the utility of the outsider (the trained social scientist) can hardly be taken for granted. The most that can be said is that the trained social scientist might be able to help the insider, without sacrificing his calling, but that it remains to be proved.

The distortions produced by individual and organizational biases can never be completely eliminated. In addition to the inadequacies of the State Department, this is a formidable argument for placing a new planning staff as much outside the framework of the normal governmental bureaucracies as is possible. This argument also suggests staffing the new unit with men equipped and willing to deal intellectually with

185

practical problems—seeking the best data, comparing, evaluating, and generalizing. This should guarantee that the inherited wisdom will not reign unchallenged. One makes this judgment with more caution—and sadness—than would have been the case in 1960.

If the policymaker wants to commission a predictive study, to whom should he turn? In the next section, we shall discuss this question as it pertains to the academic world.

PREDICTION AND ACADEMIC FASHIONS

The practitioner turns to the academic for aid only when novel problems arise.[55] He would hardly do so if his existing theories or his habitual mode of behavior were adequate: presumably the outsider is called in to diagnose mysterious ailments and not to deal with the normal run of familiar problems. It would be incorrect to assume that the phones ring very often, or, more precisely, that the right phones ever ring. But suppose the inclination does arise, to whom should the practitioner turn for studies that tell him what he does not already know?

Realism, which dominated both the academic and the practical worlds for so long, is unlikely. The conception of prediction in Realism was identical to the conception of prediction fancied by the operating fraternity. Explicit prediction of unique events became the ideal, rarely attained but sufficiently compelling to divert attention from other alternatives. The possibility that the academic world would raise fundamental questions about the practitioner's mode of behavior never arose. Historical explanations for this state of affairs are understandable and partially excusable, but the result was unfortunate: a tendency to treat the assumptions and principles on which policies were based as sacrosanct.

Realism is now in the academic (but not the practical) ash can. Is there any reason to suppose that its most salient successor—that amorphous body of work normally designated "behavioralism"—would perform the debunking role of the social scientist with more success? Would a behavioralist be more likely to criticize the assumptions and biases of his practitioners? Would he be a more effective nay-sayer or "devil's advocate" within the government? Would his predictions be more useful to the practitioner than the predictions of the Realist?

Behavioral predictions would presumably be equivalent to scientific predictions. But which scientific predictions? As we have indicated, this

---

[55] Or he also seeks help to support a view to which he is committed, and believes he can obtain assistance from friendly or naïve academic circles.

is not a simple question. If we assume that only verified probability statements qualify, then behavioral predictions would be very rare. Beyond that, behavioral predictions would also be the kind of predictions—quantitative and esoteric—most likely to elicit a strongly negative reaction from practitioners.

The difficulty with extending the meaning of behavioral predictions to include some less rigorous techniques of forecasting is that it becomes less clear why these techniques are intrinsically behavioral. For example, the extrapolation of trends appears to be an enterprise eminently suited to the behavioral fascination with empirical data and quantification. Yet there is no reason to assume that behavioralists are more adept at interpreting the meaning of trends than anyone else. In other forms of forecasting, such as the "Delphi" technique, model-building, or the creation of normative utopias, the behavioralists hardly have a monopoly of good or interesting work. Thus Ernst Haas's use of developmental models as a predictive device "based on articulate assumptions, established trends, and probable logical connections between these,"[56] is not tied to any methodological norm. This venture can be performed well by any sophisticated analyst who is willing to use the best available data and who has a sharp enough theoretical sense to ask the right questions.[57]

What this suggests is that it is probably wrong or misleading to consider the issue as a sharp contrast between behavioralists and traditionalists. Either group can produce useful work if it is willing to use reliable data and to phrase its work in terms which make it interesting to the discipline. That excludes, as I indicated at the beginning of Chapter 3, only methodologists and publicists. This is a reasonable argument with one important qualification: although there is no reason to presume that traditionalists could not produce interesting work on prediction, there is little evidence that they are willing to do so. Continued commitment to

[56] Ernst B. Haas, *Collective Security and the Future International System* (Denver: The University of Denver Monograph Series in World Affairs, 1967-68), p. 4.

[57] Perhaps the utility of these efforts should be stated as a hypothesis, since the evidence is scant. Two summers ago in interviewing present and former members of the planning staff of the British Foreign Office, I found that they thought a recent attempt to develop models of "alternative futures" for Europe was helpful. The book that they had in mind was Alastair Buchan, ed., *Europe's Futures, Europe's Choices* (New York: Columbia University Press, 1969), an interesting but not very original attempt to look ahead in Europe. Although this preview could have been considerably improved by providing speculations about the normative superiority of one model over another, as well as hints about procedures, the BFO planners still thought it useful because it suggested the utility of careful thinking about the long-run implications of their present actions. In fact, long-term consequences of current decisions, some deleterious, were an apparently novel idea.

the Realist canon—which has been, but need not be, equivalent to traditionalism—guarantees an indifference to anything except immediate policy issues. Consequently, until a more sophisticated traditionalist doctrine appears, the vast majority of the prediction studies that we can get will come from the behavioralist movement.

By the time the practitioner reaches the point at which outside advice seems imperative, it is usually too late for the scholar or the theorist to be useful. It is the Realist, hawking his opinions behind a haze of metaphysics, who steps into the breach. Offering policy advice that purports to rest on the superior theoretical virtues of traditional wisdom, the Realist appears in the guise of a surrogate (and implicitly preferable) policymaker. This can be irritating to the policymaking fraternity, which cannot respond easily in public, because such advice is frequently obsolete or irrelevant before it is spoken or appears in print. The worst part is that the policymaker deserves what he gets because of his refusal to recognize what he needs and what he can get from the realm of theory.

ON TAKING PREDICTION SERIOUSLY

One reason why we *must* be concerned with the future is that we cannot make present decisions wisely without attempting to anticipate what lies in store for us. Prediction is important, indeed indispensable, not because it tells us what the future will be like, but because it helps us to establish our priorities and our preferences *now*. Thus, it is a practical function—perhaps too important to be left in the hands of the current generation of futurologists.

We need to emphasize a simple point. What we want the future to be and what the future will actually be are not entirely unrelated. We cannot determine our future any more than we can predict it precisely. But we can influence it, we can narrow the range of uncertainty, and we can expose and analyze the model of the future we carry in our heads. This is why, I believe, the idea of choice is central to any attempt to understand the utility of social prediction. Prediction enables us not just to choose our actions in the present but to do so against standards of where we want to go and where we can go. As John McHale has said, "There is, in this sense, no future other than as we will it to be."[58]

Critics of prediction tend to misunderstand these issues. For example,

[58] John McHale, *The Future of the Future* (New York: Ballantine Books, 1971), p. 10.

Robert Nisbet is amusing when he argues, "Events do not marry and have little events, etc; small changes do not accumulate directionally and continuously to become big changes."[59] But this misses the point, for the precise accuracy of the prediction is not the main issue: we are not in a horse race in which we must put our money down on a winner. In contrast to an (honest) horse race, making the prediction almost guarantees that the future will be different because of human interventions. What social prediction attempts to do (if I use the same metaphor) is to sensitize the decision-maker to the consequences that racing might have and to compel him to assess his response according to a standard less arbitrary than the play of transitory political configurations.[60]

One point must be given to the critics. The quality of much of the work currently being done on prediction is abominable.[61] Too many futurologists are content with listing or extrapolating trends, perhaps because they believe that simple projections will be more accurate or significant than the evidence of previous efforts would suggest.[62] Beyond this, perhaps the major difficulty with such studies is a reluctance to match technological projections with normative concerns. If we hope to influence the creation of a desirable future, what might be must be joined to speculation about what we think ought to be. The normative dimension is indispensable in a policy context, for without it a knowl-

[59] Robert Nisbet, "The Year 2000 and All That," *Commentary* 45 (June 1968): 66.
[60] Winston Churchill, I believe, said that the course of history is always being altered by something or other. Nisbet and other critics use this notion as an argument against the possibility of predicting accurately. Though true, I believe it misses the reason why we predict. No one could possibly deny that it would be both aesthetically and practically pleasing if our predictions were more precise. But the fact that they are not does not mean that they are useless. I might also add that Nisbet and his fellow critics tend to underestimate the significance of the range of what things are *not* affected by random events. For the latest version of the argument about random events see Robert Nisbet, "Has Futurology a Future?" *Encounter* 37 (November 1971): 19-28.
[61] McHale's *The Future of the Future* is one place to begin examining the "futurology" literature; Alvin Toffler's *Future Shock* (New York: Random House, 1970) summarizes extensive material, but has few other virtues; Herman Kahn and Anthony Wiener, *The Year 2000* (New York: Macmillan, 1967), are fascinated, not to say obsessed, with lists of words that purport to mean something, and illustrate what the critics are complaining about.
[62] For example, see the comments by Herbert York on the inaccurate prediction in Kahn's *On Thermonuclear War:* "Every one of these errors in prediction arose out of the twin false assumptions that the immediate past was typical and that the technological future could be predicted by simple extrapolation. These errors are also illustrative of what happens when analysts use sophisticated methods but poor or nonsensical inputs." *Race to Oblivion* (New York: Simon and Schuster, 1970), p. 158.

edge of trends or a list of likely alternatives provides little guidance or insight.[63]

More explicit political prediction has not fared much better. Forecasting that uses structural models of the international system to elucidate likely classes of events and the types of policies suitable for dealing with these events is feasible and interesting. But it is also very abstract and rarely innovative enough to be truly exciting.[64] Much of the remainder of the work done on political forecasting is too conservative and traditional to be very helpful. Most of this work has verified the argument that we tend to see too much continuity in trends and tendencies: this will undoubtedly remain true so long as we continue to predict within the framework of the traditional model of interstate relations.[65]

Sensible decision-making is impossible without a serious commitment to planning, and planning is impossible without a serious commitment to prediction. The potential implicit in planning and prediction will never be realized unless we begin to educate practitioners in a different way, and unless theorists see some value in thinking about practical problems and worrying about what they are passing on to future practitioners. This is not meant to imply that planning and prediction have been done very well or that we can guarantee competent performance in the future. It *is* meant to imply that we have no choice but to attempt to plan and predict as well as we can, for the alternative is not to eliminate the need for planning and prediction but to do them without skill, without commitment, and without understanding.

---

[63] One crucial, short-range task to improve the quality of forecasting is the quest for reliable social indicators. Without such indicators, it is difficult to have much confidence—especially enough psychic security to *act* on the implications of projections—in the accuracy of any prediction. Given the perspective adopted here, I doubt that the loss of accuracy is as important as the psychological insecurities. For work on social indicators, see Raymond A. Bauer, ed., *Social Indicators* (Cambridge, Mass.: The M.I.T. Press, 1966).

[64] For comments on this kind of work, see Klaus Knorr and Oscar Morgenstern, *Political Conjecture in Military Planning* (Princeton, N.J.: Center of International Studies, Memorandum no. 35, 1968), pp. 23-25; for an argument about the relationship between the type of regime and type of policy, see Wayne Wilcox, "Forecasting Models and Foreign Policy," in Wolfram F. Hanreider, ed., *Comparative Foreign Policy* (New York: David McKay, 1971), pp. 385-402.

[65] Zbigniew Brzezinski, *Between Two Ages: America's Role in the Technetronic Era* (New York: Viking, 1970), is a recent illustration of the tendency to see more continuity than change in the future. Perhaps that work reflects Brzezinski's service on the Policy Planning Council, which also had trouble imagining that anything different would happen.

CHAPTER 5

Conclusions

PLANNING IN A REVOLUTIONARY WORLD

Planning has never been a very successful or important enterprise in foreign affairs. This is hardly surprising for it is difficult to imagine an area in which the obstacles could be more formidable. Whether we look at the political system, the bureaucracy, the attitudes of the planners, or the patterns of professional behavior by theorists and practitioners, we note the same result: planning is granted a very low priority, if it is not ignored altogether. These obstacles are so pervasive and so profound that challenges appear quixotic.

It would make very little difference if our resources were unlimited, if our errors were self-correcting or if their costs were always supportable, and if our faith in a future that is both beneficent and manageable persisted. We have lost the feeling that muddling through makes sense, that we can correct our errors before they begin to accumulate, and that the problems we face in the future will be sufficiently like those of the past to be handled on an ad hoc basis by a corps of unskilled generalists. We need to know that we are in control of events, that we are not simply drifting aimlessly from crisis to crisis. A serious effort to plan—actually the *first* such venture in foreign affairs—may be our only alternative, however formidable the obstacles.

The central argument against planning, so much fancied by the operating fraternity, that the only thing predictable about international relations is its unpredictability, has always rested on a hidden assumption: that the range of unpredictable behavior would fall within the range of diplomatic experience. Thus, the impossibility of precisely predicting any individual case was not too incapacitating, for the unpredictable was never the unexpectable. The failure to plan in this context was not surprising, or probably very costly, for stable systems in which the same events continue to recur do not appear to pay too high a price for survival by ad hoc improvisation. After all, the occasion and the improvisation tend to be familiar enough to mute any inadequacy. We have just begun to discover the long-run costs engendered by this attitude.

The development of nuclear weapons, coupled with the emergence of several different kinds of states—totalitarian, revolutionary, underdeveloped—should have destroyed any lingering belief that postwar international relations could be understood in the light of principles extrapolated from the history of the European state system. The revolutionary implications of the new state system were too salient to be missed. Yet, in the manner of General Staffs preparing to fight the last war again, we accepted an intellectual frame of reference that was designed to avoid repeating the errors and omissions of the Chamberlains and the Daladiers. Realism succeeded in turning attention away from major structural alterations in the international system toward concern with tactical questions about the distribution of power; consequently, planning in order to anticipate and deal with a different range of state behavior was still perceived as irrelevant.

The international system is again altering, perhaps even to a revolutionary degree. The salient event marking the emergence of a new system may no longer be the end of a major war—as has so often been true in the past—but the accumulation of a number of trends, some dealing with security issues, some with other issues, into a major shift in perspectives, purposes, and procedures. Where we are going remains unclear: we are only beginning to sense the shifts that are occurring. But it is very clear that the growing interdependence of the international system makes long-range planning imperative. It is the only process that offers us hope of beneficially controlling or directing these trends. Growing interdependence, in both the security and nonsecurity fields, is not necessarily equivalent to an increased likelihood of peace and cooperation: it may increase the number of antagonistic contacts within the system and ensure that all conflicts will be system-wide. The central point is that we cannot simply assume that all these trends are propitious—we must work to make them so. And that means we must plan.

CHALLENGING THE OBSTACLES TO PLANNING

No one has ever made a serious effort to challenge the obstacles to planning and to turn planning into a meaningful function. Periodic attempts to reform the planning staff have only sought—without success—

to make it more influential on matters of the moment, and not to make it a true planning unit. No more could be expected from men whose fundamental professional beliefs assert the irrelevance of planning and the impossibility of predicting anything of importance. This is why I have argued that it is necessary to carry the argument beyond the analysis of obstacles in Chapter 2: we must also attempt to understand *why* these obstacles appear so natural, and why it appears so futile to challenge them. This has required an examination (in Chapter 3) of the nature of basic beliefs about proper professional behavior within a social discipline, and speculations about the way in which those beliefs could be altered to make cooperation in planning seem useful and productive.

We have gone down complex, unusual paths, but the general direction in which we have been heading should be clear. Planning is an activity that requires—or should require—close cooperation between theorists and practitioners within a common discipline. Without that cooperation, planning will either not take place or, as we have seen in the Policy Planning Council, it will be so rudimentary as to be indistinguishable from any other staff activity. The absence of cooperation must be explained by more than the nature of the political system and the bureaucracies that populate it. As we have already said, these impede the possibility of useful planning, but they hardly explain why no one—on either side of the fence—has evinced more than rhetorical interest in real cooperation. The essential reason for this state of affairs is the existence of images of proper professional behavior that make cooperation in planning seem impossible or irrelevant.

We have challenged these images in Chapter 3. We have begun by attempting to refute the argument that the relationship between theory and practice can be understood in elegant dichotomies—for example, the quest for truth versus the quest for success, or the clash between sharply different vocational cultures. These arguments are partially true, but they miss or obscure as much as they reveal. It would perhaps be useful if all discussions of the relationship between theorists and practitioners in the social world began with the assumption that they cannot escape each other: the details may vary, but some relationship *of significance* always exists. This would make unexamined analogies with scientific disciplines more suspect than they currently are.

When we look at what theorists and practitioners actually do, we can begin to understand why simple dichotomies do not suffice. The practitioner must make decisions within a context that demands unique skills; but before he reaches the point of decision, he must make some intellectual judgments about the nature of the issues he confronts. The social theorist, because of the intrinsic limitations of all theories in the social sciences, cannot offer the practitioner any *direct* help at the point of decision. (Thus, the argument that theory is useless because it cannot tell us what to do in Vietnam tomorrow is misleading: it attacks a straw man, for this is not how social theory is meant to be used.) If the practitioner was just a chooser—if he worked only in what I have called treatment, and not diagnosis—we could say little, for theorists and practitioners would be involved in wholly disparate activities. Since this is not so, however, the grounds for cooperation become clear. The social theorist can help the practitioner to organize his cognitive world, to think about the nature of the problems he faces, and to evaluate habitual modes of behavior. He can prepare him to make better decisions, but he cannot tell him what decisions to make. A practitioner who is a better analyst will also be a better chooser—faith in this statement is at the root of a sensible understanding of what theorists can do for practitioners. We should like to say more, but we cannot; we ought at least to make sure that we do what we can.

This argument sets clear boundaries between the activities of the theorist and the practitioner. It also allows us to understand where bridges can be built to bring them together and where they are likely to lead to dangerous dead ends. Moreover, we see why the great arena of direct cooperation must be in planning, for planning is a function that is separate from the point of decision but nonetheless should (or can) provide the intellectual grounds for specific actions. This argument is also a counsel in humility for both theorists and practitioners: for the former, in that they must recognize the limitations of the theories they produce and the advice they can give on the basis of such theories, and for the latter, in that they must recognize that they need all the help they can get in diagnosing their problems.

One reason why the practitioner is not so competent a chooser as he thinks he is resides in his reluctance to accept the fact that his role does involve important intellectual elements. This insures that his intellectual judgments will be more rudimentary and haphazard. The point is not that the practitioner does not think, but that he does it badly and superficially. The practitioner seems bent on shortchanging his role, for he refuses to recognize the range of talents it requires—and consequently makes no effort to acquire them.

This argument also explains why practitioners, especially those drawn from the Foreign Service, should not be placed on the planning staff we have argued for in Chapter 2. This planning staff is meant to be different from the planning staffs that have existed in the past: it would be committed to collecting the best possible data, doing the best possible research, and, in general, doing all that it could to improve the quality of thinking about foreign affairs. To do this with any chance of success a new planning staff needs a separate, secure status outside the State Department—but within the government. But it also must be staffed by men who are not only committed to this kind of enterprise but also capable of carrying it out. This means that for the foreseeable future—until we have a group of practitioners who have been recruited and trained in accordance with these views—the group must be staffed by academics who are willing to work for the government for several years.

The Foreign Service has been receiving a bad press for some time now—which seems justifiable to me. What does not seem justifiable is an effort to simply ignore it or to turn it into a corps of second- or third-string administrators (diplomat-managers). On the contrary, I believe we need a corps of politically sophisticated, highly educated diplomatic observers and reporters, and ultimately policy officials, but that we are nowhere near having it. When (and if) we do have this corps, it should be able to provide some of the staff for the new planning unit.[1] All this requires a Foreign Service that is a professional group, and not a bogus elite complacently celebrating its lack of skills and talent.

No one can presume that it will be easy to restructure the Foreign Service or to institute the kind of planning staff that I have advocated. Nevertheless, if we are serious about change—about creating a policy process that is capable of dealing with the problems we confront—we must make the effort. As I have already argued, I believe we need to work simultaneously on three levels. First, we must make the effort now to create a planning staff that can become the constituency for the future that our political system needs, and we must not be diverted by the assertion that planning must fail. We will know what we mean by success or failure only after we have actually attempted to plan. Second, we must make the effort to use this staff as wisely as possible, in full recognition that it will stand in mortal danger for many years of becoming a redundant and second-string operating agency. This means that the planning staff must be carefully protected against its enemies until it can protect itself—or until we know that planning is indeed impossible. Finally, we must work, over the long range, to undermine the beliefs that have made planning impossible and to create new doctrines that are more

[1] I am not advocating creating practitioners who are theorists, but rather practitioners who understand what the theorist can do for them and what they can rightfully ask of the theorist. This requires a practitioner who has intellectual training in his field and not merely the experiences of being on the job.

relevant, more flexible, and more realistic than an unexamined faith in Political Realism and muddling through.

If these three levels of interaction do not converge, successful change is unlikely. It is difficult to be optimistic. Still, the apparent loss of self-confidence and unity among our political elites in recent years does suggest that this may not be a completely hopeless time to advocate major reforms of both the policymaking system and the educational process. It would be a mistake, however, to assume that we have much time, for the desire to reassert the supremacy of the conventional wisdom is always strong within the political establishment.

This argument has been unfashionable not only in advocating planning but also in maintaining that theorists and practitioners might find cooperation mutually beneficial. It may also be unfashionable in another sense. I do not believe that we can escape the necessity of relying on expert judgment in order to make wise decisions—or even to know what we have to decide. There are great dangers in this, for we are all aware of the sins committed in the name of expertise. This issue is usually dismissed with a light-hearted reference to a well-known aphorism: the expert should be on tap, not on top. As a sentiment, this is unassailable. Sentiment, however, is not sufficient, for it is far from clear how the practitioner can remain on top when he knows little about what he has tapped. The danger that the situation will degenerate into a farce—with the practitioner merely ratifying what he does not understand—is not illusory.

This is a profound dilemma, and no simple solutions will resolve it. No one wants to create a situation in which the power of decision has slipped de facto out of the practitioner's hands. I believe, however, that there are steps to increase the possibility that the expert will be able to perform his function without usurping the practitioner's function. One such step would be to improve the quality of our practitioners by training them better; this should help them understand the expert's contribution more adequately, and perhaps even enable practitioners to make judgments about the quality of expert advice. This is one important reason why I have attempted to establish the boundaries between theory and practice with care.

This is not, however, likely to be sufficient. We also need internal controls within the expert's realm. The in-house expert needs to have his views exposed to, and challenged by, other experts—both in and out of the government. I suggested mechanisms that might facilitate this in discussing the form that a long-range planning staff might take (see Chapter 2, above). The general point is that we need to take measures that ensure a reasonable flow of ideas between those inside and outside the government so that one set of expert judgments does not reign unchallenged. This does not solve the problem, for all the experts might agree—on a wrong course of action. Joined to an effort to make us aware of the problem, this may be the best we can do. Alternatives such as ignoring expert advice or demanding that all secrecy be removed from the process of giving advice hardly seem sensible.

If Congress had easier and more consistent access to its own group of experts, the dangers of disguised control by a small group of invisible experts might be diminished—but only to a degree. The Congressional experts would increase the probability that the views of one group of in-house experts would not go unchallenged or unexamined. The ABM dispute is illustrative, for Congress could not have challenged the Executive without the aid of another group of established, but dissenting, experts. But this is still expert dominance of the policy process.

Providing Congress with increased access to its own experts would constitute an important innovation only if Congress deliberately sought advice and aid outside the normal channels of inter-expert communication. When we look back over the last two decades, it seems clear that there has been a breakdown in the "circulation of elites." That is, the problem is not simply government by experts; it is also that the same experts, with the same perceptions, have remained constantly "on tap" (and too frequently "on top"). It is, however, difficult to imagine Congress making the effort to seek out wider sources of information—or even understanding the need to do so. In fact, the new long-range planning staff which I have advocated might be the most effective institution not only to seek new sources of advice but also to expand the network of communication between inside and outside experts.

Perhaps this is the most that we can hope for in a world of complex problems, but it surely does some damage to traditional principles of representative government. At any rate, we are at least much more self-conscious about this problem than we have been, and this may be more important than any particular institutional or intellectual palliative that we can devise.

ACADEMIC FASHIONS AND THE RELATIONSHIP
BETWEEN THEORY AND PRACTICE

Commitment to a methodology or an interpretation of the meaning of theory always extracts a price. Irrespective of the approach in question, this is true, for all approaches inevitably emphasize some factors at the expense of others. This is relevant to the issues we have been discussing, for when we examine the theories that have dominated the discipline of international relations since World War II, we see that they have persistently ignored factors that would have contributed to a productive relationship between theory and practice. This is true, although in very different ways, for both Realism, which dominated the discipline throughout the 1950s, and that diverse package of contemporary approaches that we usually label as behavioralism.

From this perspective, the difficulty with Realism was its tendency to distort the relationship between theory and practice by turning the theorist into a substitute, and presumably superior, practitioner. Not realizing the limitations of Realism as a theory, and committed to the notion that it somehow provided explicit guidance for difficult choices in the real world, its advocates spent most of their time trying to tell the practitioner what decisions he ought to be making. Realism also reinforced the belief that planning was impossible in international affairs: only men of experience, armed with the traditional wisdom, could successfully operate in so chancy an environment. When Realists were appointed to planning staffs, they never made the mistake of assuming that they were there to plan beyond the next tactical move.

Realism appeared to work reasonably well during the height of the Cold War. Many perceptions of Realism corresponded with the perceptions then prevalent about the proper way to deal with monolithic, totalitarian states, and it thus seemed to have no difficulty in adapting to the postwar world. For example, neither view worried about the influence of domestic factors in foreign policy, for the dominance of the latter was taken for granted. In addition, they both stressed the necessity of using limited amounts of force quickly, even in minor conflicts, in order to forestall the necessity of using larger amounts belatedly. In effect, Realism froze the learning process and the reality-testing process by asserting that we already knew the principles of politics and could learn nothing new or important from examining the external world: it was always the same game, with a few new faces. The difficulty in refuting these views and the costs of not being able to do so illustrated the need for new doctrines that could be tested and that perceived truth as hypothetical and contingent.

Thus, Realism may have contained the seeds of the behavioral revolution in its own excesses. (Perhaps the same could be said about the way in which Realism emerged.) But the indifference of most Realists to confirming their speculations, the ritual incantation of an elusive wisdom of history, the desperate desire of some leading Realists to impose their policies on events—all this was enough to make anyone overreact. More-over, an analogy with the manner in which other disciplines had achieved success was readily available. As a result, the behavioral movement made a serious effort to justify turning away from the world of practice. One bad relationship—the Realist attempt to become a surrogate practi-tioner—was succeeded by a different but equally bad relationship—the behavioralist attempt to ignore the concerns of the practitioner com-pletely (or until the acquisition of pure theories eliminates the need for practitioners—though not engineers). It was unlikely that theorists com-mitted to these views would consider it worthwhile to worry about plan-ning or what the practitioner was or was not doing.

We can, perhaps, get a clearer picture of the effects of the behavioral revolution by examining one main component—systems theory.[2] It has entailed severe costs in facilitating the practitioner's understanding of the utility of theory. There is more to understanding this than the difficulty of an arcane vocabulary. By concentrating on macropolitical data and events, systems theory, like quantitative analysis, has contributed to the neglect of other political phenomena of equal significance but of more immediate interest to the practitioner: the impact of domestic politics on foreign policy, the nature of the policymaking process in foreign affairs, and the significance of trends that cross system lines or alter erratically.

The systems approach or the version described as analytical or abstract thus shares an important bias with the Realists: they rest on an assumption of structural dominance. Concentration on structure—on the relationships between recurring patterns of behavior—reflects a belief that international politics is not so random that the general properties of a period are beyond useful abstraction. While yielding neither predictions nor prescriptions, knowledge of structure should suggest insights about *types* of policies that are in or out of harmony with the prevailing struc-tural configuration. In short, the systems approach provides insights into the nature of a period, as well as how this period of time differs from others, but since the systems approach lacks the simplifying power of a dominant idea—such as the control of the means of production—the practical inferences drawn from research seem inconclusive and overly abstract. This is especially true because the systems approach is am-biguous when the practitioner feels the sharpest need for expert advice:

[2] In a narrow sense, the systems approach is not behavioral. It has been conven-tional, however, to treat the systems approach in this fashion; this does not seem harmful so long as we recognize that we are using "behavioral" loosely—somewhat equivalent, in this context, to contemporary research strategies designed to over-come the epistemological and methodological deficiencies of Realism.

when an old system is breaking down and a new one is emerging fitfully and asymmetrically.[3]

Perhaps the difficulties that practitioners have in understanding the systems approach are related to its attractiveness for academics.[4] It may also be popular because it is amorphous; the failure to establish ground rules with a minimum of operational clarity frequently means that the use of the term "system" is as fashionable as it is significant. Another reason may account for the popularity of the systems approach (or its vocabulary) in international politics. Although its insights or methodologies may not be very attractive, the systems approach delineates an area that is indisputably international. In a discipline unsure of its boundaries, and existing in uneasy tension with potential imperialists in comparative politics and other neighboring fields, any analytical approach concentrating on unique aspects of *international* politics is attractive. These phenomena constitute repeated patterns of behavior by states within the system: they can also be analyzed as aspects of behavior within systems that are not international. But a residue of behavior is international, in that it can be measured, evaluated, and understood *only* on the presumption that it occurs because states act as if an international arena exists. This is a neutral point and is a partial explanation for the affinity of some strange bedfellows for the systems approach; an area of interaction with rules and styles of its own is indispensable.

These comments indicate some difficulties that have arisen because of the new style of theorizing within the discipline. The significance of this, however, can be misunderstood, if we assume that there is something intrinsically wrong with theoretical concentration on approaches such as systems analysis. Degrees of emphasis are what is important. An emphasis on macropolitical phenomena, to the exclusion of all else, could be justified only according to the results. But the theoretical and practical results have been meager. Consequently, it may be useful to expend *some*

[3] The more concrete or historical form of systems analysis appears to avoid some problems of the abstract systems approach. The historical form of systems analysis is less dominated by structural determinism, more open and dynamic in analysis, and more able to deal with a wider range of factors (differences in goals sought and differences between various types of actors, like Small Powers, Great Powers, and Super Powers, who do not perceive structural imperatives identically). Such analysis, however, cannot predict or prescribe behavior, and is limited to explicating typological differences between actors, areas, issues, and weapons. Done well, this is a useful, important way of ordering, and thus thinking about, a complex environment.

[4] This might follow from an extreme interpretation of some standard arguments about how the discipline ought to relate to the world of practice. Anything that sharply differentiates what the theorist is doing from what the practitioner is doing looks appealing.

effort on producing research (and ultimately theories) that concentrates on micropolitical phenomena or on analyzing major practical problems. This is true especially in light of the evidence indicating that research on political problems may have a profound impact on the development of theory.

From the practitioner's point of view, the systems approach has a different significance. He must come to understand that the systems approach is indicative of what the major part of the discipline will concentrate on, and that it is useful to him insofar as it helps to organize his cognitive world and to diagnose the problems he faces. To the practitioner who does understand such things, theoretical approaches that fail to provide solutions or even to predict the future will be more useful than comments on current events or the pseudo-profundities of Realism. This presupposes that a practitioner has been trained to understand the intellectual aspects of his activities and the relationship between his work and that of theorists. If the academic discipline accepted the change of emphasis advocated, it might be easier to train such practitioners. But even if the academic discipline adjusts more slowly than its practitioners—which is not unlikely—it is still important to expend effort on broadening the intellectual perspectives of the operating fraternity.

Perhaps the planning staff that we have advocated could be a useful bridge. We have suggested staffing it with men who have made a contribution to the academic discipline—not simply another group of in-and-outers—and who are willing to spend a few years working on policy problems. The presumption has been that they would work on current issues and be free to use their academic skills; they would *not* be just another staff grinding out speeches and instant analysis for tomorrow's headlines. Enough people and staffs are already doing this. The new planning staff might make a different kind of analysis respectable within government—as RAND made thinking about military issues respectable. If such a staff were successful, there might be ancillary benefits: government service would begin to look more attractive, and the academic discipline might understand that its virtue will not be compromised if its best people work on practical issues.

RELEVANCE AND RESPONSIBILITY

What relationship does the argument in this book have to the current demand for a more relevant political science? Relevance is an ambiguous standard, and any kind of research can be described as relevant in a particular time frame. The notion, enthusiastically shared by many radical critics of contemporary social science, that relevance is equivalent to taking a stand on pressing social problems is dangerously misleading. Although we may have difficulty in establishing a definition of what relevance is, we do know that it must be more than a euphemism for expressing opinions about current problems.

The dictionary offers two definitions of relevance. The first is "bearing upon the matter at hand." The second may be more useful: "affording evidence tending to prove or disprove the matters at issue." This definition is pertinent for a social science, for it clearly implies that relevance is inseparable from accepted professional standards that allow us to say what constitutes evidence. We are not being relevant just because we work on current problems; we are relevant only when we examine and submit them according to the best possible professional standards.[5] In effect, political science can only *be* relevant by being disciplined.

This does not mean that the legitimacy or adequacy of professional standards cannot be attacked. We must accept, however, the necessity of maintaining standards, for the alternative is to be left without the possibility of discriminating between good, bad, or indifferent pieces of work—except in terms of ideological purity. Since we know that relevant work must be disciplined work, then it follows that relevant work is professionally acceptable. A sharp line ought to be drawn between such work and what is now called policy research—which rarely meets any standard except topicality. The social scientist ought to decline involvement in this work, or indicate that his conclusions have no more importance than those of any other educated citizen. Honesty in these matters is imperative if we wish to avoid further disasters such as the efforts to sell the theory of counterinsurgency by various professorial types during the Kennedy administration.

ON EDUCATING AND MISEDUCATING PRACTITIONERS

One of the by-products of the academic desire to isolate itself from the concerns of the practitioner has been a corresponding indifference to the question of how we ought to be educating students who intend to enter a career in public service. This is unfortunate, for the academic world shares a major part of the responsibility for creating the kind of practi-

---

[5] This is not a plea for either behavioralism or traditionalism. It is, rather, an appeal for research and analysis that is committed to creating a body of reliable knowledge about international politics—and ultimately recognized and useful theories—by whatever methods are imposed according to the problem to be researched and the state of the art in methodology.

tioner who makes the split between theory and practice necessary. This vicious circle can only be broken by an effort to analyze what future practitioners ought to be getting from the discipline: we cannot go on insisting that the solution is better men, without trying to understand how to get them and how to train them. The only way we can justify a rhetorical response to this issue is by the assumption that our only responsibility is to educate and train future theorists—and that is a very dangerous, irresponsible position.

One reason why we have not faced the problem of educating practitioners should be clear from the preceding discussion. If we assume that the realms of theory and practice are separate—are two different vocational cultures—then each realm ought to set its educational standards in isolation from the other. I have argued that the two realms can help each other, and that the nature of the problems confronting us makes the need for cooperation imperative. Thus, an educational process that facilitates mutual understanding is imperative. I have also argued that the creation of a long-range planning staff will be meaningful only if the men who are on the staff, and those who appoint and consult them, alter their current beliefs about planning. The most effective place to make these changes is in the educational process.

The absence of concern with this issue has had predictable results. Prolonged exposure to courses on immediate policy problems has become the norm, and this has inevitably created the need to draft former practitioners as instructors—who better knows how we got into Vietnam, or what our policy toward France happens to be, or whether we should or should not invest in ABMs and MIRVs? These courses tend to combine superficial analysis of current events, via published sources, with the self-interested revelations of the instructor.[6] Even courses designed to elucidate the background of current problems have merely described past policy conflicts. This is not surprising, for what else can such instructors pass on? What is missing is a course that would help the student to understand how and why to raise questions about the environment he will confront. Many instructors in policy courses have indeed considered it a virtue that the courses they teach are anti-theoretical—theory, by definition, being useless because it does not provide solutions to today's problems.

[6] My favorite example is a course on Soviet policy given by a government official in which the students were asked to submit papers no longer than a typed page—for the ostensible reason that no one in government had time to read anything longer. In any case, the instructor did not, nor did he understand the issues of prediction and planning.

The fundamental error in this approach lies in the assumption that experience can be taught. Presumably, by some mysterious process, a combination of anecdotes, hearsay, the back files of *The New York Times,* and the latest memoirs of former officials is sufficient education for the next generation of practitioners.[7] After all, it was for the last generation.

I do not mean to imply that this approach to educating practitioners applies in all cases. I do believe that it is far too prevalent, especially in schools explicitly created to train future practitioners—which is the worst place. None of these schools, however, appear to have made a serious effort to understand the problem of training future practitioners, and have simply done what seems natural. They have not been challenged by their academic brethren, who are content to respond to the question with contempt or indifference.

In order to avoid misunderstandings, we should reemphasize that we are not arguing that policy questions ought not to be studied. We have already emphasized that a planning unit staffed with academics, and working on current problems, ought to be created, and that it might lead to useful results *both* practically and theoretically. This position rests on the notion that such work meets intellectual standards more rigorous than those of the Policy Planning Council and more realistic (not indifferent to the nature of the issue about which one seeks understanding) than those demanded by more extreme methodological metaphysicians. However, in order that practitioners understand these issues, they must be trained in more than current events.

Indifference to the question of how to educate practitioners could be interpreted as a sophisticated, somewhat cynical, argument about the nature of practical activity. If the latter cannot be formally learned, but must be imparted on the job (as Oakeshott has argued),[8] then nothing useful can be taught to practitioners within the framework of an academic course. Thus, it makes no difference what they are taught; there is no point in forcing them to learn anything as difficult and time-consuming as a theoretical approach to their subject. Who would deny that reading all the latest exposés of how we got into Vietnam is less demanding than reading a serious study of, for instance, the nature of the concepts by which we organize the international environment or the relationship between the structure of the international system and

[7] Experience, even if teachable, would be persistently out-of-date. Stressing the continuing relevance of experience is an instance of unplanned obsolescence (or of a built-in intellectual lag).

[8] See above, p. 143.

the types of policies it implies? Concentration on current events also provides somewhat gainful labor to out-of-work practitioners waiting for the phone to ring—a new form of indoor relief for those who guessed wrong at the last election.

It is doubtful that anything this sophisticated has occurred to many practitioners. If it had, it probably would have been rejected out-of-hand, for many practitioners feel that the policy courses to which they have been exposed have been useful. For some, such courses provide more knowledge of current events or time to think about marginal alternatives to prevailing policies. For others, who seem wiser, it is an insight into the way the system actually functions and the style of behavior appropriate to mastering it. This is one reason why the insider's courses on bureaucratic politics remain so popular, despite the low level of insight they offer—summarized, perhaps, by the unexciting observation that different institutions and different men view problems from different perspectives. The greatest practical danger, I believe, in the current fascination with bureaucratic politics is that it tends to concentrate attention exclusively (especially in the hands of less sophisticated devotées) on the process of politics or the play of personality. Once again, this turns attention away from the substance of issues, which rarely appears important, and appears to justify the assumption that the only way to train practitioners and politicians is on the job. But the critical question is whether this is all that an educational system ought to be passing on to potential practitioners.[9] We ought at least to be trying to do more.

[9] The analysis of bureaucratic politics is currently the most fashionable approach to the study of foreign affairs. If academics can continue to get access to classified documents and if the outpouring of memoirs and exposés by former bureaucrats persists, new insights, perhaps even theoretical propositions, may possibly be developed. For the moment, however, we seem to be getting only an adaptation to foreign affairs of standard propositions about informal bureaucratic behavior: there are different personality types within the bureaucracy; self-interest and organizational interest frequently clash with more general interests; and there is much intra-bureaucratic conflict.

Not that this work is uninteresting or unimportant, but it may be regressive. First, the emphasis on process, on "how" questions, can create the feeling—as it has among many former bureaucrats and in-and-outers—that "what" and "why" questions are visionary and irrelevant. Second, there is danger of fostering another conspiracy theory of politics. Radical critics of our foreign policy and many students of bureaucratic politics see the bureaucracy as the *only* cause of many current problems. But no single-factor explanation of our problems makes much sense: students of bureaucratic politics should try harder to indicate that they are talking about only *one* influence on our policymaking process. Note, for example, the ease with which Nixon and Kissinger have managed—on Vietnam, China, and the SALT talks—in spite of, or in indifference to, the reservations of the bureaucracy. Bureaucratic influence is dependent on many factors and is not the independent variable that determines all policy outcomes.

The central point that practitioners must understand is that the art of judgment, which is central to their activities, is both intellectual and practical. The hard-headed practitioner, intent on manipulating his environment, need not also be empty-headed. Of course, he is not, but the tendency to ignore or depreciate the cognitive phase of his activities merely means that they are carried out in an inconsistent, rudimentary, unreflective fashion. We can no longer afford to cater to the prejudices of the practitioner by reciting a few incantations about the differences between being in and being out every time a discussion of theory and practice begins; differences there are, but they are not the whole story. The academic world is responsible not only for analyzing the intellectual aspects of the practitioner's world but also for making him aware of its significance, helping him to improve his performance, and evaluating the results.

The manner of educating future practitioners must be changed so that the academic world does not share the responsibility for clogging the political system with premature bureaucrats who desire only to avoid heresy or innovation. Concentration on immediate policy issues, or on the intricacies of survival in the bureaucratic game, should be radically deemphasized. The practitioner who cannot learn what passes for conventional wisdom in a few weeks on the job is in the wrong business. And unless he knows something other than the conventional wisdom, he can do nothing but perpetuate it. What he needs is not an education in another's experiences, which are always out-of-date, or in procedural style, which leaves men helpless when the style becomes obsolete, but an education in the way we think about foreign affairs, the concepts we use, and the assumptions we try to hide. This education cannot be obtained on the job, and it is the only kind of education that will give us practitioners who have an alternative to repeating their mistakes.

Indicating precisely what should be in a new educational process is very difficult. We can be much clearer on what will not work. Simply adding to the list of course offerings is hardly sufficient; the fact that a future practitioner has had a few courses on methodology or contemporary theoretical approaches will be meaningless unless he also understands what these methods and approaches can do to clarify practical problems. We need to experiment with ways in which this might be done. Perhaps it would be useful to run joint projects, in which future practitioners, current practitioners on temporary leave, and theorists of various persuasions attempt to analyze a practical problem together. Rather than the normal teacher-student relationship, one might envisage here a cooperative, continuing learning process. This would be an improvement over the existing situation, in which each group watches the other as a spectator sport. An effort must also be made to provide more opportunity for practitioners to periodically return to the academic world. The fundamental point is that we need a new vision of the proper way to educate practitioners so that what they know is not always obsolescent.

Can we improve the quality of our practitioners in this manner? We have never attempted to do so, primarily because of the influence of professional beliefs that assume we cannot train men to be better practitioners. It is not absolutely clear that it will be possible to do so, but it is worth making the effort. Educating practitioners is a task well within the power of the academic discipline, and even if it fails, the effort may exert a beneficent influence. With luck, this attempt may make us understand that the relationship between theory and practice is profoundly important and that it is never wise to stop worrying about it; that we are not limited to rhetorical demands for better people in attempting to improve the conduct of practice, for we possess intellectual resources that may be far more effective; and that, in what is only apparently an instance of serendipity, theoretical involvement with practical concerns may even improve the practice of theory.

Index

Books on Related Subjects

Written under the Auspices of
The Institute of War and Peace Studies,
Columbia University

Defense and Diplomacy by Alfred Vagts; *Man, the State and War* by Kenneth N. Waltz; *The Common Defense* by Samuel P. Huntington; *Strategy, Politics and Defense Budgets* by Warner R. Schilling, Paul Y. Hammond, and Glenn H. Snyder; *The Politics of Military Unification* by Demetrios Caraley; *NATO and the Range of American Choice* by William T. R. Fox and Annette Baker Fox; *The Politics of Policy Making in Defense and Foreign Affairs* by Roger Hilsman; *Inspection for Disarmament* edited by Seymour Melman; *To Move a Nation* by Roger Hilsman, jointly sponsored with the Washington Center of Foreign Policy Research, Johns Hopkins University; and *The Origins of Peace* by Robert F. Randle. Institute studies now in press include *German Nuclear Weapons Policy* by Catherine M. Kelleher and *European Security and the Atlantic System* edited by Warner R. Schilling and William T. R. Fox.